VIKING SOCIETY FOR NORTHERN RESEARCH
TEXT SERIES

GENERAL EDITORS
Anthony Faulkes and Richard Perkins

VOLUME XIV

FOURTEENTH-CENTURY ICELANDIC VERSE ON THE
VIRGIN MARY

DRÁPA AF MARÍUGRÁT
VITNISVÍSUR AF MARÍU
MARÍUVÍSUR I–III

# Fourteenth-Century Icelandic Verse on the Virgin Mary

Drápa af Maríugrát
Vitnisvísur af Maríu
Maríuvísur I–III

Edited by

KELLINDE WRIGHTSON

VIKING SOCIETY FOR NORTHERN RESEARCH
UNIVERSITY COLLEGE LONDON
2001

© Viking Society for Northern Research 2001

ISBN: 0 903521 46 6

The cover picture is based on a dragon drawn at *Maríugrátr* 41.4 in AM 713 4to (see p. xxiii)

Printed by Short Run Press Limited, Exeter

# PREFACE

The five skaldic poems in this volume are among the finest examples of medieval literature composed in the vernacular in honour of the Virgin Mary. They are part of an extensive corpus of Old Icelandic Marian texts which is significant not merely for its size, but, more importantly, for its contribution to our understanding of the cult of the Virgin in Western Europe. Dated to the late fourteenth century, the lamentation poem *Drápa af Maríugrát* and the miracle poems *Vitnisvísur af Maríu* and *Maríuvísur I–III* are among the earliest extant evidence of Old Icelandic Marian poetry.

There has been no lack of attention paid to these texts by scholarly editors publishing in languages other than English, from Jón Þorkelsson's Danish edition of extracts from the poems in 1888, to Bernhard Kahle and Hans Sperber's German editions in 1898 and 1911 respectively, through to Finnur Jónsson's Danish edition and translation in 1912–15 and Ernst A. Kock's Swedish edition in 1946–49. While valuable in their particular ways—for instance, both Kahle and Sperber discuss the metrical features in detail—these editions have not addressed the main issues associated with this group of Marian vernacular poems.

These five skaldic poems, for example, have never been edited as a set on their own, separate from other religious poetry, yet, like so much Marian literature, especially the miracles, these Old Icelandic texts lend themselves to such treatment. Nor did any of the past editions include a glossary for these texts, which contain many words and phrases associated with the Mary cult and the monastic culture in which they appear to have been composed. Perhaps most significantly, no attempt was made by the past editors to place these poems in a broader European context, to trace at least some of the source texts which make up the textual history of *Drápa af Maríugrát, Vitnisvísur af Maríu* and *Maríuvísur I–III*, and to find a legitimate place for this Old Icelandic contribution in the cult of the Virgin across Western Europe. The present edition aims to fill these needs by providing a reliable and accessible text of the five poems, while the editor is planning to publish more comprehensive studies of the sources and analogues in article form, and is also completing a new critical edition with English translations and commentary of some of the related miracle stories about the Virgin Mary in medieval Icelandic prose (see pp. xx and x below).

While the bulk of the work for this edition was carried out at the University of Sydney in Australia, the editor has made several research visits abroad to Stofnun Árna Magnússonar in Reykjavík to transcribe the manuscripts afresh, and to University College London and the British Library to research the textual history of the miracle poems against a European background. This research was made possible with the generous financial support of the Australian Vice-Chancellors' Committee together with the Sir Robert Menzies Centre for Australian Studies, University of London, the Australian Federation of University Women (S.A. Inc.) and the University of Sydney. Suggestions for improvements have been generously offered by many scholars, namely Peter Foote and Richard Perkins in London, Anthony Faulkes in Birmingham, Jónas Kristjánsson in Reykjavík and Margaret Clunies Ross in Sydney to whom this volume is dedicated for her continued guidance and friendship.

K. W.

# CONTENTS

| | |
|---|---|
| Introduction | ix |
|   I. Marian Literature in Medieval Iceland | ix |
|   II. Preservation and Textual History | xi |
| *Drápa af Maríugrát* | 1 |
| *Vitnisvísur af Maríu* | 27 |
| *Maríuvísur I* | 40 |
| *Maríuvísur II* | 55 |
| *Maríuvísur III* | 67 |
| Glossary and Index | 83 |
| List of Kennings | 135 |
| Bibliography and Abbreviations | 143 |

# INTRODUCTION

## I. Marian Literature in Medieval Iceland

Most scholars agree that the cult of the Virgin Mary reached its peak in the eleventh and twelfth centuries in Western Europe, although there is, of course, ample evidence that veneration of the Virgin flourished much earlier in some parts of the West. Mary Clayton's study (1990) of the cult of the Virgin in Anglo-Saxon England, for example, has shown that there was a good deal of interest in and devotion to the Virgin there as early as *c.*700. For the most part, though, the widespread cult of the Virgin climaxed somewhat later than this, on the cusp of what we call the 'Dark Ages' and the 'Middle Ages' (eleventh to twelfth centuries). The situation in Iceland does not, however, fit in with this general scheme of things. There is evidence that the cult was only beginning to peak there during the thirteenth century, and continued to do so well into the fourteenth.

Iceland, therefore, appears to have been a late starter where the Mary cult is concerned, reflecting its comparatively late conversion to Christianity in *c.*999. In the first century after the conversion, the Mary cult, which by this time was certainly reaching its peak elsewhere, could have only just begun in medieval Iceland. The conversion and the writing of literature, records and other texts to support the new faith did not occur overnight. The first Icelandic bishops, the father and son, Ísleifr Gizurarson and Gizurr Ísleifsson, were consecrated in 1056 and 1082 respectively, though there were missionary bishops sent to Iceland in the first half of the century. Part of the responsibility of these early bishops was to educate the laity and it is this Christian education that influenced much of the extant literature of medieval Iceland. Moreover, the foundation of monastic establishments, from where so much Christian literature often emerged, only began in the early 1100s, around 130 years after the conversion, with the founding of the first Icelandic monastery at Þingeyrar in 1133 and the first convent at Kirkjubær in Síðu in 1186. Several monasteries, and one other convent, were established during the remainder of the twelfth and early thirteenth centuries.

The Virgin was among the first saints to be venerated in Iceland and if one views the surviving evidence for the development of the Mary cult, one can see a gradual increase in veneration of the

Mother of God through, for instance, prose and poetic literature, records of vows and offerings, and dedications of churches and monastic houses for which she was the patron or co-patron saint (see Cormack 1994, 126–29). The main evidence for veneration of her in the first century, or possibly the second, after the conversion is a collection of miracle texts dated to c.1050–1200 and surviving in AM 234 4to, compiled at Skálholt around 1340, and AM 232 4to, compiled in c.1350 at the northern Benedictine monastery of Munkaþverá. Evidence for the cult from the 1100s also includes the recording in *Prestssaga Guðmundar Arasonar* of Mary's aid being sought by a priest on behalf of a ship's crew during a storm (*Biskupa sögur* 1858–78, I 421; see also Kålund 1906–11, 136 and Stefán Karlsson 1983, 41–42), a fairly common scenario in miracle literature, and the composition of a poem on the Virgin called *Maríuflokkr*, which now survives only in fragmentary form (*Skj* B, I 634).

On the whole, however, the extant material points to a flourishing of Marian veneration during the next two centuries. It was not until the 1200s that the Ave Maria, a prayer which was often promoted in the miracle literature and which was gradually to form so central a part of Catholic devotion in the Rosary, became obligatory knowledge for Christians. Out of 51 miracle stories in the collection referred to above, for instance, the Ave is mentioned only nine times as opposed to its frequent appearance in the Norse collections dated to the 1200s and 1300s. Perhaps indicative of the increase in popularity of the Mary cult, these later collections contain around four times the number of Marian miracle stories found in the earlier collection. Altogether there survive around 400 Marian miracle stories in Old Icelandic. Also during the course of this period, Mary's *vita*, or *Maríusaga* (see *Ms*), was composed around 1215 and *Líknarbraut* (*Skj* B, II 160–74) was composed around the end of this century. In the 1300s numerous poems were composed in the Virgin's honour, including the miracle poems in the present volume *Vitnisvísur af Maríu* and *Maríuvísur I–III*, the famous *Lilja* (*Skj* B, II 390–416) dedicated to God, Christ and the Virgin, and the poem documenting Mary's sorrow at the crucifixion called *Drápa af Maríugrát*, also edited in this volume.

In view of the amount of extant material, the Icelanders appear to have been particularly keen to honour of the Mother of God in their native poetry and prose. Yet there has been a tendency to view the Old Icelandic Christian texts as not as interesting in content or as good in literary value as the older literature, for instance, the heroic poems or family sagas.[1] The miracle poems presented in this volume alone support the view that the Norse Marian literature is far from dull. One might cite, for instance, the stories known as 'Mother-in-law and Son-in-law', 'Jilted Fiancée' and 'Ave on the Tongue', versions of which are found in *Maríuvísur I*, *Vitnisvísur af Maríu*, and *Maríuvísur III* respectively. These tales present a range of scenarios from that of a woman who has her innocent son-in-law killed because of a rumour that she was having sex with him, to a young woman's efforts to get back her man, who has left her for a better match, to an unchaste, bad-tempered, and, by most standards, alcoholic cleric who narrowly escapes damnation despite having broken almost every rule in the book. Stories like these are in fact quite common among the Marian miracle literature and must have been just as entertaining for medieval audiences as they are for those in the twentieth century accustomed to similar scenarios in, for instance, popular literature and television soap-operas.

Today, Icelandic Marian literature is winning the attention of more scholars than in the past. This is partly because there has been a general change of attitude to medieval literature, particularly concerning women's devotion, the role of women in a religion with a male deity, and gender issues, which are all of contemporary interest. Moreover, the contribution of the Icelandic material to the field of Marian studies is slowly gaining recognition. Not only is there a vast amount of surviving literature and records, but there are some texts which are missing from the major miracle collections in the Middle Ages and can only be found in Old Icelandic manuscripts, such as *Vitnisvísur af Maríu*.

## II. Preservation and Textual History

There are three medieval manuscripts which contain the majority of extant Old Icelandic Marian poetry: AM 622 4to, AM 713 4to,

---

[1] The main exception is the enormous amount of research published by Ole Widding and Hans Bekker-Nielsen, particularly on the contents, style and sources and analogues of a great many of the Marian miracles. See, for example, Widding 1961; 1967; 1969; 1995 and Widding and Bekker-Nielsen 1961. Other references can be found in Wrightson 1994, 149 n. 2.

and AM 721 4to (see further *KLNM* XI, 379 and Kålund 1889–94, II 34–37, 128–31, 149–50). *Drápa af Maríugrát, Vitnisvísur af Maríu,* and *Maríuvísur I–III* are preserved in the last two of these manuscripts, both of which have particular associations with the north of Iceland and the religious and political events that preceded the Reformation. AM 713 and AM 721 are books of sacred Christian poetry, consisting almost entirely of poems in honour of the saints, the apostles and the Holy Cross. These two codices are similar in structure and content, both having *drápur* about Guðmundr, bishop of Hólar, as well as the poems *Milska* and *Meyjadrápa* at or near the beginning of the compilations and both containing Jón Arason's *Krossvísur*, poems in honour of St Óláfr, St Cecilia, St Peter, the Apostles and the Virgin Mary, *Boðunarvísur* and *Boðunardiktur*.[1]

These manuscripts were compiled sometime between 1500 and 1550 and consist of a mixture of older poems composed in the fourteenth and fifteenth centuries and contemporary verse from the sixteenth century. A number of these texts point to a connection between AM 713 and AM 721 and the northern see of Hólar. Take, for instance, the fourteenth-century poem in honour of St Guðmundr, bishop of Hólar, which was composed by Árni Jónsson, abbot at Munkaþverá 1370–79 (found in both manuscripts), the poems written by the bishop of Hólar, Jón Arason (also found in both manuscripts), a poem dedicated to the Holy Cross at Kaldaðarnes in the south-west of Iceland (in AM 713), and a great many poems in honour of the Virgin Mary (in both books) and St Andrew (in AM 713 only), who were both strongly venerated in the north of Iceland.

During the first half of the sixteenth century in Iceland, particularly the 1530s and 1540s, the well-known events that finally led to the nation-wide acceptance of Lutheranism unfolded, culminating in the beheading the last Catholic bishop of Iceland, Jón Arason, bishop of Hólar, and two of his sons on 7th November 1550. The northern see of Hólar was not only the site for the religious and political resistance to Lutheranism and the Danish authorities that

---

[1] Some of the poems in these manuscripts are available in modern editions. See, for instance, Finnur Jónsson's edition of early and late skaldic poetry (*Skj*) and his edition of Jón Arason's religious poetry (1918). See also Jón Helgason's edition of poems from the later Middle Ages on the Virgin, the Apostles and Saints (1936–38), and Jón Þorkelsson's edition and discussion of fifteenth- and sixteenth-century Icelandic poetry (1888).

were advocating it, but it also appears to have had strong associations with the veneration and cult of the Virgin Mary (Cormack 1994, 126–29), not to mention the compilation of most of the Old Icelandic saints' lives in the northern monasteries of Þingeyrar, Helgafell, Munkaþverá and Möðruvellir in the late thirteenth and fourteenth centuries (Kalinke 1996, 38).

Sometime during these decades, when the veneration of and belief in saints was being questioned by supporters of Lutheranism, a priest called Ari Jónsson and his two sons Tómas and Jón, from Staður in the north of Iceland, compiled or copied the book of poetry in honour of the saints now known as AM 713 (Jón Helgason 1932, 168; Stefán Karlsson 1970, 139). It is possible that the manuscripts from which Ari and his sons worked were from the Augustinian monastery of Möðruvellir or the Benedictine monastery of Munkaþverá. Although AM 713 does not preserve *vitae* as such, it consists almost entirely of poems in honour of St Catherine of Alexandria, St Guðmundr, St Peter, St Andrew, St Cecilia, St Óláfr, St Mary Magdalene, St Christopher, the Virgin Mary, the Apostles and the Holy Cross. Given the contents of the book, it appears to have been compiled for the edification and entertainment of monks, though at which monastery is uncertain.

Around the same time in the north of Iceland, AM 721 was compiled by an unknown scribe or scribes who copied fourteenth- and fifteenth-century Christian poems on the saints from older Icelandic manuscripts, now lost, together with a selection of poems from their own era, namely Jón Arason's *Krossvísur* and several endrhyming poems on the Virgin Mary all called *Maríukvæði*. Like AM 713, this book preserves poems about St Guðmundr, St Cecilia, St Peter, St James, St Magnús of Orkney, St Nicholas, St Óláfr, St Bartholomew, the Virgin Mary, the Apostles and the Holy Cross. AM 721 is also likely to have been part of a monastic culture, with texts that were used in the liturgy or the refectory. It was probably compiled at one of the northern monastries mentioned above.

Among its many hagiographic poems, AM 713 preserves an Old Icelandic poetic version of the enormously popular Latin religious work *Liber de passione Christi et doloribus et planctus matris eius*, by the Italian abbot Ogerius de Locedio, called *Drápa af Maríugrát* (*Mg*), found on ff. 123–29. The anonymous Icelandic poet who composed *Mg* did not work directly from any known Latin version of the *Liber de passione Christi*, but rather worked from the Old Icelandic prose translation of it called *Planctus siue lamentacio beate Marie* (*Ms* 1003–12). Given the contents and themes of *Mg*, there is no doubt that this is a meditative text in the style of the Rosary which was composed for the instruction of monks, or perhaps clerics, on devotional matters relating to the Virgin, especially the recitation of the *Ave Maria* and meditation on the joys and sorrows in the lives of Mary and her Son. *Mg* was written with a male monastic audience in mind and the poet added motifs and altered parts of the *Planctus siue lamentacio* that did not suit his audience, particularly the references to a female monastic audience, and his strictly didactic purpose (see further Wrightson 1997a and 1997b).

Also preserved in AM 713 on ff. 83–87 is a set of two Marian miracle stories, *Vitnisvísur af Maríu* (*VM*), about a young woman who enlists the help of the Virgin to get her fiancé back, a version of the 'Jilted Fiancée' story, and *Maríuvísur II* (*MvII*), an Icelandic version of a popular miracle tale about a child who is brought back to life known as 'Child Revived'.[1] Unlike *Mg* and the *Planctus Mariae* genre, which is by its very nature subdued and serious, these miracle poems are both entertaining and edifying. Like many collections or sets of miracles or legends of the saints in western Europe, the miracle stories in this edition had the dual purpose of entertaining monastic audiences in the refectory and of providing suitable exemplary material for homilies.

The remaining two miracle tales in this edition, *Maríuvísur I* (*MvI*), a very popular story about an allegation of incest between a mother-in-law and her son-in-law, aptly called 'Mother-in-law and Son-in-law', and *Maríuvísur III* (*MvIII*), about a drunken and unchaste cleric entitled 'Ave on the Tongue', are preserved together with *VM* and *MvII* as a set on ff. 10v–14r (*VM* and *MvI–II*) and 15v–16v (*MvIII*) in AM 721. On ff. 14r–15r and 15r–15v, however, occur two poems, *Brúðkaupvísur* (Jón Helgason 1936–38, II 127–36;

---

[1] This title, and those of *MvI* and *MvIII*, are the English versions of the titles assigned to these particular miracle stories in scholarship on the Marian miracle collections. See Wrightson 1997c for a discussion of the change of title of the miracle story told in *VM* from Ole Widding's 'Untrue Lover' to the present editor's 'Jilted Fiancée'. For more information on the contents of and background to both these poems and *MvI* and *MvIII*, see Wrightson 1994 and 1995.

Jón Þorkelsson 1888, 98) and *Allra postola minnisvísur* respectively, which are not considered to be part of this set of Marian skaldic miracles and are not included in this edition. *Allra postola minnisvísur* can be easily excluded on thematic grounds, since it is not a Marian miracle poem. Although *Brúðkaupvísur* is a skaldic poem about a miracle of the Virgin Mary, it is not included here because it was most likely composed in the mid or late fifteenth century, considerably later than the poems in this volume and almost certainly by a different poet.

For the past hundred years since Bernhard Kahle first edited these poems, *VM* and *MvI–III* have been viewed as a set of Marian miracles that stands apart from any other such texts, including *Brúðkaupvísur*. Considering all the evidence put forth by the first editor of *VM* and *MvI–III*, and in 1911 by Hans Sperber, it is possible and indeed likely that these poems were composed by one and the same poet and should be grouped together, without *Brúðkaupvísur*, as they are in the present edition. *Brúðkaupvísur*, although similar in subject-matter to *VM* (both tell of a dispute between a fiancé and fiancée), does not belong to this group.

As is the case with a great many texts from the Middle Ages, the authors of these fourteenth-century poems remain anonymous, perhaps as they were meant to be. There is no explicit identification of the poets in the texts themselves, nor is there any known external evidence. As Hans Schottmann has pointed out (1973, 349) regarding the miracle poems, an observation which may also be applied to *Mg*, 'weder die Überlieferung noch die Gedichte selbst gestatten über allgemeine Erwägungen hinaus Schlüsse auf die Autoren oder die Bedingungen, under denen ihre Verse lebten'.

From internal evidence in *Mg* we know that the poet, whoever he was, was a member of a monastery. In stanza 42 the poet reveals that he will hear the five joys of the Virgin and the Ave Maria and then he will teach and recite these words to *lærðir menn*, that is, monks. In addition, the didactic theme running throughout the poem (for example, 23.7–8, 31.7–8, 40.1–8 and 50.1–3) suggests it was the product of a monastic culture (Wrightson 1997a and 1997b). There is internal evidence pointing to one author for the four miracle poems. Kahle (1898, 17) and Sperber (1911, xi) both believed that *VM* and *MvI–III* were composed by the same poet and offered supporting evidence based mainly on similarity in the treatment of the subject matter, the subject matter itself (Marian miracles), diction, and the invocation of *Andréas* which occurs in all four poems.[1]

Schottmann (1973, 352–53), however, examined the evidence put forward by Kahle and Sperber and rejected the notion of single authorship on the grounds that 'keins der Argumente besitzt . . . wesentliches Gewicht'. In a similar vein, Finnur Jónsson pointed out (1920–24, III 17 n. 5) that 'ejendommeligt for dette digt og de 3 første [*VM* and *MvI–III*] er, at forfatterne påkalder Andreas. At slutte deraf, at de alle er digtede af en og samme mand, er overilet'. While this is sensible, especially if this invocation alone is used as evidence for single authorship, and while Schottmann's rejection of single authorship is well argued, the occurrence of an invocation to *Andréas* in all four poems is striking. The two obvious reasons why the poet would have invoked this saint are, first, that he himself was called Andréas, which is first recorded as a personal name in the thirteenth century (Cormack 1994, 79), and, second, that he may well have been a member of a monastery or church dedicated to the saint, as Kahle suggested (1898, 17). If these poems were composed by four different poets the chances of them all having been in either or both of these situations must be small.

It is also possible that the invocation to *Andréas* may be nothing more than formulaic. These invocations occur consistently in the second stanza, are the only references to *Andréas* in each poem, and are not found in the prose analogues in the miracle collections in *Ms*. This aside, however, the remaining internal evidence of similarities between these poems as put forth by Kahle and Sperber points to single authorship and, despite the cautions of Finnur Jónsson and Schottmann, there is no evidence to the contrary. *VM* and *MvI–III* were most likely originally intended to be read as a set of Marian miracle poems connected not simply by their veneration of St Mary and their common subject matter, but also by their unusual invocation of St Andrew.

---

[1] The suggestion by Sperber that all four miracle stories are derived from the same Marian miracle collection is, however, improbable (see discussion and tables below on sources and analogues). His suggestion that the poems are schematically similar and therefore likely to have been composed by one and the same poet is also dubious as evidence for single authorship. Many of the features he points to are more properly assigned to the genre of miracle texts rather than the style of a particular poet.

Whoever the poets of *Mg, VM* and *MvI–III* were, there is no doubt that they were working in the latter part of the Middle Ages and produced what are now among the last of the medieval skaldic poems. When Finnur Jónsson compiled *Skj* (1908–15), he placed *Mg, VM* and *MvI–III* among those poems composed in the fourteenth century and in his *Den oldnorske og oldislandske litteraturs historie* (1920–24, III 16) he allowed for the possibility that these poems could have been composed a little later again, around the turn of the century. Jón Þorkelsson (1888, 41) also suggested as a date of composition 'enten tiden omkring eller efter år 1400' and Kahle (1898, 3) agreed with this, adding 'vielleicht noch vom Ende des 14. Jahrhunderts'.

Although there is no conclusive evidence for dating these poems, there is no doubt that on metrical, stylistic and linguistic grounds, *Mg, VM* and *MvI–III* were composed in the latter part of the Middle Ages. They are among the late Christian skaldic compositions, and the last of the skaldic verse, from the late fourteenth and early fifteenth centuries. Finnur Jónsson (1920–24, III 16) pointed to some evidence in the metre and language of these poems and other anonymous religious poems, saying that 'med fuld bestemthed hører dertil kun nogle digte, der er affattede i drotkvædet, hrynhent eller et afstumpet versemål, hvis sprogform også henviser til forholdsvis gammel tid'. In relation to *Mg*, Hans Schottmann (1973, 507–08) has identified and discussed its lexical and syntactic features, arguing that it properly belongs among the late skaldic poems.

The few linguistic features which can be used for dating these poems, that is, those features which can be assigned to the proposed time of composition *c.*1400 rather than the time of manuscript compilation *c.*1500–50, include vocabulary and metre. Like many other late medieval Icelandic religious poems, *Mg* shows signs of influence from the mid-fourteenth-century classic *Lilja* (*Skj* B, II 390–416). Take, for instance, the lexical correspondences between *Mg* 14.1–4, 28.3, 45.3, 47.4 and *Lilja* 49.1–4, 31.5, 1.7, 99.8, some of which are so close they are probably due to direct influence. The choice of metre for *Mg* was no doubt also influenced by the popular *Lilja* which, like *Mg*, is a *drápa* composed in *hrynhent*, also known as *liljulag*. The references to St Andrew at the beginning of the miracle poems *VM* and *MvI–III* support a late fourteenth-century composition date since the cult of this saint was well established by this period. The cult of St Andrew in Iceland is attested by the beginning of the fourteenth century and continues thereafter, although references to him are found as early as 1213 (Cormack 1994, 78–80).

Given that the composition of poetry in skaldic metre had largely died out during the course of the fourteenth century, it is unlikely that *Mg*, *VM* and *MvI–III* were composed much later than 1400. There is, however, so little evidence to go on that the most definite one can be is to say that these are late Christian skaldic poems from the fourteenth century, or, possibly the early fifteenth century. The situation is similar in relation to provenance. As already mentioned, there are numerous indications that the manuscripts in which these poems survive, AM 713 and AM 721, were compiled in the northern diocese of Hólar. The provenance of *Mg*, *VM* and *MvI–III* is, however, uncertain beyond saying that they were composed 'somewhere in Iceland'. The references to St Andrew and St Anne in the miracle poems, and for that matter the veneration of St Mary in all five poems, may point to a northern provenance given that some aspects of the cults of these saints had particular associations with the north of Iceland. On St Andrew and St Mary see Cormack 1994, 80 and 129, and for St Anne see further Wolf 1994, 872–73.

According to current dating, around 150 years passed before *Mg*, *VM* and *MvI–III* were copied into the vellum manuscripts in which they survive today, AM 713 and AM 721, and another 150–200 years later they were copied again into the paper manuscripts known as AM 711a 4to, AM 1032 4to, and AM 920 4to. At the beginning of the eighteenth century, AM 711a and AM 1032 were compiled for the famous Icelandic scholar in Denmark, Árni Magnússon, while AM 920 was written mainly by Steingrímur Þorsteinsson with some assistance from Þorvaldur Bjarnarson and Benedikt Gröndal in the nineteenth century (Kålund 1889–94, II 125–26, 262, 299–300). Judging by the frequent lexical similarities between the versions of *Mg*, *VM*, and *MvI–III* in AM 713 and AM 721 and these three paper manuscripts, there is little doubt that the scribes of the latter worked directly from the medieval codices.[1] As far as can be determined using extant evidence, the textual history of *Mg*, *VM*, and *MvI–III* in medieval Iceland, then, is as follows:

---

[1] It is possible, however, that the version of *Mg* in AM 920 may have been copied from another manuscript now lost, or that the scribes of AM 920 edited the poem themselves.

## Introduction

| Mg | VM | MvI–III |
|---|---|---|
| *Liber de passione Christi et doloribus et planctus Matris eius* (Latin prose analogue of *Mg*; *PL* 182: 1133–42 and Mushacke 1890, 41–53) 12th/13th c. Italian origin | | Numerous Latin and vernacular analogues of *MvI–III* (see below) |
| \*Derivative text(s) 12th/13th c. | | \*Derivative text(s) 12th/13th c. |
| *Planctus siue lamentacio beate Marie* (OI prose analogue of *Mg*; see *Ms* No. CXCIII pp. xv–xviii and 1003–12) 13th c. | *Ms* No. XXXVIII (88) pp. 298–306 (OI prose analogues of *VM*) | *Ms* No. 84 and LX, CLXXXI, XLV, pp. 277–79, 1201–04, 977–79, 604–08 (OI prose sources and analogues of *MvI–III*) 13th c. |

\*Derivative texts
13th/14th c.

Non-extant 14th c. mss.
(*Mg, VM, MvI–III*)

| AM 713 16th c. (*Mg, VM, MvII*) | | AM 721 16th c (*VM, MvI–III*) |
|---|---|---|
| AM 1032 18th c. (*Mg*) | AM 711a 18th c. (*VM, MvII*) | AM 1032 18th c. (*MvI, MvIII*) |

AM 920
(*Mg*) 19th c.

It is certain that the Latin *Liber de passione Christi* and the Old Icelandic *Planctus siue lamentacio beate Marie* are part of the textual history of *Mg*. That is, it is certain that in terms of structure, content and style *Mg* is so similar to these older texts that it must have been copied from a text or texts ultimately derived from the *Liber de passione Christi* via the vernacular *Planctus siue lamentacio beate Marie*. In fact, there are so many textual similarities between *Mg* and the *Planctus siue lamentacio beate Marie* that it is difficult not to conclude that the poet worked directly from either this very text as it is now preserved or a close parallel of it which is now not extant (Wrightson 1997a).

It is equally certain that *VM* is a miracle story unique to Old Icelandic manuscripts. If this story did originally have a source outside medieval Iceland there is no trace of it now. In the absence of non-Icelandic sources, and given that of the three versions of 'Jilted Fiancée' which survive down to the present century, the two prose texts *Ms* No. XXXVIII and 88 were written before the poem, it is likely that the *VM*-poet based his version, however loosely, on *Ms* No. XXXVIII and 88 (Wrightson 1994).

According to the seminal study by Adolfo Mussafia of the origins and development of Marian miracle collections in the Middle Ages, all such works can be traced back to just four Latin collections, which Mussafia (1886–98, III 55–61) designated *HM* (eleventh century, of unknown origin), *Elements-series* (eleventh century, of English origin), *TS* (twelfth-century, of English origin) and *Pez* (twelfth-century, probably of French origin; see also Crane 1925). The complete details of known sources and analogues for the miracle poems *MvI–III* are too extensive for the scope of this Introduction. Suffice to say, however, that the history of *MvII* and *MvIII* can be traced back as far as two of the earliest known collections identified above, *TS* and *Pez*. Unlike the tale of the jilted young woman in *VM*, the miracle stories contained in *MvI–III* are firmly rooted in the twelfth-, thirteenth- and fourteenth-century collections of northern France and England.

Although textual histories are notoriously difficult, if not impossible, to compile, the extant material currently available provides a sense of the background to *MvI–III*. Versions of 'Mother-in-law and Son-in-law', 'Child Revived' and 'Ave on the Tongue' eventually found their way to Iceland in the late twelfth and thirteenth centuries, to be copied into the Marian miracle collections now edited in *Ms*.

Subsequently these stories were transferred directly from these prose collections into the poetic renditions now surviving in *MvI* and *MvIII*, or, as is probably the case with *MvII*, indirectly from a non-extant derivative work based on these collections.

For the sake of brevity, the table below lists only those collections or works which fall into the direct line of descent from the earliest known versions of 'Mother-in-law and Son-in-law', 'Child Revived' and 'Ave on the Tongue' through to the composition of the Icelandic prose renditions of these tales in *Ms* and the poetic versions in *MvI–III*. Of the many other works which also contain analogues for *MvI–III*, which are not listed below, some are quite well known, such as *Les miracles de la sainte Vierge* by Gautier de Coincy (1857, 233–38), the *Speculum historiale* by Vincent of Beauvais (1624, IV, Bk. 7, 90) and the *Legenda aurea* by Jacobus a Voragine (1890, 594–95), all of which contain texts loosely analogous to *MvI*, as well as John of Garland's *Stella Maris* (1946, 96–97) where can be found a version of 'Child Revived' similar to that in *MvII*.

## Introduction

| MvI 'Mother-in-law and Son-in-law' | MvII 'Child Revived' | MvIII 'Ave on the Tongue' |
|---|---|---|
| *Auctarium Ursicampinum* Sigebert of Gembloux (*PL* 160:359,405) Latin source of *Ms* No. 84, 12th c. Northern France | *Pez* collection No. 24 (Crane 1925, 29–30) Latin source of *Ms* No. CLXXXI 12th c. Northern France | *TS* collection No. 8 (Neuhaus 1886, 58–60) Latin source of *Ms* No. XLV 12th c. England |

*Liber de Laude Sanctae Mariae*
Guibert de Nogent
(*PL* 156:564–68)
Latin analogue of *Ms*
No. LX, 12th c.
Northern France

\*Derivative text(s) 12th/13th c.　　\*Derivative text(s) 12th/13th c.　　\*Derivative text(s) 12th/13th c.

*Ms* No. 84 (pp. 277–79) OI source of *MvI* 13th c.

*Ms* No. LX (pp. 1201–04) OI analogue of *MvI* 13th c.

*Ms* No. CLXXXI (pp. 977–79) OI analogue of *MvII*, 13th c.

*Ms* No. XLV (pp. 604–08) OI source of *MvIII*, 13th c.

\*Derivative text(s) 13th/14th c.

Non-extant 14th c. mss.
(*MvI–III*)

Of the two medieval manuscripts which contain *Mg, VM* and *MvI–III*, AM 713 is the better preserved, with fewer lacunae and less general deterioration, more legible script, and, in relation to the poems in this edition, fewer scribal errors than AM 721. Unlike AM 721, AM 713 contains decorated capitals, some with animalia, at the beginning of the poems. For instance, the capital graph 'D' at the beginning of *MvII* has a fœtus-like quadruped inside it, the 'O' at the beginning of *Mg* has a man's face with a beard inside it (perhaps the face of the Lord or the scribe), and *Katrína drápa* opens with a large illuminated 'D' inside which is a bird. *Mg* also has other instances of illumination, namely the marginal crosses inserted next to the refrains in stanzas 16, 20, 24, 28, 32, and 36 probably for the purpose of marking a change of topic for meditation (see Wrightson 1997a, 290), and two dragons, one upside-down with its mouth open swallowing the word *minnast* in 41.4 (see the illustration on the cover of this edition) and the other consisting of the head only, again with the mouth open swallowing the last two graphs of the word *fúlir* in 50.7. In AM 721, at *VM* 6.4, there is a leaf (fol. 11) containing a part of *Af heilogum meyjum* (*Skj* A, II 526–39; B, II 582–97). This is probably due to a mistake in the ordering of the leaves when the manuscript was bound.

The dates of compilation of AM 713 and AM 721 are roughly the same, both having been compiled sometime in the first half of the sixteenth century. To be more precise than this is not possible, nor, therefore, was it possible to select the earlier manuscript as the base manuscript for this edition. Instead, the better preserved manuscript, AM 713, was used for *Mg*, which only survives in this manuscript, and *VM*, which is found in both AM 713 and AM 721 though in better condition in the former. *MvI–III*, however, were edited from AM 721, even though the middle poem, *MvII*, survives in AM 713, because these three miracle tales are preserved in AM 721 as a set just as they probably were in the 'original' fourteenth-century manuscript. A comparison between *MvII* as it is preserved in AM 713 and AM 721 shows that there are no real advantages to using the former manuscript in this case. The text in AM 713 is admittedly easier to read, being clearly written and well preserved, but the AM 721 text is legible enough and the manuscript is free of major lacunae in the section where this poem occurs.

These late fourteenth-century poems have been edited conservatively with as little emendation as possible and with normalised orthography in order to present them as they most likely would have looked when they were first rendered into Old Icelandic around 1400. The previous editions of these poems present either diplomatic texts, as is the case in Kahle 1898, or texts normalised to a thirteenth-century standard, as in Finnur Jónsson's edition, creating the false impression that these poems are older than they actually are. *Mg, VM* and *MvI–III* are among the last skaldic poems to have been written and to have survived as complete texts down to the present century. Their late fourteenth-century orthographical features, which can be gleaned from the manuscript texts, are part and parcel of that inheritance and ought to be preserved and in some instances restored.

The texts preserved in AM 713 and AM 721 present a reasonably consistent picture of late fourteenth-century orthography, consistent enough to produce normalised texts without major difficulties. Based on dominant forms, and in some cases metrical evidence, for instance, final *-ð* is preferred to *-t* in weakly stressed words like *það, að, ið* (definite article neuter), and other words with a final dental like neuter past participles and adjectives. The voicing of final *-k* to *-g* is adopted (for example, *eg, og, mig, þig, sig, mjög*). Although *-vó-/-vo-* is preferred to *-vá-* (for instance, *svó, kvón, vóndr, vón*) following the majority manuscript spellings, both *-vó-* and *-vo-* are equally supported by rhyme, making an arbitrary decision necessary (*-vó-*). Initial *v-* does not appear before an originally rounded vowel in the majority of cases (namely, *urðu* and *orðinn MvI* 8.7, 18.3 and *MvII* 9.2), and is absent even where it ought to appear for alliteration in *MvII* 4.7 (then restored in this edition). Accordingly, manuscript *Uoxx* in *MvI* 6.1 is presented as *Óx*. The *rs > s* (or *ss*) reduction is maintained (for instance, *fyst, vest, vess, þassem*), and in the few cases where it does not occur in the manuscripts after a short vowel (such as *huerssu Mg* 29.2) and in *kærst* (*MvI* 3.6, where it is required by the rhyme) it is silently adopted.

The occurrence of *-je-* (or *-ie-*) in the manuscripts is much higher than that of *-e-* for *-é-* (96 occurrences of *-je-/-ie-* as opposed to 43 of *-e-*), and the former is adopted throughout (for example, *mjer, þjer, hjer, rjeð, ljet*). *Dróttinn* is preferred to *drottinn* on the basis of rhyme, though they are not distinguished in the manuscripts. Where appropriate manuscript *au, ð* and *ǫ* are normalised to *ö*, for instance, in *öðlingr, sönn, gjörðir, öllum, sögðu, mönnum* etc. Both *æ* and *œ* appear as *æ* in the manuscripts and are not distinguished in the edition. Similarly, *gjöra*, not *gera*, is used consistently in both manuscripts and so in the edition. The diphthongisation and lengthening of vowels before *-ng*, however, reflected in the consistent manuscript spelling of *eingi* for *engi*, for instance, is not indicated in this edition, since it would result in a large number of words being spelled differently from the standard spellings of both Old and Modern Icelandic. The form *eptir* as opposed to *eftir* occurs consistently, and the only occurence of *aftr* (*MvII* 18.7) is silently changed to *aptr*. The dominant form of the feminine third person pronoun is *hún* rather than *hón*.

All manuscript occurrences of the preposition *fyr* are abbreviated $f^i$, though the adverbs *fyrr* and *fyrri* appear in full as *fyr Mg* 2.8 and 38.4 and *fyrre VM* 11.4 and *MvI* 24.6. The short *fyr*, rather than *firir* or *fyrir*, is supported in the majority of cases by metrical evidence. The middle voice suffix *-st/-zt* occurs far more frequently in the manuscripts than *-z* and is adopted throughout. The instances in the manuscripts of Modern Icelandic *-i* for present and preterite first person subjunctive (and indicative of weak verbs), instead of Old Icelandic *-a*, are maintained without comment in the textual notes (for example, *unni Mg* 25.5, *skyldi Mg* 37.7, *fæddi Mg* 44.2). There are, of course, exceptions to these rules and in some instances a non-dominant form is used for metrical reasons.

Compound words have been joined, without hyphenation, whether or not they are so joined in the manuscripts, in most cases reflecting the usual practice in dictionaries of Old Icelandic. Hyphenation of compound words or kennings only occurs where alliteration requires separation of the compound elements, such as, *hús-frú MvI* 8.3, *silki-Sólu MvI* 12.5, and *bragar-bót MvII* 1.3. Strophe division and punctuation reflect the scribal practices of the manuscripts, which are, for the most part, consistent in the use of the double virgula at the end of each stanza, and, in the case of *Mg*, the single virgula at the end of each half stanza. In this edition, each half stanza is normally marked by a semi-colon (or colon, if not a full stop) and each full stanza by a full stop, except where the sense continues over the stanza or half-stanza break (e.g. *Vm* 5.8, *Mv II* 6.4, 15.8, 18.4, *MvIII* 12.4). The scribes also consistently used a punctus at the end of each stanza line, which is not reflected in the edition. For ease of reference the stanzas and lines within them are numbered, which is, of course, not a feature of the manuscripts. The base-manuscript and variant manuscripts for each text in this edition are identified at the beginning of each poem. The *stef* (refrains) are marked by vertical lines in the margins.

The footnotes consist of both textual and explanatory notes, including explanations of emendations made in this edition and, where possible, those made in past editions. For the sake of brevity in the footnotes, abbreviations are used for manuscripts.

Square brackets [ ] are used to indicate graphs which appear to have been in the base manuscript at one point but are now illegible due to damage or wear. These graphs are supplied from the manuscripts listed at the beginning of each poem, or from a previous edition as noted in the footnotes. Pointed brackets ‹ › are used for graphs which were omitted by the scribe for whatever reason, and are now supplied from other manuscripts or editions. Graphs altered from the reading of the base manuscripts are italicised and accompanied by explanatory comment in the footnotes. An asterisk indicates that one or more graphs have been omitted from the edition. The principle of emendation, as already mentioned, has been to provide better sense and grammatical structure only where the existing text is incomprehensible as it stands and where a suitable alternative reading is possible.

In a great number of cases, Finnur Jónsson and Kock emend the text to increase or reduce the syllable count to fit in with their understanding of the particular metre used in each poem (*hrynhent* in *Mg*, *dróttkvætt* in *VM* and *MvI*, and *hálfhnept* in *MvII–III*; see further Kahle 1898, 3–4, and Sperber 1911, v–ix). On the whole, their approach is not adopted in the present edition since the apparent inconsistencies do not necessarily mean that the scribes have represented the author's text wrongly. Many of these late poems tend to relax the strict requirements of the usual rules for *aðalhending* and *skothending*, and occasionally incorporate end-rhyme (for instance, *MvIII* 1.1–2, 25.1–3), and *skothending* is sometimes lacking. The pattern of internal rhyme in *MvIII* 28 has a variation similar to those in *Háttatal* st. 47 and 48. Cf. also *MvI* 27.1–2.

## Drápa af Maríugrát

*AM 713 ff. 123–129; AM 920 ff. 205r–211r; AM 1032 ff. 57r–79v.*
*This text is from AM 713.*

1   Orðin gef þú mjög til mærðar
    minn lausnari skáldi þínu
    þinnar móður mildi kunnrar,
4   mála örr, og hjálpa sálu;
    einn sýndir þú Áróns frænda,
    aldri brann þó viðrinn kaldi;
    lát þú kveikjast loginn dróttins
8   leiptra skríns í hjarta mínu.

2   Gjarna vilda eg hilmis hlýrna
    hróðr dýrligan að finna móður;
    vænti eg hryggr að verkann þiggi
4   vandað sæti heilags anda;
    umgaupnandi allrar skepnu,
    orðið gef sem eg mun krefja,
    eitt eða tvau, svó að yrkja mætti eg
8   enn sem fyrr til dýrðar henni.

My Redeemer, generous with speech, give the words to your skald very much for the praise of your mother, renowned for kindness, and save his soul; you showed Aaron's kinsman [Moses] one, yet the cold tree never burnt; let the flame of the lord of the shrine of lightnings [heaven; God; the Holy Spirit] be kindled in my heart.

I eagerly wished to compose a glorious praise-poem about the mother of the ruler of sun and moon [Christ; the Virgin]; sorrowful, I hope that the beautifully made repository of the Holy Spirit [the Virgin] accepts this work; you who hold all creation in the palm of your hand, give me the word, one or two, which I shall crave so that I might compose again as before to her glory.

**1.4** *örr*] *aur* taken with *mála* to form a kenning for poetry meaning '"Erde der Reden" oder . . . "Flüssigkeit der Reden" = Poesie?' BK (103). **1.5** *einn*] object of *sýndir* with *við* 'tree' understood (see HS n.). It refers to the burning bush (Exod. 3: 2), which is a type of the Virgin; just as the bush burned but was not consumed, so the Virgin conceived Jesus but did not lose her virginity.
**1.7** *loginn*] HS; *lõginn* all mss.; *lögin* Skj B; *lágina* EK.   *dróttins*] drottinn 920.

3   Er svó komið, að ætla eg meira,
    öðlingr, þjer, bjartra röðla
    ítarligr, er öllum veitir
4   yndis gnógt, ef hafna syndum;
    verð eg mjer að öngu orði
    einhlítr, nema þið vilið beina
    sannr Guð o[g e]n sælsta móðir;
8   s[ýta mun eg og] iðra[st lýta].

4   Al[lopt] beiddi enn elskufulli
    Augústínus m[eð bænum fögrum]
    Maríu öllu fegri og frægri
4   fyldr af [spekt að vitrast] skyldi;
    kunna vildi af harmi hennar
    hann að skýra [þjóð eð sanna]
    þeim, er hún fekk, að þengill himna
8   þoldi nauð og písl t[il] da[uða].

So the time has come, magnificent prince of the bright sun and moon [Christ], that I intend more for you who give an abundance of delight to all if they give up their sins; I cannot become self-sufficient with any word unless you both, true god and the most blessed mother, are willing to assist me; I shall grieve over and repent of my faults.

With beautiful prayers, the charitable Augustine, filled with wisdom, very often asked Mary, more beautiful and more famous than anything, to manifest herself; he wanted to be able to explain to people the truth about that sorrow of hers which she received when the prince of the heavens [Christ] endured distress and torture to death.

3.7 *og e-*] 1032; *ok hi-* 920. 3.8 *-ýta mun eg og*] 1032 and 920. *-st lýta*] 1032 and 920. 4.1 *-lopt*] 1032 and 920. 4.2 *-eð bænum fögrum*] 1032; *-ed bænum at vitrast* 920 with *fögrum* after *bænum* crossed out. 4.3 *öllu*] *ollum* 920. 4.4 *spekt að vitrast*] 1032 and 920. 4.6 *þjóð*] 713 illegible, only a lobe is visible, possibly part of a 'b' or a 'þ'; *bioð* 1032, 920 and BK, i.e. *bjóð n.* 'tray, small table' does not fit semantically; *boð* BK n. with *skýra*, referring to the Virgin's sorrow at the foot of the cross; *þióð* HS, Skj B and EK makes the best sense ('he wished to be able to explain to people the truth about her sorrow'). *eð sanna*] 1032 and 920. 4.8 *písl*] *pislir* 920. *-il*] 1032 and 920. *-uða*] 1032 and 920. 5.1–2 *göfugr gætir góðra klerka*] Saint Augustine. 5.2 *-óður*] 1032

5   'Veitum lof,' kvað göfugr gætir
    góðra klerka, 'dróttins m[óður],
    l[ær]ðir menn og lýða ferðir,
4   laugum brár og kinnr í tárum.'
    [Mætust] bið eg að mjer skuli veita
    móðir dróttins alt eð góða,
    jungfrú [glöð, er] Jesús fæddi,
8   enn að lýsa heiminn þenna.

6   Guðs son drakk þín brjóstin bæði,
    blessuð mær, að tóktu að færa
    tírargjörn af tung[u] fornri
4   taldra daga í musterið valda;
    máttugt víf og m[óðir] dróttins
    mætan ofrar himna gæti;
    son þinn taldi Símeón þenna
8   sannan Guð og en helga Anna.

The noble guardian of good clerics [bishop] said, 'Let us, learned and lay people, give praise to the mother of the Lord; let us bathe our eyelashes and cheeks in tears.' I pray that the most excellent mother of the Lord, joyous Virgin, who gave birth to Jesus, shall grant me all that is good in order to illumine this world again.

The son of God drank from both your breasts, blessed Virgin, until in accordance with the Old Testament you, eager for glory, went and brought the ruler into the temple after the fixed number of days; mighty woman and mother of the Lord, you offer the excellent keeper of the heavens [Christ]; Simeon and the holy Anna reckoned this son of yours the true God.

and 920. **5.3** *lærðir*] all eds.; *l..ða* 713, 920 and 1032. The nom. pl. ending is required, since the adjective appears to belong with *menn*. *menn*] *manna* 920. **5.5** *mætust*] 1032 and 920. **5.7** *glöð er*] 1032 and 920. *Jesús*] *Jesum* 920. **6.3** *tungu*] 1032 and 920. *fornri*] with *tungu* 'old language' (i.e. the Mosaic law in Lev. 12: 2–8, concerning the process of purification for women after childbirth). **6.5** *-óðir*] 1032 and 920. **6.5–8** For the corresponding gospel account, see Luke 2: 25–38. **6.8** *Anna*] HS, Skj B and EK; *anda* all mss. *Anna* is written above *anda* 713 and 1032 in eighteenth- or nineteenth-century hands, and is the preferred reading on semantic and theological grounds. It is unlikely that *anda* could refer to the Holy Spirit, and it must be a scribal error.

7   Flýðir þú með son þinn síðan
    svanninn undan Heródes fundi,
    vóðamaðrinn v[il]di dauða
 4  vinna honum ef næði að finna;
    fróni á í faðmi þínum
    fögnuðinn bartu allra brag[na]
    full miskunnin frægri öllu,
 8  fæddir María hann og klæddir.

8   Branda hlynr má engi undra,
    Augústínus rjeð slíkt að tína
    lýða sveit, að mær og móðir
 4  mildum lausnara fylgja vildi:
    'Treysti eg því og trúi það, prestar,
    tiginn valdr, að skildist aldri
    ágætt sprund, er júðar píndu,
 8  eingason við, himna þengil.'


Afterwards, woman, you fled with your son to escape an encounter with Herod; that terrible man wanted to bring death to Him if he managed to find Him; on earth, you, our full mercy, more famous than anything, bore the joy of all mankind [Christ] in your arms; you, Mary, fed Him and clothed Him.

No maple-tree of swords [man] can wonder that the virgin and mother wanted to accompany the kind Redeemer; Augustine chose to say this to a host of people: 'Priests, I, a noble ruler, rely upon it and believe it that the excellent woman never parted from her only son, the prince of the heavens [Christ], when the Jews tormented him.'


**7.1–4** For the corresponding gospel account, see Mt. 2: 13–14.  **7.3** *-il-*] 1032 and 920.  **7.6** *-na*] 1032 and 920.  **7.7** Cf. the almost identical line 22.3.  **8.5** *það*] though *trúa* normally takes the dat., Fr. (s.v. *trúa* 3) has examples of the acc.; otherwise *það* could perhaps be taken with *ágætt sprund*, line 7; *kvað* Skj B and EK.   *prestar*] i.e. the priests whom St Augustine is addressing; *presta* HS n., Skj B and EK.  **8.6** *tiginn valdr*] may also be vocative.  **9.3** *drottin*] refers to St Augustine; *drottins* HS, Skj B and EK, part of the kenning

9   Blíð og fögr sem björt og tigin,
    brúðrin sæt og drottning mætust,
    drottin kom með dýrð að hitta,
  4 dægra sætis, munka gæti;
    sýndist móðir sunnu grundar
    siklings þá, með ljósi miklu,
    ítarlig, með ilm og sætu,
  8 Augústínó, í skrúða fögrum.

10  María kvaddi mítra stýri:
    'Mætr vinr ertu engla gætis,'
    miskunnar, 'og minn að sönnu.'
  4 Móðir talar svó við blessuð fróðan:
    'Biðr þú það sem öngva aðra
    áðr hefir fýst á grýttu láði;
    háleit skal eg með helgum vilja
  8 hylli lýðs þinn gjarna fylla.

The sweet bride and most excellent queen of the seat of days and nights [heaven; the Virgin], gracious and beautiful as well as luminous and noble, came with glory to meet the lord, the keeper of monks [bishop]; then the magnificent mother of the prince of the sun-field [heaven; Christ; the Virgin] showed herself to Augustine with great light, with perfume and sweetness, in beautiful apparel.

Mary greeted the controller of mitres [bishop]: 'You are a valuable friend of the keeper of angels [Christ] and mine in truth.' So the blessed Mother of mercy speaks to the learned one: 'You pray for what no others have desired before on this stony earth; being sublime I together with the holy favourer of mankind [Christ] shall willingly fulfil your wish.

*brúðrin drottins dægra sætis.* **9.4** *munka gæti]* St Augustine. **9.8** *fögrum] fögur* 920. **10.1** *mítra stýri]* St Augustine. **10.4** *við]* taken with *fróðan.* *við blessuð] blezut vid* 920. **10.5** *það]* all mss., *þess* Skj B and EK; but though *biðja* normally takes a gen. object, Fr. has some examples of the acc. **10.7** *háleit]* referring to the Virgin, *háleitr* Skj B. *helgum] helgun* HS, taking the abbreviation above the *g* for *-un.* **10.8** *þinn]* with *vilja; þíns* EK taken with *lýðs.*

## 6 Maríugrátr

11 Grætiligt er að inna ýtum
angr og harm, er eg fekk enn langa
frjádag þann, er fylki sunnu
4 fleinhristendr á krossinn nistu;
síðan, er mig heim á himna
heilagr leiddi skepnu deilir,
englar fyr mjer sætt lof sungu
8 síð og árla, en lokið er stríði.

12 Föstudaginn, með frægum Kristi
fyst rjeð eg, við tveimr systrum
mínum og svó Magdaljena
4 María, að fylgja dróttni vórum;
Guðs son er til dráps og dauða
dæmdi Pilátús, lýðs að vilja,
júðar lei[ddu] hann [og] hæddu,
8 hlógu og glöddust, þar með slógu.

It is distressing to tell people about the grief and sorrow which I experienced on that Good Friday when the shaft-shakers [men] nailed the king of the sun [Christ] on the cross; afterwards, when the holy dealer of destiny [Christ] led me home into the heavens, angels sang delightful praise before me late and early and distress was brought to an end.

On that Friday, beside famous Christ, together with my two sisters and likewise Mary Magdalene, I first determined to accompany our Lord; when Pilate sentenced the son of God to slaughter and death at the wish of the people, the Jews led Him and mocked Him, they laughed and were glad; they struck Him also.

**12.7** -ddu] 1032. og] 1032 and 920. **13.1** lausnara] 1032, omitted 920. sjálfan] 1032; sjálfur 920. l-] 1032 and 920. **13.3** hjálpar] hjálpir 920. herðum stólpa] omitted 920. -ólp-] 1032. **13.4** hölda trje] 1032 and 920. það] þa 920. **13.6** -dum tók eg] lacuna 920. t-] 1032. eg kro-] 1032 (kro- 920). **14.1** Gyðing-] lacuna 920. Gyðinga-] 1032. **14.2** á] honum under-

## Maríugrátr 7

13 Lausn[ara sjálfan l]opts og himna
   leit eg vísliga bera til píslar
   hjálpar sjer á herðum st[ólp]a,
 4 [hölda trje], það er júðar völdu;
   ljetta eg honum sem mest eg mátta,
   mundum [t]ók [eg kro]ssinn undir,
   helgum Guði var eg fús að fylgja
 8 fram mínum til staðarins pínu.

14 [Gyðing]afólk með grimd og háði
   gengu að og hræktu á lengi,
   [bundu m]eiddu börðu og hæddu
 4 bæði mann og Guð vórn sannan;
   virðar grimmir [vísi d]ýrðar
   völdu allskyns písla fjölda;
   bjart gjör eg að mitt brjóst [og her]ðar
 8 bar það angr, að eg mátta ei ganga.

Unmistakably I saw the Redeemer of the sky and heavens [Christ] Himself carry to His torture the pillar of salvation [cross], the tree of humankind [cross], on His shoulders, which the Jews had chosen; I relieved Him as best I could, I put my hands under the cross, I was eager to accompany my holy God on to the place of punishment.

The Jewish people went up with cruelty and scorn and spat on Him for a long time; they bound, injured, beat and mocked the one who is both man and our true God; fierce men chose a multitude of all kinds of tortures for the prince of glory [Christ]; I make this clear that my breast and shoulders bore that sorrow to the extent that I could not walk.

stood; omitted 920. **14.3** *bundu*] 1032. *m-*] 1032 and 920. **14.5** *vísi d-*] 1032. *-ýrðar*] *-yrðir* 920. **14.7** *bjart*] *breitt* 920. *og her-*] 1032 and 920. *herðar*] refers implicitly to Christ's shoulders bearing the cross as well as to the Virgin's shoulders bearing her sorrow.

15  Halir á krossinn hilmi* sólar
     hófu, en keyrðu í ristr og lófa
     stinnoddaða af stáli gadda;
  4  stórlig öngvit á mig fóru:
     hvergi mátti eg fyr harmi og sorgum
     hræra mig, sem dauð eg væra,
     angri fyld og lá eg svó lengi,
  8  laugaðig brár og kinnr í tárum.'

16  Stillir, heyrðu, stjörnuhallar,
     stef væri eg þjer búinn að færa
     einkar mætt, ef eg má hitta
  4  orðagnógt að vilja dróttins.
     Öllum hlutum er æðri og sælli
     eilífligastr skepnu deilir,
     honum sje dýrð á himni og jörðu;
  8  hann er hærri en gjörvalt annað.

Men lifted the ruler of the sun [Christ] onto the cross and drove stiff-pointed spikes of steel into his insteps and palms; a great state of unconsciousness overcame me; I could not move myself at all because of affliction and sorrows as if I were dead and I lay in this way, filled with grief, for a long time; I bathed my eyelashes and cheeks in tears.'
 Listen, controller of the star-hall [heaven; God], I would be ready to bring you a very excellent refrain if I can come upon an abundance of words by the will of the Lord. More noble and blessed than all things is the most eternal dealer of destiny [God]; glory to Him in heaven and on earth; He is higher than everything else.

**15.1** *hilmi*] 920, BK n., Skj B and EK; *hilmir* 713, 1032 and HS, but an acc. object is required. **15.6** *væra*] *væri* 920. **15.8** *laugaðig*] *laugaði* 920. **16.2** *færa*] so 1032; altered to *hefja* in margin in an eighteenth- or nineteenth-century

17   Maríu orð er mörg að skýra
     mjög grætilig þjóð, en sæta,
     máttuligrar móður dróttins,
4    meir enn hrein rjeð slíkt að greina:
     'Því líkast var mjer sem mækir
     mundi bjartr í gegnum hjarta
     standa mitt, er eg Jesús undir
8    allar leit með benja sveita.

18   Hjálpar fúss, er hjekk á krossi,
     hýrliga til mín engla stýrir
     leit og bað mig ljetta gráti:
4    "Lítumst við á deginum þriðja;
     efalaus vertu, að upp mun eg rísa,"
     öðlingr talar svó bjartra röðla,
     "móðir trú því mín, af dauða,
8    minnig vertu, að þig skal eg finna."'

There are very many distressing words of Mary, the mighty mother of the Lord, to explain to people and the virtuous woman proceeded to tell still more of such things: 'It was just as if a shining sword should stick through my heart when I saw all Jesus's wounds in addition to the blood from His injuries.

Eager to help, the ruler of angels [Christ] looked at me kindly as he hung on the cross and asked me to stop weeping: "We will see each other on the third day; be without doubt that I will rise up," so speaks the prince of the bright sun and moon [Christ], "believe it, my mother, from death; be mindful that I shall meet you."'

hand 713; *hefja* is adopted in HS, Skj B and EK, but is not significantly better than the original ms. reading.   **17.1** *er*]   all mss., *eru* EK; but the verb is impers. and *orð* is the object of *skýra*.

19  Píndr var Kristr barðr og bundinn,
    blóðið stökk á Jesús móður;
    gjörvöll leit þá sæl og sætust
 4  sárin dróttins blessuð María;
    enskis manns fær orkað tunga
    syndugs nein fyr þjóð að greina
    stríð og eymd er mær og móðir
 8  *mætust bar þá engla gætis.

20  Ítarligr er öllum betri
    engla grundar blessaðr þengill;
    lýðr er allr leiptra stillis
 4  lofi dýrligstu skyldr að ofra.
    Öllum hlutum er æðri og sælli
    eilífligastr skepnu deilir,
    honum sje dýrð á himni og jörðu;
 8  hann er hærri en gjörvalt annað.

Christ was punished, beaten and bound, blood spurted on the mother of Jesus; then the holy and sweetest, blessed Mary saw the entire wounds of the Lord; the tongue of no sinful person can manage to describe before people the grief and misery which the most excellent virgin and mother of the keeper of angels [Christ; the Virgin] bore then.

The magnificent, blessed prince of the ground of angels [heaven; Christ] is better than all; all people have a duty to extol the most glorious praise of the controller of lightnings [God]. More noble and blessed than all things is the most eternal dealer of destiny [God]; glory to Him in heaven and on earth; He is higher than everything else.

**19.6** *syndugs*] does not alliterate, yet if it is to be replaced with a disyllabic word beginning with a vowel, the word can only be guessed at: *iarðligs* HS, *andar* Skj B, *yndis* EK. The ms. reading, though not ideal metrically, is perfectly clear and legible as well as being acceptable semantically and grammatically.
**19.8** All mss. (and BK) have *er* at the beginning of this line, but it is clearly

21 'Þegnar gjörðu þröngva og harða
    þyrnis kórónu stilli hlýrna;
    buðu honum þá með blygð og háði
  4 bannaðir Júðar slíkt og annað;
    hjarta mitt, er eg horfða á þetta,
    hrærast tók, ‹því› son minn kæri
    dýrligr virði miklu meira
  8 mína eymd en píslir sínar.'

22 Bragnings talar svó brúðrin signuð
    byrjar hvólfs af sinni álfu
    full miskunnar fr[æg]ri a[llri]
  4 fljóða sveit við skírðar þjóðir:
    'Hvar viti þjer það er harm ber m[eiri
    heimli]gt fljóð en dróttins móðir?
    Að sönnu er mjer sem stálið stinna
  8 [standi bjart í gegnum hjart]a.

'The soldiers made a tight and hard crown of thorn for the controller of sun and moon [Christ]; then the cursed Jews offered this and other things to Him with shame and scorn; my heart began to be moved when I looked at this because my dear glorious son regarded my misery much more than His own torments.'

For her part the blessed bride of the prince of the wind-vault [heaven; Christ], merciful, more famous than all womankind, speaks thus to baptized people: 'Where do you know of that mortal woman who bears greater sorrow than the mother of the Lord? Truly it is as if the shining, stiff steel is stuck through my heart.

redundant; omitted in HS, Skj B and EK. **20.5–8** not written out in full (cf. p. xxvi). **21.5** *horfða*] *horfði* 920. **21.6** *því*] 920, omitted 1032, *enn* HS, Skj B and EK. **22.3** *-æg-*] 1032 and 920. *-llri*] 1032. **22.5** *meiri*] *Maria* 920. *-eiri*] 1032. **22.6** *heimli-*] 1032; *heila-* 920. **22.8** *standi . . . hjart-*] 1032 and 920.

23 \*Kristnum á sig lýð til lausnar
lofðung⟨r⟩ hauðrs tók písl og dauða
sólar, tók að sínum vilja
4 syndalauss með fullu yn[di;
ætti] Guði að þakka þetta
þjóðin öll,' kvað dróttins móðir,
'lærðir menn t[il lofs og] dýrðar
8 löngum prýddi hann ýms*um* söngu*m*.'

24 Guðs sonar minnist dráps og dauða
dróttin skírð við hry[gð og ótta]
f[rjá]dag hvern, m[eð vóndra] vörnun
4 verka, í söng og tárum sterkum.
Öllum hlutum er æðri og sælli
eilífligastr skepnu deilir,
honum sje dýrð á himni og jörðu;
8 hann er hærri en gjörvalt annað.

The prince of the land of the sun [heaven; Christ] took torment and death upon Himself for the salvation of Christian people; being sinless He took it by His own will with complete delight; all people ought to thank God for this,' said the mother of the Lord, 'learned people have adorned Him for a long time with various songs to His praise and glory.'

Every Friday let baptized people remember the killing and death of the Son of God with sorrow and fear, in song and sincere tears, with abstinence from evil deeds. More noble and blessed than all things is the most eternal dealer of destiny [God]; glory to Him in heaven and on earth; He is higher than everything else.

**23.1** All mss. have *fyr* at the beginning of this line; omitted in Skj B and EK. It is unnecessary both syntactically and metrically, and no other stanza in *Mg* begins with a preposition or other unstressed word. **23.2** *lofðungr*] 920 and Skj B; *löfðung* 713, 1032, BK, HS and EK; but a nom. subject is required. *tók*] the repetition of this word in line 3 emphasises the theme of Christ taking His own death willingly (*að sínum vilja* 23.3, cf. 39.7). **23.4** -*di*] 1032 and 920. **23.5** *ætti*] 1032. **23.7** -*il lofs og*] 1032 and 920. **23.8** *hann ýmsum söngum*] BK n. and HS; *honum ymsa saungua* Skj B and EK; *hann ýmsa*

25  Heyrið það er heilög María
   hjálpar gladdan Jesúm kvaddi:
   'Skjöldungr, lát mig skilja aldri,
 4 skýja hauðrs, við þig lífs nje dauðan;
   er það vón að unni eg meira
   eingetnum syni, Kristi hreinum,
   en þau sprund er ala með syndum
 8 eldi sín með harm og pínu.'

26  Máttugr anzar mána stjettar
   móður sinni stillir þjóðar:
   'Ítrust, skal þín, jungfrú, gæta
 4 Jón postuli meðan lifir á fróni;
   grát eigi þú, móðir mætust,
   mína kvöl nje sára pínu;
   líknar fúss mun eg leysa í þessu
 8 lýð og heim,' kvað engla prýðir.

Listen to how holy Mary addressed Jesus made glad by salvation: 'Prince of the land of clouds [heaven; Christ], never let me be separated from you alive or dead; it is to be expected that I loved my only son, virtuous Christ, more than those women who give birth to their offspring in sin with sorrow and torment.'

The mighty controller of the beings of the moon-path [heaven; angels; Christ] answers his mother: 'Most glorious Virgin, John the Apostle shall take care of you while you live on earth; most excellent mother, weep not for my torment or my painful suffering; eager for mercy, I will redeem mankind and the world by this,' said the adorner of angels [Christ].

*saungua* all mss. must be emended to eliminate one of the two direct objects of *prýddi*; either emendations above are suitable, the first perhaps making better sense: 'learned people have adorned Him for a long time with various songs to [His] praise and glory'. **24.1** *sonar*] *sonur* 920. **24.2** *skírð*] *skyra* 920. *-gð og ótta*] 1032 and 920. **24.3** *-rjá-*] 1032. *með vóndra*] 1032. *vörnun*] *vorn en* 920. **24.5–8** not written out in full 713. **25.1** Cf. the similar lines 29.1 and 33.1.

27 'Ráðinn er eg að rækta móður,
rísa mun eg upp,' kvað sólar vísir,
'leiða oss til lífs af dauða,
4 lystr skal eg að sjá þig fysta;
kát vertu, því að kem á móti,
kraptfim, þjer af björtum himni,
gjarna skal eg með gleði á hlýrni
8 glæstum skipa þjer mjer eð næsta.'

28 Höll ítarlig himna stillis,
hásæti valið aldar gætis,
giptu fyld og guðdóms krapti,
4 gefi mjer orð til þinna stefja.
Yfirþjóðkóngs allra jöfra,
öllu góðu í himna höllu,
ræðr og stýrir, mær og móðir,
8 María sæl, hjá dróttni vórum.

'I am resolved to take care of my mother, I will rise up,' said the prince of the sun [Christ]; 'I shall lead us to life from death; I shall be desirous to see you first; be cheerful, you who are blessed in your powers, because I will come to meet you from bright heaven; with joy I shall willingly place you next to me in splendid heaven.'

Magnificent hall of the controller of the heavens [Christ; the Virgin], the chosen high-seat of the keeper of mankind [Christ; the Virgin], filled with success and the power of the Godhead, give me words for your refrains. Blessed Mary, virgin and mother of the supreme king of all princes [Christ], governs and directs all that is good in the hall of the heavens next to our Lord.

**27.5** *kem*] *eg* understood. **27.6** *kraptfim*] refers to the Virgin. **27.8** Cf. the almost identical line 46.4. **29.7–8** The distress which Mary feels in her breast alludes to Simeon's prophecy that a sword should pierce her heart/soul. **30.1** *er*] omitted 920. *mildingr*] *millding* 1032 and EK. **30.2** *-a*] 1032 and 920.

29 'Heyri þjóð,' kvað heilug María,
'hvessu eg gáða að orðum þessum,
mjer var æ því harmrinn hærri,
4 herra míns tók líf að þverra;
læriföðurinn lagði á síðu
Longínús fyr augum mínum;
næsta bar eg svó nóga í brjósti
8 nauð að mjer var búið við dauða.

30 Skylt er að tjá það er mildingr mælti
mána hauðrs í písl við dauð[a]:
"Þystir mig," kvað herra enn hæsti
4 hlýrna; má það aldri fyrnast;
geira lundar galli blandað
gumna þjóðir skapara bjóða
víniö súrt, en harm í hjarta
8 hafða eg rjett, sem edik krafði.

'Let people hear,' said holy Mary, 'how I paid attention to these words; for me the sorrow was ever the greater; my Lord's life began to wane; before my eyes Longinus stabbed the teacher in the side; I bore such abundant distress in my breast that I was almost at the point of death.

It is my duty to describe what the prince of the land of the moon [heaven; Christ] said in His passion on the point of death: "I thirst," said the highest Lord of sun and moon; that can never be forgotten; trees of spears [soldiers], multitudes of people offer the creator, who asked for vinegar, sour wine mixed with bile, and I truly had sorrow in my heart.

**30.5** *lundar*] *Júðar* 920. *blandað*] *i* above second *a* 920. **30.6** *þjóðir*] with *gumna,* 'people' as opposed to the warriors/soldiers referred to in *geira lundar*; *þjóðar* 920 and HS n., and *þjóða* Skj B and EK, both emendations taken with *skapara.*

31  Mæla frá eg það sikling sólar
seinast, enn sem eg má greina:
"Anda minn fel eg yðr á hendi,
4  eilífr faðir," kvað skepnu deilir.'
Lofsæll dó til lausnar öllum
lýð Jesús, sem guðspjöll þýða,
langa frjádag; l[o]f Guðs syngja
8  lærðir menn og öðrum kenna.

32  Ítarligr og öllum mætri,
ár og friðr sje skapara vórum,
máttugr gefr enn mildi dróttinn
4  móður sinni alt eð góða.
Yfirþjóðkóngs allra jöfra,
öllu góðu í himna höllu,
ræðr og stýrir, mær og móðir,
8  María sæl, hjá drottni vórum.

I heard that the prince of the sun [Christ] said that last, as I can also relate: "Eternal father, I commend my spirit into your hand," said the dealer of destiny [Christ].' Glorious Jesus died for the redemption of all people on Good Friday, as the gospels explain; learned people sing the praise of God and teach it to others.

He is magnificent and more excellent than all; may there be prosperity and peace for our Creator; the mighty and kind Lord gives all that is good to his mother. Blessed Mary, virgin and mother of the supreme king of all princes [Christ], governs and directs all that is good in the hall of the heavens next to our Lord.

**31.1** *það*] omitted 920.  **31.1–4** The speaker could be the author or St. Augustine, rather than the Virgin.  **31.7** *-o-*] 1032 and 920.  **32.5** *jöfra*] *þjóða* 920. **32.5–8** not written out in full 713.

## Maríugrátr

33  Heyri þjóð það er heilög María
    hýrlig sagði merkja stýri:
    'Skynlaus óaðist skaparans dauða
4   skepna öll með konum og körlum;
    hristist jörð en björgin brustu,
    beimar áttu dimmt í heimi,
    jafnvel mi[sti] sólin sæta
8   sína birti og mátti ei skína.

34  Lausnara vórs tók lík af krossi
    lærisveinn, og var eg þá næri,
    ítrs Krists, er Jósep heitir,
4   ástarmjúkr, og vafði í dúki.
    Fýsti oss að faðma og kyssa,'
    fróðust talar svó dróttins móðir,
    'mínar systr og Magdaljena,
8   mána hauðrs stilli dauðan.

Let people hear what kind holy Mary said to the ruler of symbols [bishop]: 'Every irrational creature, along with women and men, feared the death of the Creator; the earth shook and rocks burst; people had darkness in this world; even the sweet sun lost its brightness and could not shine. A loving disciple called Joseph took the body of our Redeemer, glorious Christ, from the cross and wrapped it in a cloth, and then I was close by. We, my sisters and Magdalene, wanted to embrace and kiss the dead controller of the land of the moon [heaven; Christ],' so speaks the most wise mother of the Lord.

---

**33.2** *merkja*] with *stýri* ('controller of signs/symbols'), referring to the official duties of a bishop (here St Augustine; see Meissner 1921, 390).   **33.5** This line contains an echo of Þjóðólfr of Hvinir's *Haustlǫng*, st. 16.2–3 (Skj A, I 19).   **33.7** -*sti*] 1032 and 920.

35  Síðan huldu lík í leiði
    laðar runnar hilmis sunnu,
    æstr var harmr, er eg Jesús mista,
  4 aldri kom mjer neitt að haldi;
    leið svó fram,' kvað lofðungs móðir
    'langa stund, að eg mátta ei ganga;
    hvílast vilda eg himna veldis
  8 heiðar tjalds við stillis leiði.

36  Efalaus var eg að upp mundi rísa
    ein þvóttdaginn Kristr enn hreini.'
    Þjóðir halda því nú síðan
  4 þenna dag til dýrðar henni.
    Yfirþjóðkóngs allra jöfra,
    öllu góðu í himna höllu,
    ræðr og stýrir, mær og móðir,
  8 María sæl, hjá drottni vórum.

'Afterwards the bushes of the metal plate [men] concealed the body of the ruler of the sun [Christ] in a tomb; my sorrow was intensified when I lost Jesus; nothing at all gave any support to me; so it went on for a long time,' said the mother of the prince [the Virgin], 'that I could not walk; I wanted to rest by the tomb of the controller of the tent of the heath [heaven; Christ], the controller of the heavenly kingdom [Christ].

I alone was without doubt on that Saturday that the virtuous Christ would rise up.' Therefore since then people hold this day in her honour still. Blessed Mary, virgin and mother of the supreme king of all princes [Christ], governs and directs all that is good in the hall of the heavens next to our Lord.

**35.1** *huldu*] HS, Skj B and EK; *huldi* all mss. and BK. Pl. is required with the subject *runnar*.    **35.2** *laðar runnar*] is clearly a kenning for 'men', though none of the known meanings of *löð* seems appropriate; *laufa runnar* Skj B and EK, 'trees of the sword', is a commoner type of man-kenning.    *runnar*] *runnur* 920.    **35.3** *Jesús*] *Jesúm* 920, 1032.    **35.8** *stillis*] forms the base word

37  Veiti hilmir vænnar stjettar,
    viðrkvæmilig orð í slæminn;
    þetta kvæði þinnar móður
  4 þekk kjósi smíð, bjartrar sólar.
    'Enn hlýð mjer,' kvað Jesús móðir,
    'Augústínus, er tárin fögru
    gæzkumild, að greina skyldi eg,
  8 gaft út, fyr þjer leynda krapta.

38  Ræsir prúðr, er reis af dauða,
    regna borgar, páskamorgin,
    sýndi mjer öll sár og undir
  4 sín, en glöð varð eg, fyrr en öðrum;
    gráti mínum gleði á móti
    Guð vildi svó skipa enn mildi,
    geymir vagns á grundu og himni
  8 gefr mjer alt það er eg vil krefja.

May the ruler of the beautiful path of the bright sun [heaven; Christ] grant suitable words for the concluding part; may an agreeable structure be pleased to invest this poem of your mother's. 'Keep listening to me, Augustine,' said the mother of Jesus, 'you who gave forth the beautiful tears full of goodness so that I should reveal to you secret deeds of power.

The splendid prince of the stronghold of rains [heaven; Christ], who rose from the dead on Easter morning, showed me before others all his hurts and wounds, and I became happy; so our kind God wanted to grant me joy in place of my weeping; the keeper of the Wain [Christ] gives me everything I wish to ask on earth and in heaven.'

for two kennings: *stillir tjalds heiðar* and *stillir veldis himna*; unless *tjalds heiðar* goes with *lofðungs* line 5. **36.2** *ein] einn* 920 and BK. **36.5** *jöfra] þjóða* 920. **37.4** *bjartrar] bjartur* 920. **37.7** *gæzkumild]* could be taken with *móðir* line 5. *eg]* omitted 920. **37.8** *gaft] er gaft* 920. **38.2** -*morgin] morgin* with *i* written above *u* 920.

## Maríugrátr

39 Grátinn minn,' kvað jungfrú ítrust,
'öld vórkynni mjer, með tárum
yndið er með iðran synda
4 yðvart líf,' segir gimsteinn vífa.
Náðarjenus fyr nauðsyn yðra
náði Jesús dauða bráðum,
sólar kóngs, að sínum vilja,
8 syndalausnar biðið og yndis.

40 Prúðlig verk fyr píslar marki
pátris dei formið gráti;
sonar Guðs opt í söng og bænum
4 sára minnist þjóð með tárum;
hneigið yðr fyr lærðum lýðum
langa stund með skriptagangi;
beiskr‹ar› iðranar úr brjósti klökku
8 bragnar laugi kinnr og augu.

The most glorious Virgin said, 'May mankind forgive this my lamentation; your joy is life with tears and repentance of sins,' says the gemstone of women [the Virgin]; Jesus of Nazareth obtained a sudden death by his own will because of your need; pray for redemption of sins and joy from the king of the sun [Christ].

Perform noble deeds by weeping before the sign of the passion [cross] of God the father; let people remember often the wounds of the son of God with tears in song and prayers; bow down before learned people for a long time in confession; may people bathe their cheeks and eyes out of a tearful breast of bitter repentance.

**39.5** *Náðarjenus*] *Náðarinnar* 920.   **39.5–8** This speech could be assigned to the Virgin; in *Ms* Mary asks humankind to pity her because her Son died for the sake of their sins (1011.17–19).   **39.7** *kóngs*] is not necessarily wrong though the emendation *konung* HS and Skj B ('pray the king of the sun for redemption of sins and joy') is clearer.   **40.1** *marki*] *merki* 920.   **40.7** *beiskrar*] 920, with *iðranar* 'bitter or painful repentance'; *beiskr* 713 and 1032 does not fit into the context; *bekkr* (nom. sg. m. 'brook') all eds. is problematic because

41 Mána strandar munki einum
  móðir birti dróttins fróðum
  fagnaði sína fimm, er þegnar
4 frægðarsvinnir jafnan minnast;
  líkn og hjálp tók lýðs að reikna
  lyndishrein, með gleði og yndi,
  þýð og mild, fyr þessum bróður.
8 Þetta greinir sú er eyðir meinum.

42 Hvern dag fimm vil eg heyra snemma
  höfuðfagnaði, grams kveðju
  móð[ur], bið eg að mínir lýðir
4 minnist þeira orða svinnir;
  kenna mun eg þá alla, og inna —
  orð sönn eru — það lærðum mönnum,
  næsta er skylt að nemi sem flestir
8 nýtar bænir kristnir ýtar.

The mother of the Lord of the shore of the moon [heaven; Christ; the Virgin] revealed to a certain learned monk her five joys which men of renowned wisdom always remember; the mercy and salvation of mankind [the Virgin], virtuous, kind and mild, began to reckon them with joy and pleasure before this brother; she who destroys sins describes this.

Early every day I wish to hear the five chief joys, (and) the greeting of the mother of the prince [the Virgin; the *Ave Maria*]; I pray that my wise people remember those words; I will teach them all — these are true words — and recite it to learned people; it is virtually obligatory that as many Christian people as possible should learn beneficial prayers.

*bragnar* (nom. pl.) line 8 must then be taken with the other clause or emended to gen. pl. *bragna* (so Skj B and EK). **42.2** *höfuðfagnaði*] Skj B and EK is the only sensible emendation that provides the acc. pl. to go with *heyra*; *hofut fagnaðar* all mss., BK and HS. **42.3** *móður*] Skj B, EK is the logical reading, since gen. sg. is required; *moðer* 1032, BK and HS; lacuna 920. **42.4** *svinnir*] *svinnrar* 920.

43 'Fystan tel eg þann fögnuð hæstan:
fann engill mig sólar þengils,
hann sendi mjer helgan anda
4 háleitan með gleði og teiti;
glöddumst eg, þá er skaparinn skrýddi
skýfoldar sig mínu holdi
meistari alls fyr mínu brjósti,
8 mær var eg Guðs, svó að hvern dag hræddumst.

44 Finn eg minn þann fögnuð annan:
fæddi eg Krist, er heiminn græddi,
jólanótt, að eins Guðs vilja,
4 öllum lýð til sálu prýði.
Síðan reikna eg þann enn þriðja:
þeyja borgar, páskamorgin,
ríkr og fróðr er, reis af dauða,
8 ræsir ítr, sem mátta eg líta.

'I count the highest joy first: the angel of the prince of the sun [Christ] met me; He sent the sublime Holy Spirit to me with joy and happiness; I was glad then when the creator of the land of clouds [heaven; Christ], the master of everything [Christ], adorned himself in my flesh before my breast, I was the Virgin of God so that every day I was afraid.

I find this my second joy: on Christmas night I gave birth to Christ who healed the world by the will of the one God for the embellishment of the soul for all mankind. After that I count this the third joy: the glorious prince of the stronghold of thaw winds [heaven; Christ], he is mighty and wise, rose from death on Easter morning, as I was able to witness.

**43.7** *meistari*] *meistarinn* 920.   **43.8** *að*] *ek* 920.   *hræddumst*] refers to the Virgin's fear and concern after the Annunciation; *bærðiz* Skj B (pret. 3rd pers.)

45 Guð stje upp af grýttu láði
gæzkufimr á bjarta himna,
lofaðr sitr um aldr og æfi
4 eilífr á veg skepnu deilir.
Ítarligr kom mjer á móti
minn son Guð með allri sinni
hirð ágætri himna dýrðar;
8 hann hóf mig upp á sínum lófa.

46 "Leiða skal eg þig, María móðir
mín, í dýrð," kvað skepnu tínir,
"heiðr og vald og í himna prýði
4 hæsta, skipa eg þig mjer eð næsta."
Meiri dýrð þá eg miklu af hirði
mána bryggju en nokkurt hyggi
mannligt brjóst, þótt margt gott kunni.'
8 Mætust talar svó himnesk sæta.


Ready with goodness, God ascended from the stony earth into the bright heavens; the eternal, praised dealer of destiny [Christ] sits in glory for ever and always. My magnificent son, God, came to meet me accompanied by all His excellent court of the glory of the heavens [angels]; He raised me up in the palm of His hand.

"I shall lead you, my mother Mary," said the determiner of fate [Christ], "into glory, honour and power, and to the highest splendour of the heavens; I shall place you next to me." I received much greater glory from the shepherd of the jetty of the moon [heaven; Christ] than any human breast can imagine, though it may know many a good thing.' So speaks the most excellent heavenly woman.


sg. of *bæra*) taken with *meistari alls* as subject referring to the movements of the unborn child in her womb.

47 'Gjör svó vel,' kvað göfgust María,
'gleði mig þjóð með engils kveðju,
langar mig til að á lýða tungu
4 jafnan ljeki Dómínus tjecum;
lítið hjer að laun á móti
lúkast skulu, ef beðið er sjúkum
himna gæti heilsubótar;
8 heit* eg yðr að líkn skal veita.'

48 Mönnum eru slík heitin hennar
harðla væn, en tár og bænir
helgar láti hverr maðr fylgja
4 hjarta klökku og iðran bjarta;
regnsals skulu vjer ræsi tigna
rausnsaman oss til syndalausnar,
honum gjöri dýrð á himni og j[ör]ðu
8 hvesskyns þjóð og dróttins móður.

'Please,' said the very magnificent Mary, 'may people make me happy with the greeting of the angel, I long for *dominus tecum* always to play on the tongue of mankind; they shall be paid in return for this a small reward, if a prayer is made to the keeper of the heavens [Christ] for the cure of the health of the sick; I promise you that mercy will be granted.'

Such promises from her are very good for people, but let every person add tears, holy prayers and shining repentance to a tearful heart; we shall honour the splendid prince of the hall of rain [heaven; Christ] for our redemption; may all kinds of people glorify Him and the mother of the Lord in heaven and on earth.

**47.2** *engils kveðju*] the *Ave Maria.* **47.5** *lítið*] all mss. Skj B emends to *lítil* to agree with pl. *laun*; but if *skulu lúkask* can be taken as equivalent to the pass., *lítið* is perhaps the object: 'they shall be paid little as a reward in exchange for this'. Alternatively, *skulu* might be emended to *skala* 'shall not'. **47.8** *heit*] Skj B and EK is required to form the pres. 1st pers. sg., though very occasionally the wk. form is found in this meaning (see Noreen 1923, §532.2); *heite* all mss., BK and HS. **48.7** *-ör-*] 1032 and 920. **48.8** *móður*] 920, Skj B and EK,

## Maríugrátr

49  Þurt er mjer í hring um hjarta,
    hvarma lón þótt renni af sjónum,
    svik eru slíkt og syndaauki
 4  sárr, ef hrósa eg slíkum tárum;
    hlotnast láttu hjálpar vatnið
    hreggskríns jöfurr, svó nægi mínu;
    hrynji sú mjer með helgum bænum
 8  hvarma laugin út af augum.

50  Dýrka skyldi af allri orku
    almætastan himna gæti,
    skylda er það fyr skírðar aldir;
 4  skapari sannr er hann allra manna;
    veittu mjer þá enn dýrsti dróttinn
    dýrðar grein, að hitti eg hreina
    fjörtjóns stund, svó að fúlir andar
 8  fyndi öngvar með mjer syndir.

It is dry around my heart though the lagoons of my eyelids [tears] run from my eyes; this will be falsehood and bitter increase of sins if I praise these tears; prince of the storm-shrine [heaven; Christ], let the water of salvation [tears] be allotted so that I shall have sufficient for my (heart); may the bath of my eyelids [tears] stream out from my eyes with holy prayers.

One should worship the most fully excellent keeper of the heavens [Christ] with all one's strength; it is a duty for baptized people; He is the true creator of all humankind; most precious Lord, grant me then a portion of glory that I may meet with a clean hour of death so that foul spirits may have found no sins in me.

*moðir* 713 and 1032. The clause makes better theological sense as 'may all kinds of people glorify Him and the mother of the Lord in heaven and on earth' rather than 'may all kinds of people and the mother of the Lord glorify Him in heaven and on earth'. **49.6** *mínu*] i.e. *hjarta* (line 1); it is possible that *nægi* is from *ná* rather than from *nægja*, 'so that it may reach my (heart)'. **50.7** *fjörtjóns*] all eds.; *fiortuns* 713 and 920, *fiortons* 1032 (literally 'life town's') makes no sense. *svó*] omitted 920 and 1032.

51  Bið eg þig, Kristr og blessuð móðir,
bæði ykkr að þetta kvæði
laun‹ið› mjer, er lífi týni eg;
4 lærifaðirinn statt þá næri;
ítr leittu mig Jesús dróttinn
undan hörðum djöfla fundi,
mun eg þá kjósa mærðar launin,
8 mína sál í gæzku þína.

52  Sæll hjálpa mjer sólar stillir
sóma prýddr á efsta dómi,
ýtum bið eg þig öllum veita
4 alt gott með þjer, lofaðr drottinn;
allir bið eg menn að minnist
Maríu vess og lesi með tárum,
móður Guðs og dróttins dauða,
8 dreyra þess, er grátinn heyra. Amen.

I pray to you both, Christ and your blessed mother, that you will reward me for this poem when I lose my life; teacher, stand by me then; glorious Lord Jesus, lead me out of the harsh meeting with devils, my soul into your grace, then I will choose rewards for my praise-poem.

Blessed honour-adorned controller of the sun [Christ], save me at the Last Judgement; praised Lord, I ask you to give all that is good with you to all mankind; I pray that all people who hear this lamentation remember Mary's verse [the *Ave Maria*] and read it with tears and remember the mother of God and the death of the Lord and His blood. Amen.

**51.3** *launið*] Skj B and EK gives a more straightforward meaning ('that you [Christ and Mary] will reward me for this poem when I die') than *launi* all mss., BK and HS which would mean 'that this praise poem should reward me when I die'.  **51.5** *mig*] written superscript with insertion signs 713; *þá* Skj B makes better sense, though *mig* can be taken as in apposition to *mína sál* line 8.  **52.8** *þess*] *þins* 920.

# Vitnisvísur af Maríu

AM 713 ff. 83–85; AM 721 ff. 10v and 12; AM 711a ff. 52–74.
This text is from AM 713.

1   Heyrðu til upphafs orða
    alls vinnandi minna
    þrennr og einn í þinni
4   þrenning, er Guð kennist;
    láttu líkna*r* dróttinn
    lausnari minn, af þinni,
    greiðast göfgað kvæði,
8   góðr, háleitri móður.

2   Stýrðu Andrjeás orðum
    yfirskínandi mínum
    ást, því að eg vil treysta
4   jafnan þínu nafni;
    því að, Maríu meyjar,
    móður Guðs, í óði,
    enn vilda eg inna
8   jarteign, fyrðum, bjarta.

Listen to my opening words, maker of all things, threefold and one in your Trinity, who is acknowledged as God; Lord of mercy, my Redeemer, being good, let an honoured poem be uttered about your sublime mother.

Andrew, overshining love, direct my words, because I will always rely upon your name; because I again would like to relate to people an illustrious miracle of the Virgin Mary, the mother of God, in poetry.

**1.5** *líknar*] JÞ, HS, Skj B and EK, taken with *dróttinn* 'the Lord of mercy', fits well theologically and makes considerably better sense than *liknað* all mss. and BK taken with *kvæði*, 'merciful poem'. **2.5** *því að*] *það* 721. **2.7** *eg*] 721 omits. **2.8** *fyrðum*] *firum* 721, HS, Skj B and EK provides a short syllable (see HS n.). But cf. 6.8, 12.8, and 23.8.

## Vitnisvísur

3 Rjeð í ríki góðu —
ritning ber svó vitni —
kóngr, sá átti unga,
4 óttlauss, frama dóttur;
fæddist upp með Fríði*
falds á bernsku aldri
svinnr í sögðu ríki
8 sveinn af kynslóð hreinni.

4 Blíðu barnaæði
brátt kveikjast þar leikar
enn með ungamanni
4 ótt og konungs dóttur;
sjá má sveinn af meyju
sjaldan nær eða aldri,
það varð í ást af ástum
8 áfengt, er þau gáfust.

So written authority bears witness: a fearless king ruled in a good kingdom who had a young, outspoken daughter; in the above-mentioned kingdom, a clever young man from a good family line was brought up with the Fríðr of the head-dress [girl] in their childhood.

With a friendly child-like nature, games were furthermore quickly, speedily kindled there between the young man and the king's daughter; the lad can seldom or almost never take his eyes off the girl; it became a powerful cause of love from the loves which they gave each other.

3.5 *Fríði*] 721, BK, HS, Skj B and EK; *friðre* 713 and 711a. 3.7 *ríki*] *ranni* 721 (*ri* followed by a superscript graph which could be one or two minims, *i* or *n*, i.e. *riki* or *rani*) and HS; this provides *skothending* with *svinnr*, but the meaning of *í sögðu ranni* is uncertain since no house is mentioned in the preceding stanzas. HS refers to an analogue in *Ms* where the word *garðr* is used (298.13). 3.8 *af*] 721 omits. 4.1 -*i*] -*u* 721. 4.6 *aldri*] 721 omits. 4.7 *í ást*] read as *jast* 'yeast' in HS with *ástum,* presumably referring to an intoxicating drink of love or a love potion and subject of *varð áfengt.* Schottmann

*Vitnisvísur* 29

5   Síðan nam sætar ástir
    seggr við sprund að leggja,
    Hlín má hrings af sveini
4   hvítust sjaldan líta;
    eina stund með yndi
    hann var staddr hjá henni;
    talaði svinnr við svanna
8   sveinn, í kirkju einni:

6   'Ann eg fyr allar kvinnur
    ágætust þjer sæta;
    vórr er víst svó fjarri
4   vili við yðr að skilja.'
    Hún kvað sjálfrátt sveini
    sett að styrkja þetta,
    trú gaf tignarmeyja
8   tállaust, festarmálum.

Afterwards the man developed a sweet passion for the woman; the most pure Hlín of the ring [girl] can seldom take her eyes off the young man; one time he was standing by her with pleasure in a church; the clever young man addressed the woman:
'I love you most excellent lady above all women; so my wish to part from you is certainly distant.' She said it was placed within the young man's power to confirm this with a betrothal; the noble maiden gave him her troth without deceit.

agrees (1973, 377). **5.4** *hvítust sjaldan*] *huit varliga* 721, HS, Skj B and EK is an alternative reading with much the same meaning. **5.5** *stund*] *stun* 721. **6.8** *tállaust*] seems preferable to *tal með* 721; the latter, presumably to be understood as *tál með* 'with deceit', if referring to the girl, does not fit the general portrayal of her character. Alternatively, *með* could be construed with *festarmálum*, and *tal* read as the n. noun 'talk, speech', and taken with lines 5–6: 'she said it was within the young man's own power to confirm his speech with a betrothal'. *Tal*, however, does not provide *aðalhending* with *málum*.

7   Drengr anzaði ungri:
    'Eg þori slíkt að segja
    enn fyr öngum manni.'
 4  Auðbrík svarar ríkust:
    'Víst eru vóttar traustir
    vel nær, ef þau bæri:
    sitr hjer móður mætrar
 8  minn Guð í knjám sinnar.'

8   Þá tók hann í hennar
    hand með elsku bandi,
    fram greiðandi fríðust
 4  festarorð á lesti:
    'Þú skalt, mektug meyja,
    mín innilig kvinna,
    virðist okkr að verða
 8  vóttr María og dróttinn.'

The boy answered the young person: 'I dare not yet say this in front of anyone.' The very mighty panel of riches [woman] replies: 'In truth there are trustworthy witnesses very near, if they would bear (witness): here sits my God in the lap of his excellent mother.'

Then he took hold of her hand with a ring of love, uttering at last the most beautiful words of betrothal: 'You, mighty maiden, shall be my dear wife, if Mary and the Lord deign to be witness for us.'

**7.3** *öngum*] *ðgum* 721.   **7.7** *mætrar*] *mætri* 711a.   **8.5** *mektug*] illegible 721.
**9.8** *nú*] *þá* 721.   **10.6** *dóttir*] 721, HS, Skj B and EK; *drottir* 713 and 711a 'people' or 'followers' of the king is not as plausible as the 721 reading, be-

## Vitnisvísur 31

9   Leið um langar tíðir;
    lundr fór burt frá sprundi
    auðs, því að arfrinn fríði,
4   alsæmdr, honum tæmdist;
    burgeiss var hann í borgum
    brátt og nógligt átti
    gull, en guðvefs þellu
8   gleymdi hann nú, með eymdum.

10  Brátt nam, mikill að mætti,
    meyjar faðir að deyja;
    tóku tign og ríki
4   tiggja frændr að þiggja;
    eptir erfða skipti
    óttast kóngsins dóttir*
    mein og meðferð sína,
8   minkast auðr, í nauðum.

A long time passed; the universally honoured tree of riches [man] left the woman because the fine inheritance fell to him; soon he was a person of status in the towns and had abundant gold, but he forgot now about the pine of costly cloth [woman], unhappily.

Soon the young woman's father, who had great power, died; the king's kinsmen received the status and realm; after the distribution of the inheritance, the king's daughter is terrified of harm and how she would be treated in her distress; her wealth is decreased.

sides which the *dróttir* do not otherwise feature in the story. It makes better sense in the context for the king's daughter to be the one who is concerned about her future.

11  Vitjar veglig sæta
    virktafríð um síðir
    sinn elskuga sannan,
 4  svó spyrr, er var fyrri:
    'Hví vartu so, hirtir,
    hverflyndr að *ei* fyndumst,
    mjög reynir þú, manna,
 8  mín, unnustu þína?'

12  Rekkr með reiðiþokka
    rjóðr anzaði fljóði:
    'Legg þú niðr enn leiða
 4  lygð á mig til blygðar;
    blóms ætla eg bríma
    brík að fastna ríka,
    en fjelausa fýsast
 8  fald‹reið› skal eg *aldri.'


At last the truly beautiful, honourable woman visits her true love, as he had formerly been, then asks: 'Why were you, controller of people [lord], so fickle-minded regarding me that we did not see each other? You try your loved one a lot.'
The man, red in the face, answered the woman with angry thought(s): 'Stop telling a repugnant lie to shame me again; I intend to betroth a rich panel of the flower of fire [gold; woman], but I shall never desire a wealth-lacking carrier of head-dress [woman].'


**11.2** *virkta*] in the margin at beginning of this line 713; BK takes this word with *elskuga* 'intimate lover', while HS takes *virkta* as the object of *vitjar* 'she sought friendly care'. Skj B's reading makes the most sense and is preferred here: *virkta* intensive with *fríð* 'very beautiful'. **11.6** *ei*] Skj B; *við* all mss. The neg. is necessary to the sense. **12.5** *blóms*] *bríms* HS, Skj B and EK. The kenning *brík blóms bríma* (not listed in *LP*) is semantically odd: 'the panel of the flower of fire' = 'the panel of gold' = 'woman'. While *brík* does occur in woman-kennings and *bríma* in gold-kennings, just how *blóms* fits in is uncer-

13  Brátt nam byskup hitta
    brúðr, er sorgin knúði,
    satt og segir til votta,
 4  sár, og flóar í tárum:
    'Met þú hve mikil er hætta
    mann ef eg fær annan,
    en fastúðigr festi
 8  formaðr konu aðra.'

14  Spurði hringa hirði
    herra ríkr að slíku;
    sætu sögn í móti
 4  sór hann eiða stóra;
    Guðs fyr nýtar náðir,
    nefndr byskup stefndi,
    vænn, til vótta sinna,
 8  virkr, í Maríu kirkju.

Soon the woman, whom the grievous sorrow oppressed, went and met the bishop and spoke the truth about the witnesses and was bathed in tears: 'Judge how great is the danger if I take another husband, and my previous man, unshakeable in his resolution, should betroth another woman.'

The powerful lord asked the keeper of rings [man] about all this; he swore great oaths against the woman's story; by the beneficial grace of God, the above-mentioned bishop, noble and dutiful, summoned him before his witnesses in the church of Mary.

---

tain. BK reads *brima* (although the metre requires a long vowel) with *blóms* to form a gold-kenning 'fruit of the surf', and interprets *brík blóms brima* as 'the tablet of gold' = 'woman'. **12.8** *reið*] 721, HS, Skj B and EK; 713, 711a and BK omit, clearly a scribal slip. 713 and 711a add a redundant *þig* after *eg*. **13.4** *flóar*] *floir* 721. **13.5** *hve*] *huat* 721. **13.8** *formaðr*] *formann* 721. **14.5** *Guðs*] HS n., Skj B and EK, with *nýtar náðir*; *guði* all mss. and BK is grammatically impossible. **14.8** *í*] 721 omits.

## 34  Vitnisvísur

15  Brimg‹l›óða fór bæði
    brík og maðrinn ríki
    í musterið mesta;
 4  mannfjöldi kom hölda;
    brúðr af treganum tjáði
    tilkall við hal snjallan;
    prætir þegar á moti
 8  þegn af öllu megni.

16  'Veiztu að vóttar æztir
    vóru hjá, þá er fóru
    festarorð, en firðist
 4  flokkr kaupmála okkarn;
    rjett hygg eg að þá þætti
    því ráðið vel báðum.'
    Línband* kvað hann lengi
 8  ljúga hvert orð drjúgum.

Both the panel of sea-embers [gold; woman] and the powerful man went into the very great church; a large crowd of people came; out of her sorrow the woman described her claim on the clever man; immediately the man contradicts her with all his might. 'You know that the highest witnesses were present when the words of our betrothal were spoken, but people were absent from our contract; I think that the agreement seemed well and properly made to both of us at the time.' He said that for a long time the band of linen [woman] had thoroughly lied about every word.

**15.1** *Brimglóða*] all eds., taken with *brík* to form a woman-kenning, 'panel of sea embers' is an unavoidable emendation; *brim goða* all mss. makes no sense.
**15.7** *á*] *i* 721.  **16.1-6** This is the young woman's speech.  **16.2** *vóru*] *uor* 721.
**16.7** *Línband*] BK n. involves the least change and provides an otherwise missing subject, though the kenning is unusual; *línbands* Skj B construed

## Vitnisvísur 35

17  Grjet en göfga sæta
    gangandi nú þangað
    er skorin var skriptin skæra
 4  skýrst Maríu dýrstrar;
    laut að ljúfum fótum
    líkneski þar fesku;
    miskunn bað hún manna
 8  minnast eymdar sinnar:

18  'Veit eg að mjög er í móti
    minn Guð skipan þinni
    með sambandi synda
 4  sett jáyrði þetta;
    verð eg bert fyr borði,
    blessuð hjálp, í þessu
    enn, sem ykkr er kunnigt
 8  áðr mæðginum báðum.

Now the noble woman wept while walking to where the clearest, excellent image of most precious Mary was carved; there she bowed at the beloved feet of the beautiful image; she prayed the mercy of mankind [the Virgin] to be mindful of her misery.

'I know that this consent was made with sinful union much against your commandment, my God; blessed help, I am still clearly in a bad way in this, as is already known to you both, mother and son.

with emendation *lindi* (for *lengi*); *lín hrings* EK 'the linen of the ring' = woman; *linbanda* all mss. *lengi*] *lindi* HS (taken with *línbanda* 'the lime-tree of the band of linen' = woman) and Skj B. **17.1** *Grjet*] HS, Skj B and EK meets the metrical requirements and makes sense; *Gekk* all mss. and BK lacks *skothending* and doubles the meaning of *gangandi* line 2. **17.3** *er skorin*] *gior* 721. **18.1** *it* in margin 713 without any accompanying caret.

19   Láttu, líknarmey dróttins,
     leiðast próf, þess eg beiði
     þig, að eg þörfnumst eigi,
 4   þín, rjettinda mínna;
     sýndu, með sætleiks anda,
     sveit, er alt gott veitir,
     hvort, en hæsta birti,
 8   hefir sannara við annað.'

20   Tók María mjúkust
     mæla vörrum sælum
     orð svó að allir heyrðu
 4   áhlýðandi lýðir:
     'Rjett hermir þú, hattar,
     hvert orð, vita skorða;
     ósannindum undan
 8   jungkærinn vill færast.'

Virgin of mercy of the Lord, let your testimonies come forth; I ask you for this so that I will not be without my rights; you highest brightness who give all that is good, show people with a spirit of sweetness which one of us speaks more truthfully against the other.'
Most gentle Mary began to speak words with her blessed lips so that all the listening people heard: 'Prop of the hood-beacon [gold; woman], each word you report is right; the young man wants to escape with falsehoods.'

**19.2** *þess*] Skj B and EK, *það* all mss.; *beiða* takes the gen., though cf. *Mg* 10.5 n.   *eg beiði*] 713, 711a, BK and HS; *er beiðik* 721; *beiðik* EK; *beiði* Skj B.   **19.3** *þörfnumst*] *þaurfumst* 721.   **19.7** *hvórt*] *er* adds 721.   **20.4** *áhlýðandi*] *a hlyðanda* 721.   **20.5** *hattar*] taken with *vita* to make a goldkenning 'beacon of the hood', and with *skorða*, a woman-kenning 'the bearer

21 Þagnar sætan signuð;
    son hennar rjeð þenna
    fylla framburð allan,
4   fríð sannindi, þanninn:
    'Það vitni ber eg brúði
    bjart og gott,' kvað drottinn,
    'áðr sem mín bar móðir:
8   mær hefr satt að kæra.'

22 Varð, af vitnisburði,
    virkr lýðr í kirkju
    kveiktr til mestrar mektar,
4   móður Guðs að bjóða;
    flokkr gjörði ⟨þá⟩ þakkir
    þann veg allr með svanna:
    lofsöng unnu þau ljúfan
8   list Maríu og Kristi.

The blessed woman fell silent; her son confirmed this entire statement, the beautiful truth, thus: 'I bear this bright and good witness for the woman,' said the Lord, 'as my mother did just now; the woman has made a just accusation.'

As a result of this testimony, the dutiful people in the church became fired up to the utmost of their power to worship the mother of God; then the entire company together with the woman gave thanks thus: they eloquently made a pleasant hymn of praise for Mary and Christ.

---

of the beacon of the hood'; BK (103) reads *háttar* with *rjett*, 'Recht in Bezug auf die Art und Weise'; *handar* Skj B and EK taken with *vita* to form a goldkenning 'beacon of the hand' (i.e. jewellery) and this with *skorða* to make a woman-kenning. **21.2** *rjeð*] *tok* 721. **21.4** *þanninn*] *þanig* 721. **21.8** *að*] 721 omits. **22.5** *þá*] 721 and all eds.; 713 and 711a omit.

## Vitnisvísur

23   Runnu ríkamanni
      reiðimál og eiðar,
      beiðir gekk við brúðar
  4   borða hverju orði;
      lýsti ljúfliga ástum
      lundr silkigrundar
      auðs og unni síðan
  8   ágætt víf sem lífi.

24   Hjer mátti nú heyra
      hitnað elsku vitni,
      það er sannindin sýndi
  4   sönn fyr Guði og mönnum;
      þá, mun bjarga beimum
      blíð María tíðast,
      mest* í meinum læstir
  8   menn er þurfa hennar.

The angry words and oaths left the powerful man; the demander of shields [man] admitted to every word of the woman; the tree of riches [man] willingly proclaimed his love of the ground of silk [woman] and afterwards the excellent woman loved him as her own life.

In this it has now been possible to hear the impassioned testimony of love which showed the real truth before God and the people; kind Mary will most often help people when, locked in evil, they most need her.

**23.5** ljúfliga] uanliga 721.   ástum] astir 721.   **23.6** silkigrundar] 721 omits.
**24.5** þá] goes with mest er lines 7–8.   **24.7** mest] 721, HS, Skj B and EK; mest er 711a; mest eru 713 and BK; eru is redundant syntactically and metrically.
**25.1** margföldust] margfalldrar 721.   **25.5–8** EK takes eilífrar ástar, óflekkuð

25 Þú ert margföldust mildi,
mjúklætis hásæti,
grundin guðdóms anda
4 góð og Jesús móðir;
brjóst, eilífrar ástar,
óflekkuð gaftu drekka,
full af fögnuð öllum,
8 frú mín, syni þínum.

26 Væri eg skyldr að skýra
skínandi mey þína
dýrð jarteignar orðum
4 ynnilig, sem eg kynni;
tak þú úr sárum sektum,
sönn hjálpar vón mönnum,
andir sviptar syndum,
8 sætt víf, að eilífu. Amen.

You are the most manifold mercy, the high seat of humility [the Virgin], the good ground of the spirit of the Godhead [the Holy Spirit; the Virgin], and the mother of Jesus; you, my Lady, unblemished, full of all the joy of eternal love, gave your breast to your son to drink from.

Lovely shining Virgin, it would have been my duty to explain your glorious miracle in words as well as I could; you, the true hope of salvation for humankind, sweet woman, take souls freed from sins out of severe punishments for ever. Amen.

and *full af fögnuð öllum* as referring to *brjóst* rather than to *frú mín*. **26.5** *úr*] 721 omits. **26.6–7** *sönn . . . syndum*] HS (73) translates 'erlöse die in Sünden den Menschen entrissenen Seelen (d.h. die Seelen der in Sünden Verstorbenen) aus der Verbannung'.

## Maríuvísur I

*AM 721 ff. 12v–13v; AM 1032 ff. 81v–94v.*
*This text is from AM 721.*

1   ⟨M⟩jer gefi hljóð, sá er heyrir
    hjarta mitt, og bjarta
    orðasnild, um aldir,
4   auðgreinandi, hreina;
    Guð vil eg göfgan biðja,
    Guðs vild er það mildust,
    að hann miskunnar minnist,
8   minn, á skepnu sinni.

2   Ástvin Guðs enn æsti,
    Andrjeás, bið eg að standi,
    nefndr, með nógleiks orðum
4   nafn þitt hjá mjer jafnan;
    svó að sælli meyju,
    sætt hreinlífið, mætti
    inna jarteign sanna
8   áhlýðandi lýðum.

May the distributor of riches [God], who for ever hears my heart, give me a hearing and bright, clear eloquence; I will pray to my worshipful God that He will remember mercy for His creature; it is God's most generous wish.

Most noble dear friend of God called Andrew, I pray that your name will always be close by me with plenty of words, so that, sweet chastity, I may relate to attentive people a true miracle of the blessed Virgin.

**1.1** *Mjer*] 1032; with a space for the capital 721.   **1.4** *auð-*] *auðar* 1032. *hreina*] *hreins* 1032.   **2.5** *sælli*] *sællar* BK n., HS n. and Skj B (which also emends *meyju* to *meyjar*; the phrase in all three is then gen. with *jarteign sanna*). While this improves the sense and grammar of this clause, the ms. reading is not incomprehensible: *sælli meyju* (dat.) with *jarteign sanna* means 'a true miracle performed by the blessed Virgin' (cf. the similar construction

3   Rjeð í borg svó breiðri
    brúðr fyr garði prúðum,
    siðlátust hjelt sæta
 4  sönn miskunnar dæmi;
    næst kærligum Kristi
    kæst elskaði hæsta
    Maríu drottning dýra
 8  drós, í verkum ljósum.

4   Áðr var *eigin* brúðar
    andaðr í því landi;
    átti hún eina dóttur,
 4  unnandi, vel kunna;
    hennar bað með heiðri
    heiðrsmaðr, og greiðist
    mundrinn, fyldist frændum
 8  frægð, en tókust mægðir.

So, there was a woman who ruled over a stately establishment in a large town; this most virtuous, true woman honoured the example of mercy [Virgin Mary]; after beloved Christ, the very dear woman loved Mary, the highest precious queen, in virtuous deeds.

The woman's husband had previously died in that land; she had a very knowledgeable daughter; an honourable man proposed to her with honourable intentions and the dowry is paid; renown was achieved for the relatives and the marriage took place.

29.3–4). **4.1** *Áðr*] *Auðs* HS. *eigin brúðar*] Skj B (spelled *eiginn*) taken with *unnandi* 'the woman's own husband' involves little emendation and improves the sense; EK *eiginbrúðar* ('wedded wife'?); *ægir bruðar* both mss., BK and HS, 'the sea of the woman' is an odd kenning not attested elsewhere; HS emends to *auðs ægir*, also not attested elsewhere. **4.5** *hennar*] i.e. the daughter.

5  Unni ærlig kvinna
auðgætanda mætum
sætt af sinni dóttur;
4 syndlaust var það yndi;
en fyr illsku manna
upp smíðaðist síðan,
angr vann aumlig tunga,
8 orð á silkiskorðu.

6  Óx hræðilig huxan,
hitt, er allir kvitta,
myndar* margvíss fjandi,
4 milli fólksins illa:
sagði sveit að lagðist
seimkennandi að henni,
því mundi svó sendi
8 sár‹s› kunnum frú unna.

The honest woman dearly loved the excellent keeper of riches [man] on account of her daughter; that pleasure was sinless; but because of the wickedness of people, a rumour was invented then about the silk-prop [woman]; a miserable tongue brought about sorrow.

A frightening thought grew among the wicked people, which everybody spread; a very cunning devil creates that: people said that the gold-wearer [man] had sex with her, because the lady must love the famous wound-sender [man] so much.

**5.3** *sætt*] (adv.) can also be an a. with *yndi* line 4. **6.3** *myndar*] all eds.; *meyndar* both mss. appears to be a scribal error. **6.7** *sendi*] HS, Skj B and EK, involves little emendation and makes sense; *semdi* 721 and *somði* 1032 and BK are not attested elsewhere as nouns. **6.8** *sárs*] HS, taken with *sendi* 'sender of the wound'; Skj B and EK emend to *sax*, also taken with *sendi* 'sender of the sword'; *sár* both mss. does not fit into the context. **7.3-4** *sœldar sprakki*] BK (97) interprets 'die selige Maid', though it is difficult to see why she would

7   Hjer kom, orð það heyrði
    húsfrú fríð um síðir;
    sig skildi þá sældar
 4  saklauss vera sprakki;
    ráðtæki var ríkrar
    raungrætiligt sætu;
    kunni hún mág sinn manna
 8  mest álygi vestrar.

 8  Brann í brjósti hennar
    bæði grimd og æði
    fyld, er hús-frú vildi
 4  forðast slíku orði,
    svó að af sorgum nýjum,
    sáran dauð með fári,
    urðu illar gjörðir,
 8  affíni rjeð sínum.

It happened that the beautiful mistress of the house heard this rumour at last; then the blessed woman knew herself to be innocent; the powerful woman's solution was truly regrettable; she blamed her son-in-law most out of everybody for the worst slander.

In her breast burnt both ferocity and pent-up frenzy when the mistress of the house wanted to escape this slander, so that evil deeds arose out of new sorrows; through her hatred she contrived a sore death for her son-in-law.

be happy about such defamation of character. HS (57) suggests *sæld* in this instance means the opposite of its usual meaning. It is simpler, however, if *sæld* is taken to refer to the woman's happiness before she heard the rumour.
**8.5** *af sorgum nýjum*] is taken with *urðu illar gjörðir* both here and in Skj B ('evil deeds arose out of new sorrows'), but can also be taken with *svó að sáran dauð með fári affíni rjeð sínum* ('thus on account of new sorrows, through her hatred she contrived a sore death for her son-in-law').

## 44  Maríuvísur I

9   Drepa ljet brúðrin bráða,
      bráð varð snót í ráðum,
      mann saklausan sinnar,
   4 sótt, af lífi dóttur;
      glóða Ná fekk græðis
      grát af bónda láti,
      en mæðandi móðir
   8 mein af sögðum greinum.

10  Deildi, krakleik köldum,
      kvinna einu sinni
      líns við lærðan kenni,
   4 leidd, svó að bæði reiddust;
      prestr varð óðr og æstist,
      eymdum lagðr og sagði,
      þassem þjóðir vissu,
   8 þenna glæp eptir henni.

The rash woman, accused, had her daughter's innocent husband struck from life; this woman was hasty with her undertaking; Ná of sea-embers [gold; woman] endured lamentation over the death of her husband, and the mother, afflicting (her daughter), experienced pains from the above-mentioned events.

One time, impelled by severe contentiousness, the woman quarrelled with a learned wearer of linen [priest], so that both became angry; the priest became furious and enraged, being weighed down with miseries, and told of this crime committed by her, although people knew about it already.

9.2 *bráð*] is the complement.   9.5 *glóða Ná*] HS, Skj B and EK, is the only sensible way to read *gloðana* 721 and BK and *gloðanna* 1032.  *grœðis*] HS, Skj B and EK involves little emendation; *greiðir* BK n.; *grœðir* both mss. does not make sense.   9.7–8 *en . . . greinum*] understand *fekk* from line 5. *mœðandi*] could be taken with *mein*.   10.3 *líns*] with *kenni* to form priest/ cleric-kenning; *linns* HS also taken with *kenni* but forms an odd man-kenning 'the wearer (or 'experiencer'?) of the serpent'. BK reads *líns kvinna* 'the woman of linen', an equally odd kenning.   11.4 *að sæta*] Skj B and EK is probable given that this clause needs an inf. construction and the sense 'to expose oneself to, be faced with' suits the context well; *a..e.a* 1032 and BK;

11  Hún fyr heimsku sína
    hrygðist viðr og iðrast
    þegar, en þorði eigi
 4  þrætu máls a[ð s]æta;
    gjörði hún öllum orðum
    angrþrútin við ganga;
    það manntíð*ni* meinar;
 8  morð er úr vígi orðið.

12  Frændr af frúinnar grandi
    fregna mannsins vegna;
    fljóðið fult af stríði
 4  fanga þeir, með angri;
    kvöl var silki-Sólu
    sett að dómi rjettum;
    [brá]tt skal bálið heita
 8  brenna líkama hennar.

She was sorry because of her stupidity and repents immediately, and dared not face contradiction of her words; swollen with sorrow, she confessed to everything; that does harm to a woman's reputation; the killing had turned into murder.

The relatives of the slain man hear of the lady's crime with grief; they took the suffering woman prisoner; a torment was set for Sól of silk [woman] according to the right judgement; soon the hot fire must burn her body.

alternatively, *að mæta* HS 'to encounter' with secondary alliteration between *máls* and *mæta*. **11.7** *manntíðni*] EK object of *meina* 'to do harm to' (cf. *NN* 1683 and 2865); the meaning of *manntíðni* (probably 'a person's popularity or reputation') is related to *tíðr* 'famous' or 'often spoken of'; *mantiðin* (or *manntiðin*) both mss. is not recorded elsewhere; *menn tíðin* BK is possible through alternative expansion of the abbreviation 'ñ'; *ment-iðinn* HS 'zealous for knowledge' referring to the priest; *manntiðin* Skj A/B is left out of the Danish translation. **12.7** *brátt*] HS, Skj B and EK, is the most likely word given that [...]*tt* in 721 would have begun with a *b* because of the alliteration and had a long vowel to form *skothending* with *heita*; space followed by *rt* 1032; ...*zt* BK.

13    Grjetu meyjar mætar,
      minnilig‹r› sem kvinna
      flokkrinn, karlmenn klökkva,
   4  kvöl barmandi arma;
      dregin var drós t[il] skógar
      döpr og mædd, svó hræddist;
      grjet sárliga sæta
   8  synd, er bálið kyndir.

14    [Öls] bað æskiselja
      angri mædd að ganga
      mörk í Maríu kirkju
   4  menn, er hana skulu brenna,
      því að mjúklátri meyju
      mild auðar Bil vildi
      sínar sorgir greina;
   8  senn veittu þeir henni.


Worthy young girls wept, as (did) the splendid host of women, men sob, pitying the wretched torment; the miserable and wearied woman was dragged to the forest so that she was afraid; she sorely lamented her sin when the fire is lit.

The desirous giver of ale [woman], exhausted with grief, begged the people, who are to burn her, that she might walk through the forest to the church of Mary, because mild Bil of riches [woman] wanted to tell her sorrows to the gentle Virgin; they granted her this at once.

**13.1** *meyjar*] *m..iar* 1032. **13.2** *minniligr*] Skj B and EK taken with *flokkrinn*; *minnilig* both mss.; *minniliga* HS. **13.5** *til*] 1032. **13.6** *svó*] *er* 1032. **13.7** *sæta*] *svarta* 1032. **13.8** *kyndir*] both mss. is, as HS noted, impersonal: 'when the fire is lit'. **14.1** *Öls*] 1032, HS, Skj A and EK. **14.3** *mörk*] 721 and EK, acc. with *ganga* 'through the forest'; *merk* 1032, BK t.n. and Skj B, a. construed

15  F[ór], sú er flóði í tárum,
    fann musterið svanni,
    sína grjet með greinum
 4  gjörð, og kraup að jörðu;
    þar sá fljóðið fríða
    *feskasta líkneskju
    þá, er Maríu meyju
 8  mynduð var til yndis.

16  Flóði á frúinnar klæði,
    fári spent, í tárum,
    og með angri nógu
 4  ófæltiliga mælti:
    'Sjáðu en mjúka móðir
    mína þörf og pínu:
    mig skulu meinum kvelja
 8  menn og eldi brenna.

The woman, who was bathed in tears, went, found the church, wept over her action with good reason and prostrated herself on the ground; there the lovely woman saw that very beautiful image, which was made for the joy of the Virgin Mary.

She (the woman) was flooded with tears over the Virgin's robe; clasped in danger and with abundant sorrow she spoke without fear: 'Gentle mother, see my need and suffering: people must torment me with injuries and burn me in fire.

with *æskiselja öls* 'the remarkable desirous giver of ale'; *mark* HS (59) construed with *kirkju* 'a remarkable church'. **14.5** *því að*] *þótti* 1032. **15.1** *Fór*] HS, Skj B and EK, forms *skothending* with *tárum* and fits grammatically; *Frú* BK (98) does not rhyme. **15.6** Both mss. have redundant *ed* (= *eð*, def. art.) at the beginning of this line; omitted Skj B and EK.

17  Því sótta eg þetta
    þitt líkneski að hitta
    mest að María treysta eg
 4  mín fulltingi þínum;
    öngvan á eg til gengis
    annan fæddra manna,
    því er eg sett í sára
 8  sorg, að mjer fái bo‹r›gið.

18  Fel eg nú, frú mín sælust,'
    fljóð mælir svó rjóðast,
    'líf‹s› orðinnar æfi
 4  enda þjer á hendi;
    gangi öll, þó að illa
    eg hafi gjört að segja,
    málin, meyja heilög
 8  mín, að vilja þínum.'

The reason I sought to visit this your image is that I rely most on your help, my Mary; I have no other born human being to turn to for support so that I may be saved, therefore I am put into sore grief.

My most blessed Lady, now I put the end of my spent life in your hands,' so says the deeply blushing woman; 'although I have poorly represented myself, my holy Virgin, may the entire case proceed according to your wish.'

**17.3** *María*] HS, Skj B and EK, taken with *mín*; *mariu* both mss. and BK does not fit the context. **17.4** *þínum*] with *fulltingi* (dat. sg. m.; see HS). **17.8** *borgið*] 1032. **18.3** *lífs*] Skj B and EK; *lífs enda* goes with *orðinnar æfi* to

19  Út gekk síðan sæta,
   sótt af mörgum dróttum,
   hún var harðri pínu
4  hreld, og leidd að eldi;
   bað hún mjúkláta móður,
   menn köstuðu henni,
   sat hún fastliga fjötruð,
8  friðar, í báli miðju.

20  Hlóðu bál að brúði,
   brann umhverfis svanna
   allr, á víðum velli,
4  viðköstr í fasta;
   vald Maríu vök‹d›ugt
   vinnr syndugri kvinnu
   bót, svó að hyrr enn heiti
8  hlífir frúinnar lífi.


Then the woman went outside, attacked by a great host; she was distressed by the severe torment and was led to the fire; she prayed to the kind mother for quarter; the people cast her in the middle of the pyre; she sat firmly fettered.

They built up a fire against the woman on an open field; a whole pile of wood burnt in flame around the lady; the mighty power of Mary brought about atonement for the sinful woman so that the hot fire spared her life.


form the phrase *enda lífs orðinnar æfi* 'the end of the spent course of (my) life'; *lif* both mss., BK and HS does not make sense.   **19.5** *hún*] in margin 721.   **20.5** *völdugt*] all eds.; *uollôgt* both mss. is meaningless.

21 Öld af fjandskap fyldist
   fljótt, er sýndi dróttinn
   vægð, og virðar sögðu
 4 villir sín á milli:
   'Eldsneyti hafa ýtar
   of lítið gjört rít*ar,*
   því hefr minst en mjóva
 8 mengrund af kvöl brunnið.'

22 Enn gjörðu þeir annan
   eld af harmi sveldir,
   hyrjar, miklu meira,
 4 mein bjó‹ð›andi fljóði;
   svó var æsilig eisa
   elds að hringa þellu
   bandið hvert, af brúði,
 8 brennr, en fjötrar renna.

The people were quickly filled with hostility when the Lord showed mercy and the erring people said among themselves: 'The pushers of the shield [men] have prepared too little firewood, therefore the slender necklace-ground [woman] has burnt very little as a result of her her torment.'

Swollen with passion, they made again another fire much bigger, presenting flame's harm to the woman; the embers of the fire were so vehement that every bond on the pine of rings [woman] burns and the fetters melt off the woman.

**21.6** *rítar*] HS, Skj B and EK, taken with *ýtar* (pl. of agent noun *ýtir* [cf. the verb *ýta* 'to push forward'] not the pl. noun *ýtar* 'men'; see Meissner 1921, 307) to form a warrior/man-kenning; *ritri* 721 and *rícri* 1032 and BK do not make sense. **22.3** *hyrjar*] gen. with *mein* but can also be taken with *eld* as in BK and HS. **22.4** *bjóðandi*] 1032. **22.7** *af brúði*] can be taken with *brennr* or *renna*; or perhaps with both. **23.7** No fully satisfactory emendation is available for the word missing in both manuscripts at the end of the line; no gap in 721 though the lack of *skothending* and alliteration as well as short syllable count suggests there is a disyllabic word beginning with *b* missing which provided *skothending* with *hosk* or *brúðr*, though since this poem is often irregular in metre and rhyme (see, for example, 2.3) the word does not necessarily have to conform metrically; the text of the ms. also has several grammatical

23  Máttr var móður dróttins
    mjög ríkr um frú slíka
    sýndr með sætleik reyndum
 4  sveit í loganum heita;
    þann gaf þessi kvinnu
    þrótt óskamey dróttins;
    hosk sat brúðr í ‹...›
 8  baugstalls um dag allan.

24  Hvergi rann á hennar
    hár í loganum sárum;
    klæðin fögr á fljóði
 4  fölna ei nje völna;
    Hildr gekk hrings úr eldi
    hæg og kyrr sem fyrri,
    naut hún Maríu mætrar
 8  miskunnar, óbrunnin.

The very great power of the mother of the Lord in relation to this woman in the hot flame, with her proven kindness, was shown to the people; the chosen virgin of the Lord gave that fortitude to this woman; the wise woman sat in... of the ring-seat [arm or shield] all day long. Not one of her hairs was touched in the severe flame; the beautiful clothes on the woman do not fade or shrivel; Hildr of the ring [woman] went from the fire, calm and collected, unburnt as before; she enjoyed the mercy of excellent Mary.

errors in the following stanzas (see below). Given the context, the missing word should mean, or relate to, 'fire', though *baugstalls* is left without a base-word and there is still no *skothending* if *báli* is supplied as in Skj B, which emends *brúðr* to *brú*, taken with *baugstalls* to form an otherwise unknown (though not impossible) woman-kenning (*brú* = resting-place); *bróður* HS is taken with *baugs hjalls* (substituted for *baugstalls*) to make a fire-kenning ('brother of Ægir'); *háska* EK is metrically better than the above suggestions; this reading involves the additional emendation of *baugstalls* to *haukstalds* 'nobleman'. **24.4** *nje*] + *brena* crossed out 721; *brena* adopted in BK. *völna*] apparently the only medieval occurrence of this word which is related to the Old English *wealwian* 'to dry up, shrivel, wither, decay', cf. Modern English 'wallow'; see *NN* 2808.

25　Sungu sætt og lengi
　　sannfróðir Guðs móður
　　lýð‹i›r lof, þá er brúði
4　litu hvíta þar sitja;
　　ljetu síðan sætu
　　seimstalls viðir allir
　　fara í friði og æru;
8　fljóð var sátt og þjóðir.

26　Hrings nam heim að ganga
　　Hlín í kirkju sína,
　　þakkar líf og lukku
4　lút þreyjandi meyju;
　　skrifa ljet baugs á brjefi
　　brík jarteignir slíkar,
　　að Maríæ meyjar
8　margfaldi lof aldir.

Sweetly and for a long time the well-informed people sang praise of the mother of God when they saw the white woman sitting there; afterwards all the trees of the seat of the gold ring [arm; people] let the woman go in peace and honour; the woman and the people were reconciled.

Hlín of the ring [woman] went home into her church; bowed down, the patient woman thanks the Virgin for her life and good fortune; the panel of the ring [woman] let these miracles be written in a document so that humankind may multiply the praise of the Virgin Mary.

**25.3** *lýðir*] HS, Skj B and EK; *lýðr* both mss. and BK. Pl. form is required as subject of *sungu* line 1.   **25.5** *sætu*] HS, Skj B and EK; *sæta* both mss. and BK. Acc. form needed for object of *ljetu.*   **25.6** *seim-*] *sioar* 1032.   *seimstalls viðir*] 'gold(ring)-seat's (i.e. arm's) trees' is a kenning for men modelled on the common type of woman-kenning *arma eik,* which in late poems is also found (with masculine tree-names) for man. Cf. Meissner 1921, 140, 269–71, 279, 419–20.   **26.4** *meyju*] HS n., Skj B and EK; *meyja* both mss. and BK. Dat. form required with *þakka.*   **27.1** *sæta sæt*] vocative, parallel to *þú* line 2.   **27.4** *svó*] supplied all eds.; lacking 1032.   *lífi*] 1032, BK t.n. and HS; *uifi* Skj

27  Heyrði sveit að sæta
    sæt leystir þú mætrar
    hold úr heitum eldi,
 4  hlífandi [svó lí]fi;
    minnstu, minnandi mestrar,
    meyja Guðs, þá er deyjum,
    þínum björtum bænum
 8  bál við vórum sálum.

28  Lúta þjer í þrautum
    þjóðir, dróttins móðir,
    bergr þú manni mörgum
 4  mest, þá er þurfa flestir;
    aldri muntu eldi
    enn vilja þann brenn*a*
    þinn, er þig hefr kunnað,
 8  þræl, María s[æla].


The company heard that you, sweet lady, freed the flesh of the excellent one from the hot fire, so saving her life; Virgin of God, while remembering this very great woman, remember in your bright prayers the fire at our souls when we die.

People pray to you in distress, mother of the Lord; you save many a person most when the majority of them need you; you, blessed Mary, will never wish this your servant, who has known you, still to burn in the fire.


B and EK. **27.5–8** *minnstu . . . sálum*] makes some sense as it stands, though *minna* in this sense is usually impers. ('virgin of God, while remembering this very great woman, remember in your bright prayers the fire at our souls when we die', i.e. save us from damnation through your prayers). The following emendations are not adopted because they involve too much tampering with the text.  **27.5** *minnstu*] *forða* Skj B;  *Firr* EK.    *minnandi*] *unnande* HS. *mestrar*] *mestar* HS; *mærrar* Skj B and EK.   **27.8** *við*] uncertain 721, *af* HS; 1032 omits.    *sálum*] BK omits.   **28.6** *brenna*] all eds.; *brenni* both mss. Inf. form needed with *vilja*.   **28.8** *sæla*] all eds.; *sæl..* 1032.

29   Nú hefi eg út fyr ýtum
     þitt [sem þ]að minti,
     inta jarteign eina
   4 alhróðigri Guðs móð[u]r;
     veittu, María, meiri
     miskunn en [vjer] kunnim
     oss, þá er andir missum,
   8 iðröndum. Guð biðjum.

Now I have told to the end before people a miracle by you the entirely triumphant mother of God, as I remembered it; Mary, give us, the repentant ones, more mercy than we know when we lose our lives. Let us pray to God.

29.2 *þitt*] *ynítt* 1032, *ynitt* BK and HS. *sem það*] *sem .at* 1032. Little sense can be made of the ms. readings here; no attempt at reconstruction is made in Skj A and B. HS n. suggests *innilega* (with *jarteign*) *sem eg minti*, and EK reads *innit þitt mik minti* 'templet ditt jag mindes' (see *NN* 1691), neither of which is completely satisfactory; *jarteign*, however, can be either n. or f., and perhaps both *þitt* and *inta eina* agree with it. Cf. *MvII* 1.6–7.   29.4 -*hróðigri*] taken with dat. *móður*.   *móður*] *moð.r* 1032.   29.6 *vjer*] HS, Skj B and EK.
29.8 *biðjum*] 1st pers. pl. imp. 'let us pray'.

## Maríuvísur II

*AM 721 ff. 13v–14r; AM 713 ff. 85–87; AM 711a ff. 81–102.*
*This text is from AM 721.*

1   ⟨D⟩ýrðar gefðu dóms vörðr
    drott*inn*, er alt gott
    veitir, að bragar-bót,
4   brögnum, gjaldi hjer þögn;
    móður þinnar, minn Guð,
    megna vil eg jarteign
    segja, það er sæl mey
8   sætu dugði ágæt.

2   Veittu að lof ljett
    líði fram á gleðitíð
    Andrjeás, að mjúk mynd
4   mærðar væri Guði færð:
    hvessu mætust mjúklát
    móðir og þrautgóð
    brúði þeiri, er bar nauð,
8   bænum krafði⟨st⟩, Guðs kvón.

Guardian of the court of glory [heaven; Christ], Lord, who gives all that is good to humankind, grant this, that silence may be paid here to the ornament of poetry; my God, I will tell of your mother's mighty miracle, in which the blessed, excellent Virgin helped a woman.

Andrew, grant that effortless praise may flow forth in a time of joy, so that an eloquent form of praise may be presented to God: (telling) how the most excellent, kind and helpful mother, the bride of God, was called on with prayers by that woman who was in trouble.

**1.1** *Dýrðar*] 713 and 711a; *with space for capital* 721.  **1.2** *drottinn*] 713, 711a and all eds. fits into the context better than *drottir* 721 'host of people'.  **2.8** *krafðist*] Skj B and EK involves little change, fits grammatically and improves the sense greatly; *krafðe* 721, BK and HS, *uafði* 713 and 711a.

3   Herra nokkurr hugdýrr
    hreinn bygði stað einn;
    kæra hans af konum bar
4   kurteis, sem frá er spurt;
    unnust *þau* hún og hann
    hjartaliga; vili bjartr
    láta ekki má í mót
8   milli þess, er hvórt vill.

4   Sýnast máttu sögð hjón
    sjúku fólki auðmjúk,
    föðurliga fagrráð,
4   fátækum örlát;
    hævesk og hugljúf
    hverjum þeim í nánd er
    vurðu þau; af velferð
8   veldi tók að þróast heldr.


There was a certain courageous, virtuous lord who lived in a town; his courteous wife surpassed other women of whom there is report; he and she loved each other sincerely; between them the good wish (of one) could not oppose that which either of the two wished.

The above-mentioned husband and wife could show themselves humble to sick people, giving wise counsel in a fatherly way, generous to the poor; they became courteous and kind to everyone who was round about them; because of their prosperity their influence began rather to increase.


**3.5** *þau*] 713, 711a, BK and HS; *sem* 721; Skj A reads *suo*. **3.8** *þess*] *það* 713 and 711a. **4.3** *fagr-*] *faugr* 713, 711a. **5.2** *við*] 713, 711a; *með* 721. *gulls*] *gull-* 713 and 711a. **6.1** *Sótti*] HS, Skj B and EK; *Sottu* all mss. and BK; sg.

5   Erfingja ógndjarfr
    öngan *við* gulls spöng
    getið hafði; góðlátr
 4  gjarna vildi ala barn;
    hennar í hvert sinn
    harmr tók að gjörast armr,
    önnur þá er frúin fann
 8  fljóðin plaga sín jóð.

6   Sótt*i* til söngs þrátt
    sorguð í höfuðborg
    kvinna, þar er kljent rann
 4  kirkja stóð Guði virk,
    musterið af múr gjört
    Maríu og stöpull hár,
    þar er að barni baugnorn
 8  bænum syrgði opt væn.

The courageous man had not begotten any heir with the plate of gold [woman]; the courteous man eagerly wanted to have a child; her sorrow began to become severe every time when the lady came across the other women nursing their babies.

The sorrowful woman constantly attended Mass in the main town, where there stood a beautiful building, a church dear to God, the minster of Mary and a high tower built with stone walls where the beautiful ring-Norn [woman] often grieved with prayers for a child.

required with subject *kvinna*. **6.4** *kirkja*] in apposition to *kljent rann* line 3. **6.5** *musterið... gjört*] The church is part of a monastery as in the analogue in *Ms* (977.14).

7 Ríkust frú‹in› tala tók
   tregafull á þann veg
   optast, þar er skorin skript
4 skærar meyjar stóð nær:
   'Sælust heyrðu mitt mál
   María og þau tár
   er sætan síst kát
8 sútafullust gefr út.

8 Sje eg það, sæl frú,
   sonu elr hver kvon;
   frjófast af því flest víf
4 fegin, nema sjálf eg;
   gleðifullan getnað
   gjaltu mjer, víf snjalt,
   meyjan, að eg mega fá
8 móður nafn og bera jóð.

This very powerful, sorrowful lady very frequently began to speak in this way where a carved image of the excellent Virgin stood nearby: 'Most blessed Mary, hear my case and those tears which this least cheerful woman, most sorrowful, pours forth.

I see this, blessed Lady, every woman bears sons; most wives are joyfully fruitful as a result, except I myself; skilful woman, Virgin, grant me a happy conception so that I can take the name of mother and bear a child.

7.1 *frúin*] 713, 711a, Skj B and EK. 8.3–4 *frjófast . . . fegin*] can be read as 'because most joyful women conceive' or 'most joyful women conceive as a result of that (i.e. of being married)'. 9.5 *hneyksl*] 713, 711a, all eds.; *hneykls*

9   Bæði fyr barnfæð
    bíða urðu mikið stríð
    faðir þinn og fögr mæðr,
 4  frúin áðr en vartú;
    brigsli og búin hneyks*l*
    berast mun á hönd mjer,
    ef eg aldri jóð mild
 8  ala mínum ver skal.'

10  Mjúkust heyrð*i* mál slík
    María og fögr tár;
    kæran varð kynstór
 4  kviðuð eptir lands sið;
    fæðingar á frumtíð
    fögr bar sinn mög,
    gjörðist þá, gullskorð,
 8  gleðitími kominn með.

Both your father and fair mother had to endure a lot of torment because of their childlessness before you, our Lady, were born; reproach and ready-made shame will be borne against me if I shall never bear gentle babies for my husband.'

Kindest Mary heard these words and beautiful tears; the high-born wife fell pregnant according to the custom of the land; in the first hour of giving birth the fair gold-prop [woman] bore her son, then a period of happiness arose with it.

721.  **10.1** *heyrði*] 713, 711a, all eds.; *heyrðu* 721.  **10.7** *gullskorð* can be taken as subject of *bar* line 6, but would perhaps be better read as dat. sg. with *kominn* line 8.

11  Vænan leggr víf svein
    í vöggu með búin plögg,
    fríðan elskar frúin nið,
 4  faðir hans og ljek að;
    móðir unni megi blíð;
    má hún varla af sjá,
    svó að brúð‹a›r Guðs góð
 8  gáði trautt, sem hefir áðr.

12  Unnandi eitt sinn
    að jóði sínu ljek fljóð;
    sjúkan kendi hún sárleik
 4  sveini gjöra lífs mein;
    sútafull í sitt skaut
    svanni lagði mög þann,
    svó að barni bani forn
 8  búinn þótti vera nú.

The woman lays the fair boy in a cradle with embroidered bedclothes; the lady loves her beautiful son, and his father played with him; the kind mother loved her son; she can scarcely take her eyes off him, so that the good one hardly heeded the bride of God as she has previously done.

One time the loving woman was playing with her baby; she noticed a severe pain delivering a mortal blow to the boy; the sorrowful woman laid the son in her lap so that it seemed the old slayer was now ready for the child.

**11.3** *nið*] *við* 711a.  **11.7** *brúðar*] 713, Skj B and EK; *bruðr* 721, BK and HS, 'so that the good woman hardly heeded God as she had previously done' is also possible, though less likely in a context of a poem about devotion to the Virgin.  **11.8** *hefir*] *hefur* 711a.  **12.3** *hún*] in margin 721.  **12.5** *sitt skaut*]

13  Síðan lá sveinn dauðr,
    sætan af trega grætr
    lengi, meðan lá ungr
  4 líkamr á börum slíkr;
    auðar þellan óglöð
    annan dag flytr hann
    þar er kirkju mikið mark
  8 Maríu í borg stár.

14  Hreina vildu huggan
    henni veita staðarmenn;
    engi mátti auðspöng
  4 eina finna feginsgrein;
    sat hún upp og sárt grjet
    sonar, það er mikil von,
    dauða, unz dagr leið
  8 dróttum en kemr nótt.

Afterwards the boy lay dead; the woman wept from sorrow for a long time, while this young body lay on the bier; the next day the unhappy pine of riches [woman] carried him to where the great buildings of the church of Mary stand in the city.

The townspeople wanted to give her sincere comfort; no one could find a single reason for joy for the plate of riches [woman]; she sat up and wept bitterly over the death of her son, which is only to be expected, until the day passed for the people and night comes.

*sinn klut* 713 and 711a.  **13.4** *líkamr*] *likame* 713 and 711a.  **14.3** *engi*] *eigi* 713 and 711a.  **14.6** *það*] *þess* 713, 711a.  *er*] 713 and 711a omit.  **14.8** *kemr*] *kom* 713 and 711a.

## Maríuvísur II

15 Mátti vera miðnótt,
    móðir sveins er upp stóð
    og í burtu barn stirt
4 af börum tók gulls Vör;
    móðurinnar dís dýr
    driptar sá hvar stóð skript;
    ljet hún niðr lítt kát
8 líkamann við orð slík:

16 'Líknarinnar lofað tákn
    líttu hjer á barn frítt
    það er minning miskunn
4 mínu holdi gaf þín;
    móður nafn og [minn] heiðr
    mist hefi eg nú tvist;
    vel máttu björt böl
8 bæta mjer frúin sæt.

It must have been midnight when the boy's mother got up and Vör of gold [woman] took the stiff child away off the bier; the goddess of snow [woman] saw where a precious image of the mother [of God] stood; with little joy, she put down the body with these words:
'Praised symbol of mercy [the Virgin], look here on a beautiful child which is a remembrance your mercy gave to my flesh; sad, I have now lost the name of mother and my honour; our luminous sweet Lady, you can well put right this misfortune for me.

**15.5** *dýr*] with either *skript móðurinnar* or *Dís*. **16.1** *lofað*] *lofuð* 713, 711a.
**16.5** *minn*] 713 and 711a. **16.7** *björt*] 713, 711a, Skj B and EK; *borit* 721, BK and HS. **16.8** *frúin*] *meyian* 713 and 711a. **17.1** *Vænni*] *-ni* unclear 721; read

17 Væn[ni] muntu vórkunn
veita fyr tár heit
brúði, þótt í barns nauð
4 bera kunni sorg hjer;
líða svó lífs nauð
láttu að eg deyi brátt,
ella græði friðar-full
8 fljóða hjálpin mitt jóð.'

18 Manna hjálp og miskunn
mátti eigi hrings gátt
lengr fyr lífs angr
4 láta bera sinn grát,
[svó] að í limu líkams
litr kom og fagrt vit;
sendist aptr sæl önd;
8 sveini gaf það mey hrein.

In return for passionate tears you will show compassion for a fair woman, since during her child's distress she was able to convey her sorrow here; let life's distress pass so that I die soon or else, peaceful help of women [Virgin], heal my baby.'
The help and mercy of mankind [the Virgin] could no longer let the door-post of the ring [woman] endure her lamentation on account of life's sorrow, so that colour and good wits returned to the limbs of his body; the blessed soul was sent back; the virtuous Virgin gave that to the boy.

*Vænuz* Skj A; *Vænne* 713 and 711a. **17.3** *þótt í*] *þotte* 713 and 711a. *barns nauð*] read as *barn-snauð* HS n. 'childlessness'. **17.5** *nauð*] *tið* 713 and 711a. **18.1** *Manna*] 713; unclear 721; *Maria* 711a and BK. **18.5** *svó*] 713 and 711a.

19 Lifna fyr lofað nafn
   lætr síðan Guð mætr,
   sá hann upp og sætt hló
 4 sína móður utan pín;
   fljóði gazt feginstíð
   farnaðar og lífs barn,
   gaf hún síðan Guði lof,
 8 grátandi og þó kát.

20 Tunga má það alls öng
   inna í brag sinn,
   hvessu móðir míns Guðs
 4 mundi heiðra göfugt sprund,
   þá er föður hrings hlíð
   hreinum færði kvikan svein,
   þann er fjörvi fjögur dægr
 8 firðr lá á börum stirðr.

Afterwards excellent God let him revive for the praised name; he looked up at his mother and laughed sweetly without pain; the woman got a joyful time of prosperity and her child alive; afterwards she gave praise to God, weeping and yet happy.

Not one tongue can relate in its poetry how the mother of my God could honour a noble woman, when the hill-side of the ring [woman] carried to the virtuous father the living boy who, deprived of life, had lain stiff on the bier for four half-days.

**19.1** *Lifna*] *hann* acc. understood.   **19.3** *hann*] i.e. the child.   **19.6** *lífs barn*] subject of *gazt* parallel to *feginstíð farnaðar*.

21  Þegar gjörðu þá mjög
    þjóðir og göfugt fljóð
    að lofa ljúft víf
 4  listuga er bar Krist;
    og með þrifum þaðan af
    þjóna tóku Guði hjón;
    þeira var blíðr burr
 8  bráðgjörr og heilráðr.

22  María ertu mey skær
    móðir og líkn góð
    öllum þeim er ákall
 4  jaf‹n›an veita á þitt nafn;
    þjóðin öll þig biðr,
    þú heitir vór frú,
    en vjer segjumst syndug,
 8  sveitir þínar, háleit.

Then the people and the noble woman immediately began to praise greatly the beloved, skilled woman who bore Christ; and from then on the husband and wife began to serve God in prosperity; their gentle son was advanced in his development and gave wise counsel.

Mary, you are a luminous Virgin, mother and good mercy for all those who always invoke your name; all the people pray to you; you are called our Lady, and, sublime one, we, your followers, declare ourselves sinful.

22.4 *jafnan*] 713 and 711a.  22.7 *segjumst*] 713 and 711a; spelled *seígumzt* 721.

23  Synda veittu, sannreynd,
    sanna, við Guð og mann,
    þótt vjer brjótum, meyin mæt,
 4  móti honum, yfirbót;
    og að sönnu son þinn
    sálir fyr lífs mál
    græðarann geti sjeð
 8  glaðan; veittu oss það.

24  Þikk‹j›umst eg í þinn flokk
    þeygi kunna, Guðs mey
    skærust, sem skylt er,
 4  skilin orð að fá til;
    verði þjer valin dýrð,
    vífa sæmdin, eilíf
    um alla heims höll
 8  haldin með Guðs vald. Amen.

Excellent Virgin, proved true to God and mankind, give true atonement of sins even though we offend against Him; and may souls be able to see your joyous son in truth, the Saviour, at the end of life; grant us that.

Most luminous Virgin of God, I do not consider myself at all capable of providing clear words for your poem as is my duty; honour of women [the Virgin], may eternal choice glory be maintained for you by the power of God throughout the entire hall of the world. Amen.

**23.2** *sanna*] with *yfirbót* line 4. **23.3** *meyin*] *meyian* 713 and 711a. **23.5** *son*] *sonr* 713 and 711a. **23.6** *fyr lífs mál*] 'at the end of life'; *NN* 3364 suggests something like 'beyond life's borderline'. **24.1** *í*] 711a omits. **24.8** *Amen*] in margin 721.

## Maríuvísur III

*AM 721 ff. 15v–16v; AM 1032 ff. 143v–157v.*
*This text is from AM 721.*

1 ⟨D⟩róttinn gef þú mjer mátt
 máttugr bragar hátt,
 svó að eg færði fögr orð,
4 faðir vórr, í einn stað;
 veittu fyr vald þitt,
 valdandi Guð um aldr
 ástar, í opið brjóst
8 óttalausa máls nógt.

2 Heyrðu svó að hrein orð
 hitti eg og gleði mitt
 æstr fyr unað best
4 Andrjeás hugar land;
 minnunst eg að mey sönn
 María, sú er líkn vór
 í hreinum vís vón
8 verkum, leysti einn klerk.


Mighty Lord, our Father, give me ability, the verse-form of poetry, so that I might put together beautiful words; God, ruler of love for ever, through your power give a fearless abundance of speech to my open breast.

Listen most noble Andrew so that I may find clear words and gladden my heart-land [breast] to my best satisfaction; I remember that the true Virgin Mary, who is our mercy, our certain hope in virtuous deeds, freed a certain cleric.


1.1 *Dróttinn*] 1032 and all eds.; with a space for the capital 721.

3  Siða geymdi sjá maðr
   sjaldan um barns aldr;
   uppi vill hann heims hopp
4  hafa þegar til gaf;
   þegninn lagði þrátt magn
   þykkjustórr í víndrykk;
   gjörðist hann við gleðiorð
8  gálauss um sitt mál.

4  Rít‹a›r gjörðist ranglátr
   rennir við yfirmenn;
   hjartað varð af sökum sárt,
4  siðir spillast þar við;
   kvinna ástin kvelr hann,
   klerkum er það mein, sterk;
   var hann úr viti nær
8  vífa fyr gleðilíf.


This man had seldom heeded morality throughout his childhood; he wanted to enjoy the merriment of the world as soon as it was on offer; the arrogant fellow put persistent effort into wine-drinking; amidst words of merriment he became careless about his affairs.

The distributor of the shield [man] became unjust towards his superiors; his heart became wounded by sins; with that his morality was corrupted; intense lust for women tormented him; that is harmful for clerics; he was bordering on insanity because of his life of merriment with women.


**4.1** *Rítar*] Skj B and EK (gen. sg.) with *rennir* 'distributor of the shield' makes better sense than HS (64) *Rita* with *rennir* 'Feind der (heiligen) Schriften'; *Ritr* 721, 1032 and BK may, however, be a gen. sg. form (cf. Noreen 1923, §417). **4.3** *hjartað*] *hiartit* 1032 and BK. **4.6** *sterk*] with *ástin* line 5, though could perhaps be taken with *mein* (pl.) as in HS. **5.1** *-st*] 1032. **5.2** One

5   Sefi gjörði[st] saurlífr,
    sárum [...] hugarfár,
    lýtanna logi heitr
4   lerkað fekk þann klerk;
    hverja nótt að hann fór
    Hrundar á gulls fund
    villr yfir vazfall
8   vóða gekk um hans ráð.

6   Ítr hafði einn hlut
    jafnan fyr Guðs nafn
    Maríu, sem vitum vær,
4   vaktað, ef frá er sagt:
    hann las í hvert sinn
    hæstar tíðir Guði næst
    mjúkri við mein slík
8   móður þegar hann upp stóð.

His mind became unchaste; painfully ... evil disposition; the hot flame of his sins was able to injure that cleric with wounds; every night that, erring, he crossed a river to meet Hrund of gold [woman], he trod dangerously with his situation.

Excellent, he had always observed one thing in the name of God for Mary, as we shall see if it is related: every time when he got up he immediately recited the most sublime hours for the mother, kind regarding such transgressions, next to God.

expects a monosyllabic verb after *sárum*, but there are no clues as to what it should be; *l..tit* 1032; *var þat* HS n.; *óx* EK; *hneig* 'declined' would be possible. **5.8** *vóða*] *hann* line 5 is understood in line 8 and *vóða* (dat.) is used adverbially. **6.1** *einn hlut*] object of *hafði vaktað*. **6.3** *Maríu*] 'for Mary'. **6.4** *ef frá er sagt*] with *sem vitum vær* line 3. **6.6** *hæstar*] *hæstri* 1032.

7 Enn fór hann eitt sinn
   ofanvert nætrrof
   heiman yfir stór-straum,
4  strangan efldi fossgang;
   farið gjörði* fult nær
   flóðið, það er hann stóð;
   leynir óttast líftjón
8  lýta, ef skipið brýtr.

8 Kvíðir við kvala nauð
   klerkr fyr mein sterk;
   treysti hann á tign Krists,
4  trúandi, og biðr nú:
   'Nær vertu ‹mær› mjer
   María svó að linist fár;
   lát mig eigi, dugar drótt,
8  deyja hjer, Guðs mey.'

One time when it was nearing dawn he again went from home across the great river; the powerful flow of the tumbling stream was increased; the water which came upon him nearly filled the boat; the hider of sins is terrified of death if the boat is wrecked.

The cleric is worried about the distress of tortures because of his dire sins; he relied upon the sublimity of Christ, believing, and now he prays: 'Glorious Mary, stand by me so that the danger will be softened; Virgin of God, the company (of angels) will help; do not let me die here.'

7.4 *strangan*] with *fossgang* (see *NN* 3366), or with *stór-straum* line 3. 7.5 *gjörði*] Skj B and EK requires little change and improves the grammar and sense; or *giordizt* both mss. could be retained and *flóðið* line 6 emended to *flóði* and *það* replaced with *þar* (1032). 7.6 *það*] *þar* 1032, BK and HS. *hann*] *hafði* 1032. 8.5 *mær*] 1032; either the adjective 'renowned' with *María* or the noun 'Virgin' in apposition. 8.7 *dugar*] an unusual form of the pres.

9   Tíða sinna tregbjóðr
    trúar hafði ei gáð nú,
    heyriliga hann hefr þær,
 4  henni boðast dýrð tvenn;
    lítið fekk hann lesið út,
    líðr svó að honum stríð;
    Áve María hann upp hóf
 8  óttafullr og dó skjótt.

10  Síðan er hann sökk niðr,
    syndafullr, og varð drektr,
    kraup hann kafadjúp,
 4  kaldr eptir liðinn aldr;
    lítr þegar líf þraut
    lokkandi djöfuls flokkr;
    fjandr gripu fast önd
 8  fleiri en telist þeir.

The reluctant preacher of the faith had not heeded his hours this time; he began them out loud; double glory was proclaimed for her [the Virgin]; he could complete only little of his recitation, so (quickly) did torment come upon him; full of fear he began the *Ave Maria* and died swiftly.

After he sank down, sinful, and was drowned, he crept through the great depth, cold after his departed life; the devil's luring flock saw when his life failed; more fiends than can be counted gripped his soul firmly.

indicative; the phrase is presumably a parenthesis, 'the host (of angels) will help'. **9.3** *þær*] refers back to *tíða* line 1. **9.8** 1032 has *í* at the beginning of this line where there is an inkblot in 721. **10.2** *syndafullr*] with *hann.* **10.3** *hann*] Skj A reports a possible *í* above the line after this word; adopted in Skj B and EK. **10.5** *lítr*] *lidr* 721.

11 Englar kómu að þeim
ofan með Guðs lof.
'Láti þjer,' kvað ljúf sveit,
4 'liggja þann er frið þiggr;
en ef þjer hatið hann,
hefndin verðr af Guði efnd;
María kallar mann sjer;
8 muni þjer að kemr hun.'

12 Hrópar hinn, er gaf glæp,
og greinir þegar klerks mein;
löstu ber á lopt fast;
4 ló hann við margt þó,
áðr himi‹n›s björt brúðr
borgið fekk hans sorg;
er af rótum rjettlát
8 runnin upp við miskunn.

Angels confronted them from above with God's permission: 'Let him rest who will receive peace,' said the beloved troop; 'but if you persecute him, vengeance will be carried out by God; Mary claims the man for herself; be aware that she will come.'

That one who gave sin [the devil] called out loudly and immediately told of the cleric's sins, firmly revealing his faults; he lied about many things though, until the luminous bride of heaven was able to relieve his (the cleric's) sorrow; that just one is filled with mercy from the roots up.

12.5 *himins*] HS, Skj B and EK; BK n. *himnes*; *himes* both mss. must be a scribal error, but cf. 14.2 and 30.1. **12.7–8** *af rótum* . . . *runnin upp við miskunn*] grown up from the roots with mercy, i.e. full of mercy from head to

13  María kom til móts þar,
    móðurliga hún hjá stóð;
    dökkr hafði djöfuls flokkr
 4  dregið hann á kvala veg;
    hrygðarfull, 'Höfuðslægð
    hverju valdi taki þjer
    meinafullir minn þjón?'
 8  mærin talar Guði kær.

14  'Hvessu máttu í hendr oss,
    himiríkis frú slík,
    þennan eigna þjer mann?'
 4  þverinn mælti kvala herr;
    'Fleygir gjörði fjarðlogs
    flest það er hann gat vest,
    svó var hann saurlífr
 8  syndafullr og harðlyndr.

Mary came to that gathering there; she stood nearby in motherly fashion; the devil's dark flock had dragged him on the path of torments; the sorrowful Virgin, dear to God, speaks: 'By what power are you harmful beings taking my servant with outstanding cunning?'

'How can you, such a lady of the kingdom of heaven, take this man for yourself from in our hands?' said the defiant host of torments [fiends]; 'the distributor of the fjord-flame [gold; man] did most things the worst he could, he was so unchaste, sinful and harsh-tempered.

toe. Cf. *Hávamál* st. 138. **14.**2 *himiríkis*] all mss. is a Norwegian form, see Fr. **14.**4 *þverinn*] *þverra* 1032.

15  Siða skyldar svó Guð
　　sannan vera hvern mann:
　　hæfilæti og hreint líf,
4  háleitt er það lögmál;
　　hjer í móti að hann fór
　　háðuliga með sitt ráð,
　　fleiri gjörði hann verk vór
8  en vili Guðs að stóð til.'

16  'Eg mun eigi það við þig
　　þræta,' kvað meyin sæt,
　　'Guðs hefr bana blóð
4  banni frá leyst hann;
　　býð eg því mens meið
　　máli og klerks sál,
　　að sönnu, fyr son minn,
8  sjer hann það er rjett er.'

God requires every person to be true in morals thus: moderation and a virtuous life, this is sublime law; on the contrary when he proceeded shamefully with his conduct, he performed more of our deeds than what God's will was directed towards.'
'I will not argue with you about that,' said the sweet Virgin, 'God's death-blood has freed him from damnation; in this case I summon the necklace-tree [man] and the cleric's soul before my son; in truth He sees what is right.'

**16.5–7** Awkward, though not incomprehensible: *mens meið* parallel to *klerks sál, því máli* adverbial, 'in this case'. Skj B and EK emend *meið* to *meiðs* so that *mens meiðs* is gen. with *því máli.* Cf. *Mg* 51.5, 8.

17   Koma fyr Krist‹s› dóm
     kvalarar, sem geta skal,
     akta þeir upp kveikt
   4 ógurliga nýtt róg:
     árar kváðu álmbör
     jafnan styggja Guðs nafn;
     sárar gengu sakir nær;
   8 sögðu þeir hans brögð.

18   Kippa þeir um klerk upp
     kyndugir höfuðsynd:
     'Siða drýgði sviptuðr
   4 sómalausan hórdóm;
     síðast, áðr lífið leið,
     líkti hann að gjöra slíkt,
     fyr þetta saka-sár
   8 sálin verðr að hafa bál.'

The tormentors came before Christ's judgement; as will be told, they frighteningly devised a new invented slander: the messengers said that the bow-tree [man] always blasphemed the name of God; dire accusations pressed upon him; they told of his tricks.

Those cunning beings dragged up about the cleric a cardinal sin: 'The destroyer of morality committed dishonourable fornication; finally, before his life came to an end it pleased him to do such things, because of this sinful blemish his soul must have fire.'

**17.1** *Krists*] HS, Skj B and EK; *crist* both mss. It is not likely that this is an example of an undeclined foreign name since *Kristr* is declined as an Icelandic word elsewhere (e.g. 8.3). **18.8** *bál*] *sál* 1032.

19 Árum veitti andsvör
   unnandi miskunn,
   heldr verndar meyin mild
4  merkiliga sinn klerk;
   ræð⟨i⟩r svó rík brúðr:
   'Rjetta hefr yðr stjett
   dáðum prýddr Davíð
8  diktað, er hann söng slíkt:

20 "Rangir vóttar ráð þung
   *rísa upp og gjöra;" slíkt
   lygi flytr reift róg,
4  rennr sú er með flærð enn;
   minnast rjeð á miskunn
   maðr sá,' [a]ð frúin kvað,
   'að sönnu las hann Síóns
8  síðast á lífs [tíð].

Loving Mercy gave answers to the messengers; the kind Virgin defends her cleric in a rather remarkable way; so the powerful bride speaks: 'David, adorned with achievements, has dictated the right attitude for you all when he sang this:
"False witnesses rise up and carry out harsh plans"; their lie spreads this slander in a lively way, which (lie) spreads further by falsehood; that man did remember Mercy,' said our Lady to them, 'for sure he recited Zion's (song) in the last hour of life.

**19.3** *meyin*] *meyia* 1032. **19.5** *rœðir*] Skj B and EK; *rœðr* both mss., BK and HS is likely to be an error. **20.1–4** Awkward grammatically and semantically and requires some emendation and explanation. **20.1–2** appears to paraphrase Psalm 34 (35): 11, and *rísa* is closer to the Vulgate *surgentes* than *reisa* Skj B and EK; *ráð þung* must be the object of *gjöra*. There is nothing for *slíkt* to go with except *reift róg*. **20.2** Both mss. have a redundant *er* at the beginning of this line; omitted in Skj B and EK. **20.4** *rennr*] Skj B and EK gives better sense than subj. *renni* both mss. (*sú er rennr* refers to *lygi* line 3). **20.6** *að*] Skj A and B and EK is the most likely word; *er* 1032. *kvað*] *bað* 1032. **20.7** *Síóns*] *söng* understood, i.e. the Ave Maria. **20.8** *tíð*] 1032 and all eds.; very faint 721. **21.1–2** *Munnr hans mart lýsist upp*] 'his mouth is lit up a lot', referring to the recitation of the Ave Maria, and allowing *björt tungan* lines

21  Munnr hans,' kvað mekt sönn,
    '[mart l]ýsist upp, björt
    tungan endi sinn söng,
 4  og sjái f[y]st hvað það má.'
    Skýja laus skö[r] ló,
    skilja má að, kóng til,
    Áve María upphaf
 8  á var þar skráð þá.

22  Árar stukku þegar þeir
    þessa heyrðu getið vess;
    síðan yrðir sæl brúðr
 4  sveitir þeira háleit:
    'Hversu máttu [hjer]
    hælast,' kvað meyin sæl,
    'þennan kalla eg mann mjer,
 8  minna sje eg að þjer vinnst.

His mouth,' said the true power, 'is lit up greatly; his bright tongue concluded its song, but first let us see what it can achieve.' The reckless flock lied to the king of clouds [Christ] about it; one can perceive that the beginning of the *Ave Maria* was written there (on his tongue) then.

Those messengers took to flight as soon as they heard mention of this verse; afterwards the blessed, sublime bride addresses the crowds of them: 'How could you boast about this?' said the blessed Virgin, 'I claim this man for myself; I see that you are winning less for yourself.

2–3 to be read literally. **21.2** *mart lýsist*] EK is a likely conjecture for the illegible graphs in 721; *mar..s..uist* 1032. *upp björt*] ..*i bi..* 1032. **21.4** *fyst*] Skj A, is the most likely here; *f..* 1032. **21.5** *skör*] HS, 721 uncertain; *sku.* 1032, Skj A. **21.6** *kóng*] abbreviated $\bar{k}$ 721 as alsewhere, read as *kom* HS and EK; but this scribe uses $\bar{ko}$ for *kom* (*MvII* 18.6) or writes the word in full (*MvI* 7.1 and *MvIII* 13.1); $\bar{ki}$ 1032. **21.8** *skráð*] 721 uncertain; *ski...* 1032. *þá*] *fá* 1032; 721 uncertain. **22.3** *yrðir*] ..*ðir* 1032. **22.5** *máttu*] after this word 721 has *i hendr oss himerikis* deleted (cf. 14.1–2). **22.5, 8** The singular pronoun is used in addressing the (leader of?) the *árar*; the pl. pron. in 23.1, 5, 7 is presumably not the 'polite' plural. **22.5** *hjer*] *hior* 1032; 721 uncertain. **22.8** *eg*] omitted 1032.

23 Ginni þjer frá Guði menn
   að gjöra það eð illt er,
   sárar fyr sakir þær
 4 síðan að þeir fái stríð;
   einatt skal yðr pín
   aktast, þá frá er sagt
   að þjer freistið fira mest
 8 og fáið eigi svikið þá.'

24 Flatir hurfu frá í braut
   fjandr, [sviptir hans] önd,
   og mistu nýtt nest
 4 nauðigir, sem Guð bauð;
   sína bað Sátán
   sveina fá stór mein,
   er þeir kómu í kvalir heim;
 8 kvað hann vera skylt það.

You entice humankind away from God to do what is evil so that afterwards they endure pain because of those dire offences; torment shall constantly be devised for you when it is mentioned that you do your best to tempt people yet do not manage to deceive them.'

The shame-faced fiends made off, deprived of his soul, and were forced to go without new meat, as God commanded; Satan ordered his servants to suffer severe pains when they came back into torments; he said that was obligatory.

23.4 *síðan*] *siðir* 1032. 24.2 *sviptir hans*] Skj A and B and EK; *sn..ir..* 1032; 721 uncertain. 24.3 *nýtt nest*] i.e. a new soul. 24.6 *fá*] *fái* 1032. 24.8 *kvað ... það*] 'he said he could do nothing else'. 25.3 *að*] 1032; *af* Skj B and EK; 721 uncertain. *að ... líf*] i.e. a life which is comfortable but not too easy,

## Maríuvísur III

25  Göfugligt Guðs víf
    gefr fyr utan ef
    [að] hófi hægt líf;
4   heimar skiptust klerk þeim;
    síðan undir sátt bauð
    sættandi fljóðið mætt
    að hann rjetti ráð sitt;
8   rausnar var það fögr lausn.

26  Þerfiliga þaðan af
    þakkir gjörði hugrakkr,
    meðan endist líf lunds
4   linna, við Guð sinn;
    og af mönnum mest ann
    maðr sjá fyr dugnað
    Maríu, sem vón var;
8   verkin bætti sjá klerkr.

The glorious bride of God gives without doubt a moderately easy life; worlds changed for the cleric; afterwards in atonement the excellent, atoning Virgin commanded that he amend his life; that was a splendidly fine remission.

Thereafter the brave man humbly gave thanks to his God while the life of the tree of gold [man] lasted; and from among mankind this man loves Mary most because of her help, as was to be expected; this cleric amended his deeds.

certainly not a lazy or slothful life. **26.**4 *linna*] with *lundr* 'tree' forms a mankenning; *linnr*, 'snake' or 'fire' perhaps means 'gold (arm)ring' here (halfkenning, = *armlinnr*?); but it could perhaps, like *ormr* occasionally, mean sword or spear; or even ship.

27 María, krjúpa menn þjer,
mætust, því að ágætr
setti þig fyr mikinn mátt
4 móður sína hreint fljóð;
enginn mun svó aumligr,
iðrandi ef þig biðr,
að hann farist, frúin skær;
8 flestra ertu hjálp mest.

28 María, ertu sköpuð skær,
skærust og Guði kær;
kæran muntu duga dýr
4 dýru fólki lofskýr;
skýrust má; sektsár
sárin láttu gróa vór;
vóra kenni eg nauð nær;
8 næri vertu Guðs mær.

Most excellent Mary, people prostrate themselves before you because the renowned one placed you, His mother, virtuous woman, in charge of great power; no one will be so wretched that he will perish if, repentant, he prays to you, our luminous Lady; you are the greatest help of most people.

Mary, most luminous and dear to God, you are created luminous; precious dear, glorious with praise, you will help precious mankind; the most glorious one is capable; let our guilt-sore sores, heal; I realise our distress is near; Virgin of God, be near us.

**27.5** *enginn mun*] *vera* understood. **28.1–8** On the linking of the end of one line with the beginning of the next by rhyme cf. *Lilja* 49.1–4, 55, 66; Snorri Sturluson's *Háttatal* 47–48. **28.5** *má*] pres. 3rd pers. sg. with *skýrust* ('woman' understood) 'the most virtuous woman is capable (of doing this)'. **29.2** *sjúkr*] i.e. both physically sick and spiritually sick from sin. **29.3** *löng pín*] probably refers to the agony of death, especially in the context of the second half-stanza

29  María, gef þú, meyin dýr
mjúkust, þeim eð er sjúkr
linun, að löng pín
4 líði, sú er vór bíðr,
því að úr heimi, hæst blóm,
hjeðan trúi eg oss kveðr
sannr Guð sonr þinn;
8 sálum hjálpi þitt mál.

30  Himiríkis hæst blóm,
hæstum Guði ertu næst,
móðir og mey prúð
4 mildinnar, fögr snild;
María legg þú dóm dýr,
diktandi, á verk slíkt;
tákna mun eg lofuð líkn
8 linna hjer við flokk þinn. Amen.

Mary, precious, most gentle Virgin, give relief to the one who is sick so that the long torment which awaits us may pass, highest bloom, because I believe that true God, your son, will call us hence out of the world; may your speech save souls.

Highest bloom of the heavenly kingdom [the Virgin], mother and splendid Virgin of kindness, beautiful eloquence, you are next to highest God; precious Mary, as you dictate, pass judgement on this work; praised mercy, I will end your poem of miracles here. Amen.

in which Christ calls us from this world; or maybe refers to the torments of Purgatory or Hell. **30.1** *Himirikes*] all mss., cf. 14.2. **30.6** *diktandi*] dictating, i.e. the Virgin is inspiring his poem, cf. *Mg* 1? LP suggests 'carefully considering' ('velovervejende') and it may be just an elaboration of *legg þú dóm á*. **30.8** *Amen*] Occurs at end of st. 29 in 721.

# GLOSSARY AND INDEX

All words in the poems are glossed, complete with references to all occurrences. Headwords are in nominative singular for nouns and first person pronouns, nominative singular masculine for adjectives, articles, demonstratives, and third person pronouns, and infinitive for verbs. The abbreviation 'n.' in an entry means that there is a note on this word in the footnotes to the texts.

## ABBREVIATIONS

| | | | |
|---|---|---|---|
| *a.* | adjective | *nom.* | nominative |
| *acc.* | accusative | *num.* | numeral |
| *adv.* | adverb(ial, -ially) | *ord.* | ordinal |
| *art.* | article | *pass.* | passive voice |
| *aux.* | auxiliary | *pers.* | person(al) |
| *card.* | cardinal | *pl.* | plural |
| *comp.* | comparative | *poss.* | possessive |
| *conj.* | conjunction | *pptc.* | past participle |
| *dat.* | dative | *prep.* | preposition(al) |
| *def.* | definite | *pres.* | present tense |
| *dem.* | demonstrative | *pret.* | preterite |
| *f.* | feminine | *pret.-pres.* | preterite-present verb |
| *gen.* | genitive | *pron.* | pronoun |
| *imp.* | imperative | *prptc.* | present participle |
| *impers.* | impersonal | *refl.* | reflexive |
| *indecl.* | indeclinable | *rel.* | relative |
| *indef.* | indefinite | *sg.* | singular |
| *inf.* | infinitive | *s-one* | someone |
| *interj.* | interjection | *s-thing* | something |
| *interrog.* | interrogative | *subj.* | subjunctive mood |
| *intr.* | intransitive | *subst.* | substantive |
| *m.* | masculine | *sup.* | superlative |
| *md.* | middle voice | *sv.* | strong verb |
| *ms(s).* | manuscript(s) | *vb.* | verb |
| *n.* | neuter | *wk.* | weak |
| *neg.* | negative | *wv.* | weak verb |

**á** *prep.* (1) *with acc.* on, in, at, to, into *Mg* 11.4, 11.5, 15.1, 15.4, 19.2, 21.5, 23.1, 29.5, 45.2; *VM* 12.4; *MvI* 16.1, 24.1; *MvII* 7.2, 9.6, 16.2, 22.4; *MvIII* 5.6, 8.3, 12.3, 13.4, 20.5 (see **minnast**), 30.6. (2) *with dat.* in, on, upon, at, to *Mg* 7.5, 10.6, 13.3, 16.7, 18.1, 18.4, 20.7, 24.7, 26.4, 27.7, 31.3, 38.7, 45.4, 45.8, 47.3, 48.7, 52.2; *VM* 3.6, 8.4; *MvI*

1.8 (for), 5.8 (about), 18.4, 20.3, 24.3, 26.5; *MvII* 2.2, 10.5, 13.4, 20.8; *MvIII* 20.8. (3) *adv.* on him *Mg* 14.2 n.; *þar á* thereon (i.e. on the tongue) *MvIII* 21.8.

**að** *prep. with dat.* (1) at *VM* 17.5. (2) to *MvI* 15.4, 19.4. (3) against *MvI* 20.1; *MvIII* 11.1. (4) upon *MvIII* 9.6. (5) with *MvI* 6.6 (see **leggja**); *MvII* 12.2 (see **leika**). (6) as *Mg* 35.4. (7) for *MvII* 6.7. (8) in regard to, concerning *Mg* 3.5; *VM* 10.1, 14.2. (9) in accordance with *Mg* 10.3, 12.6, 16.4, 22.7, 23.3, 39.7, 44.3; *MvI* 12.6, 18.8; *MvII* 23.5; *MvIII* 16.7, 20.7, 25.3 n. (10) *að eilífu* for ever *VM* 26.8. (11) *with acc.* as *Mg* 47.5 n. (*or adv. hjer að*). (12) *as adv.* with him *MvII* 11.4; to them *MvIII* 20.6 n.; see also **ganga**.

**að** *with inf.* (1) to *Mg* 2.2, 4.6, 6.2 (second *að*), 7.4, 8.2, 9.3, 11.1, 12.4, 13.7, 16.2, 17.1, 17.4, 19.6, 20.4, 23.5, 27.1, 27.4, 29.4, 30.1, 34.5, 41.5; *VM* 5.2, 6.4, 6.6, 7.2, 8.7, 10.2, 10.4, 12.6, 21.8 n., 22.4, 26.1; *MvI* 11.4 n., 14.2, 17.2, 18.6, 26.1; *MvII* 4.8, 5.6, 21.3, 24.4; *MvIII* 18.6, 18.8, 23.2. (2) in order to *Mg* 5.8.

**að** *conj.* (1) that *Mg* 2.3, 3.1, 4.4, 5.5, 8.3, 8.6, 14.7, 14.8, 18.5, 18.8, 25.5, 29.8, 35.6, 36.1, 42.3, 42.7, 47.3, 47.8, 51.2, 52.5; *VM* 11.6, 16.1, 16.5, 18.1; *MvI* 1.7, 2.2, 6.5, 17.3, 22.6, 27.1; *MvII* 1.3, 2.1, 17.6; *MvIII* 2.5, 11.8, 15.8, 21.6, 22.8, 23.7, 25.7, 27.7. (2) when, it being the case that *Mg* 4.7; *MvIII* 5.5, 15.5. (3) so that, in order that *Mg* 37.7, 50.6; *VM* 19.3; *MvI* 17.8, 26.7; *MvII* 2.3, 8.7; *MvIII* 23.4, 29.3. (4) until, after which (of time) *Mg* 6.2.

**áðr** (1) *adv.* before, previously *Mg* 10.6; *VM* 18.8 (already), 21.7 (just now); *MvI* 4.1; *MvII* 11.8. (2) *conj.* before *MvIII* 12.5 (until), 18.5; *áðr en* before *MvII* 9.4.

**af** *prep. with dat.* (1) made of *Mg* 15.3; built of *MvII* 6.5. (2) full of, (filled) with *Mg* 4.4; *VM* 25.7; *MvI* 12.3, 21.1. (3) off, from, away from, out of, with *Mg* 18.7, 27.3, 27.6, 34.1, 38.1, 44.7, 45.1, 46.5, 49.2, 49.8, 50.1; *VM* 3.8 n., 4.5, 4.7, 5.3, 15.5. 15.8; *MvI* 8.5, 9.4, 22.7; *MvII* 3.3 (see **bera**), 15.4; *MvIII* 12.7, 26.5. (4) about, concerning, regarding *Mg* title, 4.5; *VM* title, 1.6; *MvI* 12.1. (5) in accordance with, according to *Mg* 6.3, 22.2. (6) because of, on account of, as a result of *VM* 22.1; *MvI* 5.3, 9.6, 9.8, 21.8, 22.2; *MvII* 4.7, 8.3 n., 13.2; *MvIII* 4.3. (7) *with pptc.* by *MvI* 19.2; *MvIII* 11.6. (8) *as adv.* off him *MvII* 11.6 (see **sjá**), 21.5 (see **þaðan**).

**áfengr** *a.*; *n. as adv. with í* powerfully causing *VM* 4.8.

**affinis** *m.* (*Latin*) son-in-law *MvI* 8.8.

**ágætr** *a.* excellent, renowned *Mg* 8.7, 45.7; *VM* 6.2 (*sup.*), 23.8; *MvII* 1.8; *MvIII* 27.2

# Glossary and Index 85

**áhlýðandi** *a.* listening *VM* 20.4 n.; *dat. pl. -i MvI* 2.8.
**ákall** *n.* invocation *MvII* 22.3.
**akta (að)** *wv.* to take care of/to, occupy oneself with, attend to; to devise *MvIII* 17.3; *md.* to be paid attention to *MvIII* 23.6.
**ala (ól)** *sv.* to give birth to, bear, produce *Mg* 25.7; *MvII* 5.4, 8.2, 9.8.
**aldr** *m.* (1) life *MvIII* 10.4. (2) age, time, period *Mg* 45.3; *VM* 3.6; *MvIII* 3.2.
**aldri** *adv.* never, not at all *Mg* 1.6, 8.6, 25.3, 30.4, 35.4; *VM* 4.6 n., 12.8; *MvI* 28.5; *MvII* 9.7.
**álfa** *f.* side, part *Mg* 22.2.
**alhróðigr** *a.* entirely triumphant *MvI* 29.4 n.
**allopt** *adv.* very often *Mg* 4.1.
**allr** *a.* all, every, whole, entire *Mg* 2.5, 3.3, 5.6, 7.6, 16.5, 17.8, 20.1, 20.3, 20.5, 22.3, 23.6, 24.5, 28.5, 28.6, 31.5, 32.1, 32.4, 32.5, 32.6, 33.4, 36.5, 36.6, 38.3, 38.8, 42.5, 44.4, 45.6, 50.1, 50.4, 52.3, 52.4, 52.5;*VM* 6.1, 15.8, 19.6, 20.3, 21.3, 22.6, 25.7; *MvI* 6.2, 11.5, 18.5, 20.3, 23.8, 25.6; *MvII* 1.2, 22.3, 22.5, 24.7; *n. as subst.* everything *Mg* 4.3 n., 7.7, 43.7; *VM* 1.2 (*object of vinnandi*); *gen. as adv. alls öng* no . . . at all *MvII* 20.1.
**allskyns** *adv.* of all kinds *Mg* 14.6.
**álmbörr** *m.* bow-tree *MvIII* 17.5 (see List of Kennings, 'Man').
**almætastr** *sup. a.* most thoroughly excellent *Mg* 50.2.
**alsæmdr** *a.* thoroughly honoured *VM* 9.4.
**álygi** *f.* slander *MvI* 7.8.
**amen** *interj.* amen *Mg* 52.8; *VM* 26.8; *MvII* 24.8 n.; *MvIII* 30.8 n.
**andaðr** *a. pptc.* dead *MvI* 4.2.
**andi** *m.* spirit *Mg* 2.4, 31.3, 43.3, 50.7;*VM* 19.5, 25.3.
**Andrjeás** *m.* St Andrew (the Apostle) *VM* 2.1; *MvI* 2.2; *MvII* 2.3; *MvIII* 2.4.
**andsvar** *n.* answer, reply *MvIII* 19.1.
**angr** *n.* grief, sorrow *Mg* 11.2, 14.8, 15.7; *MvI* 5.7, 12.4, 14.2, 16.3; *MvII* 18.3.
**angrþrútinn** *a.* swollen with sorrow *MvI* 11.6.
**Anna** *f.* Anna daughter of Phanuel (Luke 2:36) *Mg* 6.8 n.
**annarr** *ord. num. and a.* (1) second *Mg* 44.1; next *MvII* 13.6. (2) other, another *Mg* 10.5, 16.8 (else), 20.8 (else), 21.4 (other things), 24.8 (else), 31.8, 38.4; *VM* 13.6, 13.8, 19.8; *MvI* 17.6, 22.1; *MvII* 5.7.
**anza (að)** *wv. with dat.* to answer, reply to *Mg* 26.1;*VM* 7.1, 12.2.
**aptr** *adv.* back *MvII* 18.7.

**ár** *n.* prosperity *Mg* 32.2.
**arfr** *m.* inheritance *VM* 9.3.
**árla** *adv.* early *Mg* 11.8.
**armr** *a.* wretched *MvI* 13.4; *MvII* 5.6.
**Árón** *m.* Aaron *Mg* 1.5.
**árr** *m.* messenger, servant; (fallen) angel, i.e. devil *MvIII* 17.5, 19.1, 22.1.
**ást** *f.* love *VM* 2.3, 4.7 n., 5.1, 23.5 n., 25.5; *MvIII* 1.7, 4.5.
**ástarmjúkr** *a.* full of gentle love *Mg* 34.4.
**ástvin** *m.* dear friend *MvI* 2.1.
**auðbrík** *f.* panel of riches *VM* 7.4 (see List of Kennings, 'Woman').
**auðgreinandi** *m.* distributor of riches *MvI* 1.4 n. (see List of Kennings, 'God').
**auðgætandi** *m.* keeper of riches *MvI* 5.2 (see List of Kennings, 'Man').
**auðmjúkr** *a.* humble *MvII* 4.2.
**auðr** *m.* wealth, riches *VM* 9.3, 10.8, 23.7; *MvI* 14.6; *MvII* 13.5.
**auðspöng** *f.* (metal) plate of riches *MvII* 14.3 (see List of Kennings, 'Woman').
**auga** *n.* eye *Mg* 29.6, 40.8, 49.8.
**Augústínus** *m.* St Augustine of Hippo *Mg* 4.2, 8.2, 9.8, 37.6.
**aumligr** *a.* miserable, wretched *MvI* 5.7; *MvIII* 27.5.
**Áve María** Ave Maria, Hail Mary *MvIII* 9.7, 21.7.

**báðir** (*n.* **bæði**) *a. pron.* both *Mg* 6.1, 51.2; *VM* 16.6, 18.8; *MvI* 10.4.
**bál** *n.* bonfire, pyre *MvI* 12.7, 13.8, 19.8, 20.1, 27.8; *MvIII* 18.8 n.
**band** *n.* band; ring *VM* 8.2; bond, fetter *MvI* 22.7.
**bani** *m.* (1) death *MvIII* 16.3. (2) cause of death, slayer *MvII* 12.7.
**bann** *n.* condemnation, damnation *MvIII* 16.4.
**bannaðr** *a.* cursed *Mg* 21.4.
**barar** *f. pl.* bier *MvII* 13.4, 15.4, 20.8.
**barma** (**að**) *wv.* to pity; *prptc. MvI* 13.4.
**barn** *n.* child *MvII* 5.4, 6.7, 12.7, 15.3, 16.2, 17.3 n., 19.6 n.; *MvIII* 3.2.
**barnfæð** *f.* childlessness *MvII* 9.1.
**barnaæði** *n.* child-like nature *VM* 4.1
**baugnorn** *f.* ring-Norn *MvII* 6.7 (see List of Kennings, 'Woman').
**baugstallr** *m.* ring-seat *MvI* 23.8 n. (see List of Kennings, 'Other').
**baugr** *m.* ring *MvI* 26.5.
**beiða** (**dd**) *wv.* to ask, request *Mg* 4.1; *with gen. VM* 19.2 n.
**beiðir** *m.* demander, commander *VM* 23.3 (see List of Kennings, 'Man').
**beimar** *m. pl.* men, people *Mg* 33.6; *VM* 24.5.

**beina (d)** *wv.* to assist *Mg* 3.6.
**beiskr** *a.* bitter *Mg* 40.7 n.
**ben** *f.* wound *Mg* 17.8.
**bera (bar)** *sv.* (1) to bear, carry, convey *Mg* 7.6, 13.2; *MvII* 17.4; *bera á lopt* to reveal *MvIII* 12.3; *bera af* to surpass *MvII* 3.3. (2) to endure *Mg* 14.8, 19.8, 22.5, 29.7; *MvII* 2.7, 18.4. (3) to bear (witness) *VM* 3.2, 7.6, 21.5, 21.7. (4) to bear, give birth to *MvII* 8.8, 10.6, 21.4. (5) *md. berast* to be brought *MvII* 9.6.
**berja (barði)** *wv.* to strike, beat *Mg* 14.3, 19.1.
**bernska** *f.* childhood *VM* 3.6.
**bert** *adv.* clearly *VM* 18.5.
**betri** *a. comp.* better; *with dat. of comparison Mg* 20.1; *sup. bestr* best *MvIII* 2.3.
**bíða (beið)** *sv.* (1) to await (*with gen.*) *MvIII* 29.4. (2) to endure, suffer *MvII* 9.2.
**biðja (bað)** *sv.* (1) to ask, tell, pray *Mg* 5.5, 18.3, 42.3, 51.1, 52.3, 52.5; *VM* 17.7; *MvI* 1.5, 2.2, 14.1 (begged), 29.8 n.; *MvII* 22.5; *MvIII* 8.4, 24.5 (commanded), 27.6. (2) *with gen.* to ask or pray for (something) *Mg* 39.8, 47.6; *MvI* 19.5; to ask for (a woman's hand) in marriage *MvI* 4.5; *with acc.* to ask for (something) *Mg* 10.5 n.
**Bil** *f.* name of a goddess *MvI* 14.6 (see List of Kennings, 'Woman').
**binda (batt)** *sv.* to bind *Mg* 14.3, 19.1.
**birta (rt)** *wv.* to display, reveal *Mg* 41.2.
**birti** *f.* brightness *Mg* 33.8; (referring to the Virgin) *VM* 19.7.
**bjarg** *n.* rock *Mg* 33.5.
**bjarga (barg)** *sv.* (*with dat.*) to help; to save *VM* 24.5; *MvI* 17.8 n. (*pptc. with fá*), 28.3.; *MvIII* 12.6 (relieve).
**bjartr** *a.* bright, luminous, shining *Mg* 3.2, 9.1, 17.6, 18.6, 22.8, 27.6, 37.4 n., 45.2, 48.4; *VM* 2.8, 21.6; *MvI* 1.2, 27.7; *MvII* 3.6, 16.7 n.; *MvIII* 12.5, 21.2 n.; clear *Mg* 14.7. n.
**bjóða (bauð)** *sv.* (1) to offer *Mg* 21.3, 30.6; *prptc. MvI* 22.4 n. (2) to worship, offer praise to *VM* 22.4. (3) to invite, summon, command *MvIII* 16.5, 24.4, 25.5.
**blandaðr** *a. pptc.* mixed *Mg* 30.5 n.
**blessaðr** *a. pptc.* blessed *Mg* 6.2, 10.4, 19.4, 20.2, 51.1; *VM* 18.6.
**blíðr** *a.* gracious, kind *Mg* 9.1; *VM* 4.1, 24.6; *MvII* 11.5, 21.7.
**blóð** *n.* blood *Mg* 19.2; *MvIII* 16.3.
**blóm** *n.* flower *VM* 12.5 n.; (referring to the Virgin) *MvIII* 29.5, 30.1. (See List of Kennings, 'Gold', 'Virgin Mary'.)
**blygð** *f.* shame *Mg* 21.3; *VM* 12.4.

**boðast (að)** wv. md. be proclaimed *MvIII* 9.4.
**bóndi** m. husband *MvI* 9.6.
**borð** n. side of a ship: *fyr borði* overboard, in a bad way *VM* 18.5; by metonymy = ship (or shield?) *VM* 23.4.
**borg** f. stronghold, town *Mg* 38.2, 44.6; *VM* 9.5; *MvI* 3.1; *MvII* 13.8. (See List of Kennings, 'Heaven'.)
**bót** f. betterment, remedy; atonement *MvI* 20.7.
**brá** f. eyelash *Mg* 5.4, 15.8.
**bráðgjörr** a. advanced in development *MvII* 21.8.
**bráðr** a. quick, hasty; rash; sudden *Mg* 39.6; *MvI* 9.1, 9.2 n.; *n. as adv. brátt* soon, quickly *VM* 4.2, 9.6, 10.1, 13.1; *MvI* 12.7 n.; *MvII* 17.6.
**bragð** n. behaviour, deed *MvIII* 17.8.
**bragarbót** f. ornament of poetry *MvII* 1.3.
**bragnar** m. people, humankind *Mg* 7.6, 40.8 n.; *MvII* 1.4.
**bragningr** m. prince *Mg* 22.1 (see List of Kennings, 'Christ').
**bragr** m. poetry, poem *MvII* 20.2; *MvIII* 1.2.
**brandr** m. sword *Mg* 8.1.
**braut** f. road, way; *í braut* (as adv.) away *MvIII* 24.1.
**breiðr** a. broad, large *MvI* 3.1.
**brenna (brann)** sv. intr. to burn *Mg* 1.6; *MvI* 8.1, 20.2, 21.8, 22.8, 28.6 n.
**brenna (nd)** wv. trans. to burn *MvI* 12.8, 14.4, 16.8.
**bresta (brast)** sv. intr. to break *Mg* 33.5.
**brigsli** n. reproach *MvII* 9.5.
**brík** f. panel *VM* 12.6 n., 15.2; *MvI* 26.6. (See List of Kennings, 'Woman'.)
**brimglóðir** f. pl. embers of the sea *VM* 15.1 n. (see List of Kennings, 'Gold').
**brími** m. fire *VM* 12.5 (see List of Kennings, 'Gold').
**brjef** n. document *MvI* 26.5.
**brjóst** n. breast *Mg* 6.1, 14.7, 29.7, 40.7, 43.7, 46.7; *VM* 25.5; *MvI* 8.1; *MvIII* 1.7.
**brjóta (braut)** sv. (1) to break, damage, destroy; *impers. MvIII* 7.8. (2) to offend *MvII* 23.3.
**bróðir** m. brother (of a religious order) *Mg* 41.7.
**brúðr** f. bride, woman *Mg* 9.2, 22.1; *VM* 13.2, 15.5, 21.5, 23.3; *MvI* 3.2, 4.1 n., 9.1, 20.1, 22.7, 23.7 n., 25.3; *MvII* 2.7, 11.7 n., 17.3; *MvIII* 12.5, 19.5, 22.3. (See List of Kennings, 'Virgin Mary', 'Woman'.)
**bryggja** f. landing-stage, jetty *Mg* 46.6 (see List of Kennings, 'Heaven').

búinn a. pptc. (1) ready, prepared Mg 16.2; MvII 12.8; n. with dat. var búið við s-one was on the point of Mg 29.8. (2) adorned, ornamented; embroidered MvII 11.2. (3) invented MvII 9.5.
burgeiss m. citizen, person of status VM 9.5.
burr m. son MvII 21.7.
burt adv. away VM 9.2; í burtu away MvII 15.3.
byggja (gð) wv. to inhabit, live in MvII 3.2.
byrr m. (favourable) wind Mg 22.2.
byskup m. bishop VM 13.1, 14.6.
bæði conj. both Mg 14.4; VM 15.1; MvI 8.2; MvII 9.1.
bæn f. prayer Mg 4.2 n., 40.3, 42.8, 48.2, 49.7; MvI 27.7; MvII 2.8, 6.8.
bæta (tt) wv. to make better, put right, amend MvII 16.8; MvIII 26.8.
böl n. misfortune MvII 16.7.

dáð f. deed, achievement MvIII 19.7.
dagr m. day Mg 6.4, 18.4, 36.4, 42.1, 43.8; MvI 23.8; MvII 13.6, 14.7.
dapr a. sad MvI 13.6.
dauði m. death Mg 4.8, 7.3, 12.5, 18.7, 23.2, 24.1, 27.3, 29.8, 30.2, 33.3, 38.1, 39.6, 44.7, 52.7; MvII 14.7.
dauðr a. dead Mg 15.6, 25.4, 34.8; MvII 13.1.
dauðr m. death MvI 8.6.
Dávíð m. David (psalmist) MvIII 19.7.
deila (d) wv. to quarrel MvI 10.1.
deilir m. dealer, distributor Mg 11.6, 16.6, 20.6, 24.6, 31.4, 45.4. (See List of Kennings, 'Christ', 'God'.)
deus m. (Latin) God; páter deus God the Father Mg 40.2.
deyja (dó) sv. to die Mg 31.5; VM 10.2; MvI 27.6; MvII 17.6; MvIII 8.8, 9.8.
dikta (að) wv. to dictate MvIII 19.8, 30.6 n. (prptc.)
dimmr a. dark; n. as subst. darkness Mg 33.6.
dís f. name of a norn or a common noun meaning goddess or lady MvII 15.5 (see List of Kennings, 'Woman').
djöfull m. devil Mg 51.6; MvIII 10.6, 13.3.
Dóminus m. (Latin) the Lord Mg 47.4.
dómr m. (1) judgement Mg 52.2; MvI 12.6; MvIII 17.1, 30.5. (2) court MvII 1.1 (see List of Kennings, 'Heaven').
dóttir f. daughter VM 3.4, 4.4, 10.6 n.; MvI 4.3, 5.3, 9.4.
draga (dró) sv. to drag MvI 13.5; MvIII 13.4 (pptc. with hafa).
dráp n. killing, slaughter, death Mg 12.5, 24.1.
drápa f. a laudatory poem (with refrains) Mg title.

**drekka (drakk)** *sv.* to drink (from) *Mg* 6.1; *VM* 25.6.
**drekkja (kt)** *wv.* to drown *MvIII* 10.2.
**drengr** *m.* boy, young man *VM* 7.1.
**drepa (drap)** *sv.* to strike *MvI* 9.1.
**dreyri** *m.* blood *Mg* 52.8.
**dript** *f.* snow; half-kenning for silver *MvII* 15.6.
**drjúgum** *adv.* to a high degree, much, greatly *VM* 16.8.
**drós** *f.* woman *MvI* 3.8, 13.5.
**drótt** *f.* company, host, people *Mg* 24.2; *MvI* 19.2; *MvII* 14.8; host of angels *MvIII* 8.7.
**dróttinn, drottinn** *m.* lord *Mg* 1.7 n., 5.2, 5.6, 6.5, 9.3 n., 12.4, 16.4, 17.3, 19.4, 22.6, 23.6, 28.8, 32.3, 32.8, 34.6, 36.8, 41.2, 48.8, 50.5, 51.5, 52.4, 52.7; *VM* 1.5, 8.8, 19.1, 21.6; *MvI* 21.2, 23.1, 23.6, 28.2; *MvII* 1.2 n.; *MvIII* 1.1 n. (See List of Kennings, 'Christ', 'God'.)
**drottning** *f.* queen *Mg* 9.2 (see List of Kennings, 'Virgin Mary'), *MvI* 3.7.
**drýgja (gð)** *wv.* to carry out; commit *MvIII* 18.3.
**duga (ð)** *wv. with dat.* to help *MvII* 1.8; *MvIII* 8.7 n., 28.3.
**dugnaðr** *m.* help *MvIII* 26.6.
**dúkr** *m.* cloth *Mg* 34.4.
**dýrð** *f.* glory *Mg* 2.8, 9.3, 14.5, 16.7, 20.7, 23.7, 24.7, 36.4, 45.7, 46.2, 46.5, 48.7, 50.6; *MvII* 1.1 n., 24.5; *MvIII* 9.4; *dýrð jarteignar* glorious miracle *VM* 26.3. (See List of Kennings, 'Angels'.)
**dýrka (að)** *wv.* to worship *Mg* 50.1.
**dýrligr** *a.* glorious *Mg* 2.2, 21.7; *sup. Mg* 20.4.
**dýrr** *a.* dear, precious *MvI* 3.7; *MvII* 15.5 n.; *MvIII* 28.3, 28.4, 29.1, 30.5; *sup. dýrstr Mg* 50.5, *VM* 17.4.
**dægr** *n.* half-day (period of twelve hours) *Mg* 9.4; *MvII* 20.7.
**dæma (d)** *wv.* to judge, sentence *Mg* 12.6.
**dæmi** *n. pl.* example, model *MvI* 3.4.
**dökkr** *a.* dark *MvIII* 13.3.

**eð** *rel. particle* which *MvIII* 23.2, 29.2.
**eða** *conj.* or *Mg* 2.7; *VM* 4.6.
**edik** *n.* vinegar *Mg* 30.8.
**ef** *conj.* if *Mg* 3.4, 7.4, 16.3, 47.6, 49.4; *VM* 7.6, 13.6; *MvII* 9.7; *MvIII* 6.4, 7.8, 11.5, 27.6.
**ef** *n.* doubt *MvIII* 25.2.
**efalauss** *a.* without doubt, certain *Mg* 18.5, 36.1.
**efla (d)** *wv.* to strengthen, increase; *impers. MvIII* 7.4.
**efna (d)** *wv.* to perform *MvIII* 11.6.

## Glossary and Index 91

**efstr** *a. sup.* last *Mg* 52.2.
**eg** *pron.* I *Mg* 2.1, 2.3, 2.6, 2.7, 3.1, 3.5, 3.8, 5.5, 8.5, 10.7, 11.2, 11.5, 11.7, 12.2, 13.2, 13.5, 13.6 n., 13.7, 14.7, 14.8, 15.4, 15.5, 15.6, 15.7, 16.2, 16.3, 17.5, 17.7, 18.2, 18.3, 18.5, 18.8, 21.5, 22.7, 25.3, 25.5, 26.7, 27.1, 27.2, 27.4, 27.7, 27.8, 28.4, 29.2, 29.3, 29.7, 29.8, 30.3, 30.8, 31.1, 31.2, 31.3, 34.2, 35.3, 35.4, 35.6, 35.7, 36.1, 37.5, 37.7 n., 38.3, 38.4, 38.8, 39.2, 42.1, 42.3, 42.5, 43.1, 43.2, 43.3, 43.5, 43.8, 44.1, 44.2, 44.5, 44.8, 45.5, 45.8, 46.1, 46.4, 46.5, 47.2, 47.3, 47.8, 49.1, 49.4, 49.7, 50.5, 50.6, 50.8, 51.1, 51.3, 51.5 n., 51.7, 52.1, 52.3, 52.5; *VM* 2.3, 2.7 n., 6.1, 7.2, 11.8, 12.4, 12.5, 12.8, 13.6, 16.5, 18.1, 18.5, 19.2 n., 19.3, 21.5, 26.1, 26.4; *MvI* 1.1 n., 1.5, 2.2, 2.4, 16.7, 17.1, 17.3, 17.5, 17.7, 17.8, 18.1, 18.6, 29.1; *MvII* 1.6, 8.1, 8.4, 8.6, 8.7, 9.6, 9.7, 16.6, 16.8, 17.6, 24.1; *MvIII* 1.1, 1.3, 2.2, 2.5, 8.5, 8.7, 16.1, 16.5, 22.7, 22.8 n., 28.7, 29.6, 30.7; *suffixed to vb. Mg* 15.8.
**ei** (= **eigi**) *adv.* not *Mg* 14.8, 33.8, 35.6; *VM* 11.6 n.; *MvI* 24.4; *MvIII* 9.2.
**eiðr** *m.* oath *VM* 14.4, 23.2.
**eiga (átti)** *pret.-pres.* (1) to have, to own, to possess *VM* 3.3, 9.6; *MvI* 4.3, 17.5; to experience *Mg* 33.6. (2) *subj. with inf.* ought *Mg* 23.5.
**eigi** *adv.* not *Mg* 26.5; *VM* 19.3; *MvI* 11.3; *MvII* 18.2; *MvIII* 8.7, 16.1, 23.8. Cf. **ei**.
**eigin** *a. indecl.* own *MvI* 4.1 n.
**eigna (að)** *wv.* to take possession of (*sér* for oneself) *MvIII* 14.3.
**eilífligr** *a.* eternal; *sup. Mg* 16.6, 20.6, 24.6.
**eilífr** *a.* eternal *Mg* 31.4, 45.4; *VM* 25.5; *MvII* 24.6; *n. as noun að eilífu* for ever *VM* 26.8.
**einatt** *adv.* incessantly, constantly *MvIII* 23.5.
**eingason** *m.* only son *Mg* 8.8.
**eingetinn** *a.* only (begotten) *Mg* 25.6.
**einhlítr** *a.* self-sufficient *Mg* 3.6 (with *mjer*).
**einkar** *adv.* very, extremely *Mg* 16.3.
**einn** (*n.* **eitt**) *a. and card. num.* (1) one, a, a certain *Mg* 1.5 n., 2.7, 41.1, 44.3; *VM* 1.3, 5.5, 5.8; *MvI* 4.3, 10.2, 29.3; *MvII* 3.2, 12.1, 14.4 (a single); *MvIII* 1.4, 2.8, 6.1, 7.1. (2) alone *Mg* 36.2 n.
**eisa** *f.* fire, glowing embers *MvI* 22.5.
**ekki** see **engi**.
**eldi** *n.* offspring, child *Mg* 25.8.
**eldr** *m.* fire *MvI* 16.8, 19.4, 22.2, 22.6, 24.5, 27.3, 28.5.
**eldsneyti** *n.* firewood *MvI* 21.5.

**ella** *conj.* or else *MvII* 17.7.
**elska** *f.* love *VM* 8.2, 24.2.
**elska (að)** *wv.* to love *MvI* 3.6; *MvII* 11.3.
**elskufullr** *a.* full of love, charitable *Mg* 4.1.
**elskugi** *m.* lover, loved one *VM* 11.3.
**en** *conj.* (1) but *Mg* 48.2; *VM* 9.7, 12.7, 16.3; *MvI* 5.5; *MvIII* 11.5. (2) and *Mg* 11.8, 15.2, 17.2, 30.7, 33.5, 38.4 (first *en*); *VM* 13.7; *MvI* 4.8, 9.7, 11.3, 22.8; *MvII* 14.8, 22.7. (3) than *Mg* 16.8, 20.8, 21.8, 22.6, 24.8, 25.7, 38.4, 46.6; *MvI* 29.6; *MvIII* 10.8, 15.8 (*en að* than that).
**enda (nd)** *wv.* to end *MvIII* 21.3; *md.* to last *MvIII* 26.3.
**endi** *m.* end *MvI* 18.4.
**engi/öngr/enginn** *pron. and a.* not a (one), no (one), none *Mg* 3.5, 8.1, 10.5, 50.8; *VM* 7.3 n.; *MvI* 17.5; *MvII* 5.2, 14.3 n.; *MvIII* 27.5 n.; *f. öng MvII* 20.1; *gen. enskis Mg* 19.5; *n. ekki* nothing *MvII* 3.7.
**engill** *m.* angel *Mg* 10.2, 11.7, 18.2, 19.8, 20.2, 26.8, 43.2, 47.2; *MvIII* 11.1.
**enn** *adv.* yet, still, again, further, furthermore, as well *Mg* 2.8, 5.8, 17.4, 31.2, 37.5; *VM* 2.7, 4.3, 7.3, 12.3, 18.7; *MvI* 22.1, 28.6; *MvIII* 7.1, 20.4 .
**enn, en, eð** *def. art.* the *Mg* 3.7, 4.1, 4.6 n., 5.6, 6.8, 11.2, 27.8, 30.3, 32.3, 32.4, 36.2, 38.6, 44.5, 46.4, 50.5; *VM* 17.1, 19.7; *MvI* 2.1, 16.5, 20.7, 21.7.
**eptir** *prep.* (1) *with acc.* after (of time) *VM* 10.5; *MvIII* 10.4. (2) *with dat.* (a) committed by *MvI* 10.8. (b) in accordance with *MvII* 10.4.
**er** *rel. particle and conj.* (1) who, which *Mg* 3.3, 4.7, 5.7, 11.2, 13.4, 19.7, 22.5, 25.7, 30.1 n., 33.1, 34.3, 37.6, 38.1, 38.8, 41.3, 41.8, 44.2, 52.8; *VM* 1.4, 4.8, 11.4, 13.2, 19.6, 24.3; *MvI* 1.1, 6.2, 14.4, 15.1, 15.7, 28.7; *MvII* 1.2, 1.7 (in which), 2.7, 3.8, 7.7, 20.7, 21.4, 22.3; *MvIII* 7.6, 11.4, 12.1, 14.6, 16.8, 20.4, 29.4. (2) when *Mg* 8.7, 11.3, 11.5, 12.5, 17.7, 18.1, 21.5, 35.3, 51.3; *VM* 24.8; *MvI* 8.3, 13.8, 21.2; *MvII* 15.2; *MvIII* 10.1, 19.8, 24.7. (3) where *VM* 17.3. (4) how *Mg* 25.1.
**erfð** *f.* inheritance *VM* 10.5 (*pl.*).
**erfingi** *m.* heir *MvII* 5.1.
**eyða (dd)** *wv. with dat.* to destroy *Mg* 41.8.
**eymd** *f.* misery *Mg* 19.7, 21.8; *pl. VM* 9.8, 17.8; *MvI* 10.6.

**fá (fekk)** *sv.* (1) to get, obtain *VM* 13.6 (1st pers. sg. *fær*); *MvII* 8.7; *fá til* to provide *MvII* 24.4. (2) to experience, endure, suffer *Mg* 4.7, 11.2; *MvI* 9.5; *MvIII* 23.4, 24.6 n. (3) *with pptc.* to be able to do

## Glossary and Index

s-thing *Mg* 19.5; *MvIII* 5.4, 9.5, 12.6, 23.8; *impers. pass. MvI* 17.8.
**faðir** *m.* father *Mg* 31.4; *VM* 10.2; *MvII* 9.3, 11.4, 20.5; *MvIII* 1.4.
**faðma (að)** *wv.* to embrace *Mg* 34.5.
**faðmr** *m.* embrace; arms *Mg* 7.5.
**fagr** *a.* beautiful *Mg* 4.2 n., 9.1, 9.8 n., 37.6; *MvI* 24.3; *MvII* 9.3, 10.2, 10.6, 18.6; *MvIII* 1.3, 25.8, 30.4; *comp. fegri with dat.* of comparison *Mg* 4.3.
**fagrráðr** *a.* giving wise counsel *MvII* 4.3 n.
**faldr** *m.* woman's head-dress (probably conical in shape with the tip curved forward) *VM* 3.6.
**faldreið** *f.* carrier of a head-dress *VM* 12.8 n. (see List of Kennings, 'Woman').
**fanga (að)** *wv.* to take prisoner *MvI* 12.4.
**far** *n.* vessel, boat *MvIII* 7.5.
**fár** *n.* (1) hatred *MvI* 8.6. (2) harm, danger *MvI* 16.2; *MvIII* 8.6.
**fara (fór)** *sv.* (1) to go *VM* 9.2, 15.1, 16.2 (go forth, i.e. be performed); *MvI* 15.1 n., 25.7; *MvIII* 5.5, 7.1, 15.5 (behave); *fara á* to come over *Mg* 15.4. (2) *md.* to perish, die *MvIII* 27.7.
**farnaðr** *m.* prosperity, good fortune *MvII* 19.6.
**fast** *adv.* firmly *MvIII* 10.7, 12.3.
**fasti** *m.* fire *MvI* 20.4.
**fastliga** *adv.* firmly, securely *MvI* 19.7.
**fastna (að)** *wv.* to betroth *VM* 12.6.
**fastúðigr** *a.* unshakeable in one's resolution *VM* 13.7.
**fátækr** *a.* poor; *as subst. MvII* 4.4.
**feginn** *a.* joyful *MvII* 8.4.
**feginsgrein** *f.* reason for happiness, source of happiness *MvII* 14.4; cf. **grein**.
**feginstíð** *f.* joyful time *MvII* 19.5.
**fela (fal)** *sv.* to commit *Mg* 31.3; *with á hendi* to put in s-one's hands *MvI* 18.1.
**ferð** *f.* company, troop *Mg* 5.3.
**feskr** *a.* beautiful *VM* 17.6; *sup. MvI* 15.6.
**festa (st)** *wv.* to betroth *VM* 13.7.
**festarmál** *n. pl.* contract of betrothal *VM* 6.8.
**festarorð** *n. pl.* formula of betrothal *VM* 8.4, 16.3.
**fimm** *num. indecl.* five *Mg* 41.3, 42.1.
**finna (fann)** *sv.* (1) to find, discover *Mg* 7.4, 44.1, 50.8; *MvI* 15.2; *MvII* 14.4. (2) to meet *Mg* 18.8, 43.2; *MvII* 5.7. (3) to invent, compose *Mg* 2.2. (3) *md.* to meet with one another *VM* 11.6.

**firar** *m. pl.* people *MvIII* 23.7.
**firra (rð)** *wv.* (1) *with dat.* to deprive of s-thing; *pptc. MvII* 20.8. (2) *md.* to be absent from *VM* 16.3.
**fjandi** *m.* fiend, devil *MvI* 6.3; *MvIII* 10.7, 24.2.
**fjandskapr** *m.* hostility *MvI* 21.1.
**fjarðlog** *n.* flame of the fjord *MvIII* 14.5 (see List of Kennnings, 'Gold').
**fjarri** *adv.* far off, distant *VM* 6.3.
**fjelauss** *a.* poor *VM* 12.7.
**fjórir** *num.* four; *n. fjögur MvII* 20.7.
**fjöldi** *m.* multitude *Mg* 14.6.
**fjörtjón** *n.* loss of life, death *Mg* 50.7 n.
**fjör** *n.* life *MvII* 20.7.
**fjötraðr** *a. pptc.* fettered *MvI* 19.7.
**fjöturr** *m.* fetter, bond, shackle *MvI* 22.8.
**flatr** *a.* deflated, shame-faced *MvIII* 24.1.
**fleinhristandi** *m.* shaft-shaker *Mg* 11.4 (see List of Kennings, 'Man').
**fleiri** *a. comp.* more *MvIII* 10.8, 15.7.
**flestr** *a. sup.* most *MvI* 28.4; *MvII* 8.3; *MvIII* 14.6, 27.8; *sem flestir* as many as possible *Mg* 42.7.
**fleygir** *m.* flinger, distributor *MvIII* 14.5 (see List of Kennings, 'Man').
**fljóð** *n.* woman *Mg* 22.4, 22.6; *VM* 12.2; *MvI* 12.3, 15.5, 18.2, 22.4, 24.3, 25.8; *MvII* 5.8, 12.2, 17.8, 19.5, 21.2. *MvIII* 25.6, 27.4.
**fljótt** *adv.* swiftly, quickly *MvI* 21.2.
**flóð** *n.* flood, water *MvIII* 7.6.
**flóa (ð)** *wv.* to flow, overflow, flood; *flóa í tárum* to be bathed in tears *VM* 13.4 n.; *MvI* 15.1, 16.1.
**flokkr** *m.* (1) flock, (body of) people, company *VM* 16.4, 22.5; *MvI* 13.3; *MvIII* 10.6, 13.3. (2) poem (without refrains) *MvII* 24.1; *MvIII* 30.8.
**flýja (flýði)** *wv.* to flee *Mg* 7.1.
**flytja (flutti)** *wv.* to convey; carry *MvII* 13.6; *MvIII* 20.3 (spread).
**flærð** *f.* falsehood *MvIII* 20.4.
**fólk** *n.* people *MvI* 6.4; *MvII* 4.2; *MvIII* 28.4.
**forðast (að)** *wv. md. with dat.* to avoid, escape *MvI* 8.4.
**forma (að)** *wv.* to make, perform *Mg* 40.2.
**formaðr** *m.* former man or husband *VM* 13.8 n.
**forn** *a.* old, ancient *Mg* 6.3 n.; *MvII* 12.7.
**fossgangr** *m.* tumbling stream *MvIII* 7.4.
**fótr** *m.* foot *VM* 17.5.
**frá** *prep. with dat.* (1) from, away from *VM* 9.2; *MvIII* 16.4, 23.1.

## Glossary and Index 95

(2) *as adv.* about, concerning *MvII* 3.4; about it *MvIII* 6.4, 23.6; off, away *MvIII* 24.1.

**fram** *adv.* forward, on *Mg* 13.8, 35.5; forth *VM* 8.3; *MvII* 2.2.

**framburðr** *m.* statement *VM* 21.3.

**framr** *a.* outstanding, excellent; courageous; outspoken *VM* 3.4.

**fregna (frá)** *sv.* to hear, learn *Mg* 31.1; *fregna af* hear about *MvI* 12.2.

**freista (að)** *wv. with gen.* to test, tempt *MvIII* 23.7.

**friðarfullr** *a.* peaceful *MvII* 17.7.

**friðr** *m.* peace *Mg* 32.2; *MvI* 19.8 (quarter), 25.7; *MvIII* 11.4.

**fríðr** *a.* beautiful, fine *VM* 9.3, 21.4; *MvI* 7.2, 15.5; *MvII* 11.3, 16.2; *sup. VM* 8.3.

**Fríðr** *f.* name of a goddess or giantess *VM* 3.5 n. (see List of Kennings, 'Woman')

**frjádagr** *m.* Friday *Mg* 11.3, 24.3, 31.7.

**frjófast (að)** *wv. md.* to become pregnant, conceive *MvII* 8.3 n.

**fróðr** *a.* learned, knowledgeable, wise *Mg* 10.4 n. (*as subst.*), 41.2, 44.7; *sup.* most wise *Mg* 34.6.

**frón** *n.* earth, land *Mg* 7.5 (*fróni á*), 26.4.

**frú** *f.* lady *VM* 25.8; *MvI* 6.8, 12.1, 16.1, 18.1, 20.8, 23.2; *MvII* 5.7, 7.1 n., 8.1, 9.4, 11.3, 16.8 n., 22.6; *MvIII* 14.2, 20.6, 27.7.

**frumtíð** *f.* first hour *MvII* 10.5.

**frægð** *f.* renown, fame *MvI* 4.8.

**frægðarsvinnr** *a.* illustrious or of renowned wisdom *Mg* 41.4.

**frægr** *a.* renowned *Mg* 12.1; *comp. with dat. of comparison Mg* 4.3, 7.7, 22.3.

**frændi** *m.* relative *Mg* 1.5, *VM* 10.4; *MvI* 4.7, 12.1. (See List of Kennings, 'Other'.)

**fúll** *a.* foul *Mg* 50.7.

**fullr** *a.* full *Mg* 22.3; *VM* 25.7; *MvI* 12.3; *MvIII* 7.5; complete *Mg* 7.7, 23.4.

**fulltingr** *m.* help *MvI* 17.4.

**fundr** *m.* meeting, encounter (*with gen.* with) *Mg* 7.2, 51.6; *MvIII* 5.6.

**fúss** *a.* eager (*with gen.* for) *Mg* 13.7, 18.1, 26.7.

**fylgja (ð)** *wv. with dat.* to accompany *Mg* 8.4, 12.4, 13.7; *láta fylgja* add 48.3.

**fylkir** *m.* battle-leader, king *Mg* 11.3 (see List of Kennings, 'Christ').

**fylla (ld)** *wv.* to fill; fulfil *Mg* 10.8; *VM* 21.3 (confirm); *pptc. fyldr* filled *Mg* 4.4, 15.7, 28.3; tightly compressed? *MvI* 8.3; *md.* be filled *MvI* 21.1; be achieved, increased *MvI* 4.7.

**fyr** *prep.* (1) *with acc.* (a) before, in front of, beyond *VM* 6.1; *MvII*

23.6; *MvIII* 16.7, 17.1; in charge of *MvIII* 27.3. (b) for *Mg* 50.3. (c) because of, on account of, through, for the sake of *Mg* 39.5; *VM* 14.5 (by means of); *MvI* 11.1; *MvII* 18.3, 19.1; *MvIII* 1.5, 4.8, 6.2, 8.2, 18.7, 23.3, 26.6; *fyr utan* without *MvIII* 25.2. (d) for, so as to bring about *MvIII* 2.3. (e) in return for *MvII* 17.2. (2) *with dat.* (a) before, in front of *Mg* 11.7, 19.6, 29.6, 37.8, 40.1, 40.5, 41.7, 43.7 (under); *VM* 7.3, 18.5, 24.4; *MvI* 3.2 (over), 29.1. (b) because of, for, as a result of *Mg* 15.5, 23.1 n.; *MvI* 5.5; *MvII* 9.1.

**fyrðar** *m. pl.* people *VM* 2.8 n.

**fyrnast (d)** *wv. md.* to be forgotten *Mg* 30.4.

**fyrr** *adv.* before, previously *Mg* 2.8; *fyrr en* before *Mg* 38.4.

**fyrri** *adv.* earlier, before *VM* 11.4; *MvI* 24.6.

**fýsa (t)** *wv.* (1) *impers. with acc.* s-one desires *Mg* 10.6, 34.5. (2) *md.* to desire *VM* 12.7.

**fyst** *adv. sup.* first *Mg* 12.2; *MvIII* 21.4 n.

**fystr** *a. sup.* first *Mg* 27.4, 43.1.

**fæða (dd)** *wv.* (1) to give birth to *Mg* 5.7, 44.2; *pptc.* born *MvI* 17.6. (2) to feed *Mg* 7.8. (3) *md. fæðast upp* to be brought up *VM* 3.5.

**fæðing** *f.* giving birth *MvII* 10.5.

**færa (ð)** *wv.* to bring *Mg* 6.2, 16.2 n.; *MvII* 2.4, 20.6; *MvIII* 1.3 (*with í einn stað* to bring or put together); *md. færast undan* get oneself out of it, escape *VM* 20.8.

**föðurliga** *adv.* in a fatherly way *MvII* 4.3.

**fögnuðr** *m.* delight, joy *Mg* 7.6, 41.3, 43.1, 44.1; *VM* 25.7. (See List of Kennings, 'Christ'.)

**fölna (að)** *wv.* to fade *MvI* 24.4.

**föstudagr** *m.* Friday *Mg* 12.1.

**gá (ð)** *wv. with gen.* to heed, pay attention to *MvII* 11.8, *MvIII* 9.2; *gá að* to heed *Mg* 29.2.

**gaddr** *m.* spike (i.e. nail) *Mg* 15.3.

**gálauss** *a.* careless, reckless *MvIII* 3.8.

**gall** *n.* bile *Mg* 30.5.

**ganga (gekk)** *sv.* to go, walk *Mg* 14.8, 35.6; *VM* 17.2 (*prptc.*); *MvI* 18.5 (turn out), 19.1, 24.5, 26.1; *MvIII* 5.8; *with acc.* to go through *MvI* 14.2; *ganga að* to approach *Mg* 14.2; *ganga nær* to press upon *MvIII* 17.7; *ganga við with dat.* to confess to, admit to *VM* 23.3; *MvI* 11.6.

**garðr** *m.* establishment, premises (in a town) *MvI* 3.2.

**gátt** *f.* door-post *MvII* 18.2 (see List of Kennings, 'Woman').

**gefa (gaf)** *sv.* to give *Mg* 1.1, 2.6, 28.4, 32.3, 38.8; *VM* 6.7, 25.6; *MvI*

1.1, 23.5; *MvII* 1.1, 16.4, 18.8, 19.7; *MvIII* 1.1, 12.1, 25.2, 29.1; *gefa út* pour forth *Mg* 37.8 n.; *MvII* 7.8; *impers. gefr til* there is opportunity for it *MvIII* 3.4; *md. reciprocal* to give each other *VM* 4.8.
**gegnum** *prep. with acc.* (*í gegnum*) through *Mg* 17.6, 22.8.
**geirr** *m.* spear *Mg* 30.5.
**gengi** *n.* support, help *MvI* 17.5.
**geta (gat)** *sv.* (1) to get; be able *MvIII* 14.6; *with pptc.* be able *MvII* 23.7; *md. with dat.* to be got for s-one *MvII* 19.5. (2) to beget *MvII* 5.3. (3) to mention, refer to, speak of s-thing (*with gen.*) *MvIII* 17.2, 22.2.
**getnaðr** *m.* conception *MvII* 8.5.
**geyma (d)** *wv. with gen.* to heed *MvIII* 3.1.
**geymir** *m.* keeper, guardian *Mg* 38.7 (see List of Kennings, 'Christ').
**gimsteinn** *m.* gemstone *Mg* 39.4 (see List of Kennings, 'Virgin Mary').
**ginna (nt)** *wv.* to trick, entice *MvIII* 23.1.
**gipta** *f.* success *Mg* 28.3.
**gjalda (galt)** *sv.* to grant, give *MvII* 1.4 (*impers.*), 8.6.
**gjarna** *adv.* willingly, eagerly *Mg* 2.1, 10.8, 27.7; *MvII* 5.4.
**gjöra (ð)** *wv.* (1) to do, make *Mg* 14.7, 21.1, 48.7; *VM* 22.5; *MvI* 21.6, 22.1; *MvII* 6.5, 12.4; *MvIII* 7.5 n., 14.5, 15.7, 18.6, 20.2, 23.2. 26.2; *gjör svó vel* please *Mg* 47.1. (2) *md.* to become *MvII* 5.6; *MvIII* 3.7, 4.1, 5.1 n.; *gjörðist kominn* arose *MvII* 10.7. (3) *periphrastic with inf. MvI* 11.5, 18.6; *MvII* 21.1.
**gjörð** *f.* deed *MvI* 8.7, 15.4.
**gjörvallr** *a.* absolutely all *Mg* 16.8, 19.3, 20.8, 24.8.
**glaðr** *a.* glad, happy, cheerful *Mg* 5.7, 38.4; *MvII* 23.8.
**gleði** *f.* gladness, delight, joy *Mg* 27.7, 38.5, 41.6, 43.4.
**gleðifullr** *a.* joyful *MvII* 8.5.
**gleðilíf** *n.* life of merriment or pleasure *MvIII* 4.8.
**gleðiorð** *n.* word of merriment *MvIII* 3.7.
**gleðitíð** *f.* time of joy *MvII* 2.2.
**gleðitími** *m.* period of happiness *MvII* 10.8.
**gleðja (gladda)** *wv.* to make glad or happy *Mg* 47.2; *MvIII* 2.2 (1st pers. sg. pres. subj.); *pptc. Mg* 25.2; *md.* become glad *Mg* 12.8, 43.5.
**gleyma (d)** *wv. with dat.* to forget *VM* 9.8.
**glóðir** *f. pl.* embers *MvI* 9.5 n. (see List of Kennings, 'Woman' and 'gold').
**glæpr** *m.* misdeed, crime, sin *MvI* 10.8; *MvIII* 12.1.
**glæstr** *a. pptc. of* **glæsa** made splendid *Mg* 27.8.
**gnógt, nógt** *f.* abundance, plenty *Mg* 3.4; *MvIII* 1.8.

**góðlátr** *a.* good-natured, courteous *MvII* 5.3.
**góðr** (*n.* **gott**) *a.* good *Mg* 5.2, 5.6, 28.6, 32.4, 32.6, 36.6, 46.7, 52.4; *VM* 1.8, 3.1, 19.6, 21.6, 25.4; *MvII* 1.2, 11.7, 22.2.
**gramr** *m.* prince, king *Mg* 42.2.
**grand** *n.* crime *MvI* 12.1.
**gráta** (**grjet**) *sv.* to weep, mourn, grieve (for), lament *Mg* 26.5; *VM* 17.1 n.; *MvI* 13.1, 13.7, 15.3; *MvII* 13.2, 14.5, 19.8 (*prptc.*).
**grátr** *m.* weeping, lament, lamentation *Mg* 18.3, 38.5, 39.1, 40.2, 52.8; *MvI* 9.6; *MvII* 18.4.
**greiða** (**dd**) *wv.* to prepare, put in order; *prptc. greiðandi fram* bringing forth, uttering *VM* 8.3; *md.* to be made, produced *VM* 1.7; to be paid *MvI* 4.6.
**grein** *f.* (1) condition, state; periphastic for an abstract noun (cf. **feginsgrein**), *dýrðar grein* glory *Mg* 50.6. (2) event *MvI* 9.8. (3) *með greinum* with (good) reason, in detail *MvI* 15.3.
**greina** (**d**) *wv.* to describe, relate, tell *Mg* 17.4, 19.6, 31.2, 37.7, 41.8; *MvI* 14.7; *MvIII* 12.2.
**grimd** *f.* fierceness, cruelty *Mg* 14.1; *MvI* 8.2.
**grimmr** *a.* fierce, cruel *Mg* 14.5.
**grípa** (**greip**) *sv.* to grip, grasp, seize *MvIII* 10.7.
**gróa** (**greri**) *sv.* to be healed (of wounds) *MvIII* 28.6.
**grund** *f.* ground *Mg* 9.5, 20.2, 38.7 (earth); *VM* 25.3. (See List of Kennings, 'Heaven', 'Virgin Mary'.)
**grýttr** *a.* stony, rocky *Mg* 10.6, 45.1.
**græða** (**dd**) *wv.* to heal; *MvII* 17.7; to save *Mg* 44.2.
**græðari** *m.* saviour *MvII* 23.7.
**græðir** *m.* sea *MvI* 9.5 n.
**grætiligr** *a.* distressing *Mg* 11.1, 17.2.
**Guð** *m.* God *Mg* 3.7, 6.1, 6.8, 12.5, 13.7, 14.4, 23.5, 24.1, 31.7, 38.6, 40.3, 43.8, 44.3, 45.1, 45.6, 52.7; *VM* 1.4, 2.6, 7.8, 14.5 n., 18.2, 22.4, 24.4; *MvI* 1.5, 1.6, 2.1, 25.2, 27.6, 29.4, 29.8; *MvII* 1.5, 2.4, 2.8, 6.4, 11.7, 19.2, 19.7, 20.3, 21.6, 23.2, 24.2, 24.8; *MvIII* 1.6, 6.2, 6.6, 8.8, 11.2, 11.6, 13.8, 15.1, 15.8, 16.3, 17.6, 23.1, 24.4, 25.1, 26.4, 28.2, 28.8, 29.7, 30.2.
**guðdómr** *m.* Divinity, Godhead *Mg* 28.3; *VM* 25.3.
**guðspjall** *n.* gospel *Mg* 31.6.
**guðvefr** *m.* costly cloth *VM* 9.7.
**gull** *n.* gold *VM* 9.7; *MvII* 5.2 n., 15.4; *MvIII* 5.6.
**gullskorð** *f.* gold-prop *MvII* 10.7 n. (see List of Kennings, 'Woman').
**gumi** *m.* man, person *Mg* 30.6.

## Glossary and Index 99

**gyðingafólk** *n*. Jewish people *Mg* 14.1 n.
**gæta (tt)** *wv. with gen.* to watch over, tend, take care of *Mg* 26.3.
**gætir** *m*. keeper, guardian *Mg* 5.1, 6.6, 9.4, 10.2, 19.8, 28.2, 47.7, 50.2. (See List of Kennings, 'Bishop' and 'Christ'.)
**gæzka** *f*. goodness, grace *Mg* 51.8.
**gæzkufimr** *a*. ready with goodness *Mg* 45.2.
**gæzkumildr** *a*. generous with goodness *Mg* 37.7 n.
**göfga (að)** *vw*. to honour *VM* 1.7.
**göfugligr** *a*. worshipful, noble *MvIII* 25.1.
**göfugr** *a*. worshipful, noble *Mg* 5.1; *VM* 17.1; *MvI* 1.5; *MvII* 20.4, 21.2; *sup. Mg* 47.1.

**háð** *n*. scorn, mockery *Mg* 14.1, 21.3.
**háðuliga** *adv*. scornfully, shamefully *MvIII* 15.6.
**hafa (ð)** *wv*. to have *Mg* 10.6, 30.8; *VM* 19.8, 21.8; *MvI* 18.6, 21.5, 21.7, 28.7, 29.1; *MvII* 5.3, 11.8 n., 16.6; *MvIII* 6.1, 9.2, 13.3, 16.3, 18.8, 19.6; *hafa uppi* to enjoy *MvIII* 3.4.
**hafna (að)** *wv. with dat.* to reject, shun, give up *Mg* 3.4.
**hald** *n*. help, support *Mg* 35.4.
**halda (hjelt)** *sv*. to hold, keep *Mg* 36.3; *MvII* 24.8; to keep to, follow *MvI* 3.3.
**háleitr** *a*. sublime *Mg* 10.7 n., 43.4; *VM* 1.8; *MvII* 22.8; *MvIII* 15.4, 22.4.
**halr** *m*. man, person *Mg* 15.1; *VM* 15.6.
**hanga (hjekk)** *sv*. to hang *Mg* 18.1.
**hann, hún/hun, það** (*pl.* þeir, þær, þau) *pers. pron*. he, she, it, they etc. *Mg* 2.8, 4.5, 4.6, 4.7, 7.4, 7.8, 8.5 n., 12.7, 13.5, 16.7, 16.8, 20.7, 20.8, 21.3, 23.8 n., 24.7, 24.8, 31.1 n., 36.4, 42.6, 43.3, 45.8, 48.1, 48.7, 50.3, 50.4; *VM* 4.7, 4.8 (*pl.*), 5.6, 6.5, 7.6 (*pl.*), 8.1, 9.4, 9.5, 9.8, 14.4, 16.6 (*dat. sg. n. object of ráðið*), 16.7, 17.7, 19.2 n., 21.2, 22.7 (*pl.*), 24.8; *MvI* 1.6, 1.7, 4.3, 4.5 n., 6.6, 7.7, 8.1, 10.8, 11.1, 11.5, 11.7, 12.4 (*pl.*), 12.8, 14.4, 14.8 (*pl.*), 19.3, 19.5 n., 19.6, 19.7, 22.1 (*pl.*), 24.1, 24.7, 29.2; *MvII* 3.3, 3.5 n. (*sg. and pl.*), 3.8 n., 4.7 (*pl.*), 5.5, 8.1, 8.3, 11.4, 11.6, 12.3 n., 13.6, 14.2, 14.5, 14.6 n., 15.7, 16.3 (*rel.?*), 18.8, 19.3 n., 19.7, 20.1, 21.7 (*pl.*), 23.4, 23.8; *MvIII* 3.3, 3.7, 4.5, 4.6, 4.7, 5.5, 5.8, 6.5, 6.8, 7.1, 7.6 n., 8.3, 9.3 n. (*sg. and pl.*), 9.4, 9.5, 9.6, 9.7, 10.1, 10.3, 10.8 (*pl.*), 11.1 (*pl.*), 11.5, 11.8, 12.4, 12.6, 13.2, 13.4, 14.7, 15.4, 15.5, 15.7, 16.1, 16.4, 17.3 (*pl.*), 17.8 (*pl.*), 18.1 (*pl.*), 18.6, 19.8, 20.7, 21.1, 21.4, 22.1 (*pl.*), 22.4 (*pl.*), 23.2, 23.4 (*pl.*), 23.8 (*pl.*), 24.2 n., 24.7 (*pl.*), 24.8, 25.7, 25.8, 27.7.
**hár** *n*. hair *MvI* 24.2.

**hár** *a.* high *MvII* 6.6; *comp. hærri* higher, greater *Mg* 16.8, 20.8, 24.8, 29.3; *sup. hæstr* highest *Mg* 30.3, 43.1, 46.4; *VM* 19.7; *MvI* 3.6; *MvIII* 6.6 n., 29.5, 30.1, 30.2.
**harðla** *adv.* very *Mg* 48.2.
**harðlyndr** *a.* harsh-tempered *MvIII* 14.8.
**harðr** *a.* hard, harsh *Mg* 21.1, 51.6; *MvI* 19.3.
**harmr** *m.* sorrow, grief, affliction *Mg* 4.5, 11.2, 15.5, 22.5, 25.8, 29.3, 30.7, 35.3; *MvI* 22.2 (passion); *MvII* 5.6.
**hásæti** *n.* high seat, throne *Mg* 28.2; *VM* 25.2. (See List of Kennings, 'Virgin Mary'.)
**hata (að)** *wv.* to hate, persecute *MvIII* 11.5.
**háttr** *m.* kind, type, verse-form *MvIII* 1.2.
**hauðr** *n.* land *Mg* 23.2, 25.4, 30.2, 34.8 (see List of Kennings, 'Heaven').
**hefja (hóf)** *sv.* (1) to lift, raise *Mg* 15.2, 45.8. (2) to begin *MvIII* 9.3; *hefja upp MvIII* 9.7.
**hefnd** *f.* vengeance *MvIII* 11.6.
**heiðr** *f.* heath *Mg* 35.8.
**heiðr** *m.* honour *Mg* 46.3; *MvI* 4.5 (honourable intentions); *MvII* 16.5.
**heiðra (að)** *wv.* to honour *MvII* 20.4.
**heiðrsmaðr** *m.* honourable man *MvI* 4.6.
**heilagr (helg-)** *a.* holy *Mg* 2.4, 6.8, 10.7 n., 11.6, 13.7, 25.1, 29.1, 33.1, 43.3, 48.3, 49.7; *MvI* 18.7.
**heilráðr** *a.* giving good counsel *MvII* 21.8.
**heilsubót** *f.* recovery of health *Mg* 47.7.
**heim** *adv.* home, back *Mg* 11.5; *MvI* 26.1; *MvIII* 24.7.
**heiman** *adv.* from home *MvIII* 7.3.
**heimligr** *a.* of this world, i.e. mortal *Mg* 22.6 n.
**heimr** *m.* world *Mg* 5.8, 26.8, 33.6, 44.2; *MvII* 24.7; *MvIII* 3.3, 25.4, 29.5.
**heimska** *f.* stupidity *MvI* 11.1.
**heit** *n.* promise *Mg* 48.1.
**heita (hjet)** *sv.* (1) (*pres. heitr*) to promise *Mg* 47.8 n. (3) (*pres. heitir*) to be called, be named *Mg* 34.3; *MvII* 22.6.
**heitr** *a.* hot *MvI* 12.7, 20.7, 23.4, 27.3; *MvII* 17.2; *MvIII* 5.3.
**heldr** *comp. adv.* rather *MvII* 4.8; *MvIII* 19.3.
**herðar** *f. pl.* shoulders *Mg* 13.3 n., 14.7 n.
**herma (d)** *wv.* to report *VM* 20.5.
**Heródes** *m.* Herod *Mg* 7.2.
**herr** *m.* host, army *MvIII* 14.4 (see List of Kennings, 'Fiends').

**herra** *m.* lord *Mg* 29.4, 30.3; *VM* 14.2; *MvII* 3.1. (See List of Kennings, 'Christ'.)
**heyra (ð)** *wv.* to hear, listen to *Mg* 16.1, 25.1, 29.1, 33.1, 42.1, 52.8; *VM* 1.1, 20.3, 24.1; *MvI* 1.1, 7.1, 27.1; *MvII* 7.5, 10.1 n.; *MvIII* 2.1, 22.2.
**heyriliga** *adv.* audibly *MvIII* 9.3.
**Hildr** *f.* name of a valkyrie *MvI* 24.5 (see List of Kennings, 'Woman').
**hilmir** *m.* ruler, king *Mg* 2.1, 15.1 n., 35.2, 37.1 (see List of Kennings, 'Christ').
**himinn** *m.* heaven, sky *Mg* 4.7, 6.6, 8.8, 11.5, 13.1, 16.7, 20.7, 24.7, 27.6, 28.1, 28.6, 32.6, 35.7, 36.6, 38.7, 45.2, 45.7, 46.3, 47.7, 48.7, 50.2; *MvIII* 12.5 n.
**himiríki** *n.* kingdom of heaven *MvIII* 14.2, 30.1.
**himneskr** *a.* heavenly *Mg* 46.8.
**hinn, hin, hitt** *pron.* that (one) *MvI* 6.2; *MvIII* 12.1.
**hirð** *f.* court, following *Mg* 45.7.
**hirðir** *m.* shepherd, keeper *Mg* 46.5; *VM* 14.1. (See List of Kennings, 'Christ', 'Man'.)
**hirtir** *m.* punisher, i.e. ruler *VM* 11.5 (see List of Kennings, 'Man').
**hitnaðr** *a. pptc. of* **hitna** heated, impassioned *VM* 24.2.
**hitta (tt)** *wv.* to meet, go and see, visit, encounter, come upon, find *Mg* 9.3, 16.3, 50.6; *VM* 13.1; *MvI* 17.2; *MvIII* 2.2.
**hjá** (1) *prep. with dat.* beside, next to, close by *Mg* 28.8, 32.8, 36.8; *VM* 5.6; *MvI* 2.4. (2) *adv.* nearby, present *VM* 16.2; *MvIII* 13.2.
**hjálp** *f.* help; salvation *Mg* 13.3 n., 18.1, 25.2, 41.5, 49.5; *VM* 18.6 (here a term for the Virgin), 26.6; *MvII* 17.8, 18.1; *MvIII* 27.8. (See List of Kennings, 'Virgin Mary'.)
**hjálpa (að)** *wv. with dat.* to save *Mg* 1.4, 52.1; *MvIII* 29.8.
**hjarta** *n.* heart *Mg* 1.8, 17.6, 21.5, 22.8, 30.7, 48.4, 49.1; *MvI* 1.2; *MvIII* 4.3 n.
**hjartaliga** *adv.* deeply, sincerely *MvII* 3.6.
**hjeðan** *adv.* hence, from here *MvIII* 29.6.
**hjer** *adv.* here *VM* 7.7; *MvII* 1.4, 16.2, 17.4; *MvIII* 8.8, 30.8; for this *Mg* 47.5 n. (see **að** *prep.* 11); in this *VM* 24.1; to this *MvI* 7.1; about this *MvIII* 22.5; *hjer í móti* on the contrary *MvIII* 15.5.
**hjón** *n. pl.* married couple, husband and wife *MvII* 4.1, 21.6.
**hlaða (hlóð)** *sv.* to pile up *MvI* 20.1.
**hlíð** *f.* hill-side *MvII* 20.5 (see List of Kennings, 'Woman').
**hlífa (ð)** *wv. with dat.* to spare *MvI* 20.8; *prptc. MvI* 27.4.
**Hlín** *f.* name of a goddess *VM* 5.3; *MvI* 26.2 (see List of Kennings, 'Woman').

hljóð *n.* hearing, silence; audience *MvI* 1.1.
hlotnast (að) *wv. md.* to be allotted *Mg* 49.5.
hlutr *m.* thing *Mg* 16.5, 20.5, 24.5; *MvIII* 6.1.
hlýða (dd) *wv.* to listen to *Mg* 37.5.
hlynr *m.* maple-tree *Mg* 8.1 (see List of Kennings, 'Man').
hlýrn *n.* heavenly body; *in pl.* sun and moon *Mg* 2.1, 21.2, 30.4.
hlýrnir *m.* heaven *Mg* 27.7.
hlæja (hló) *sv.* to laugh *Mg* 12.8; *MvII* 19.3.
hneigja (gð) *wv.* to bow; *hneigja sig* to bow down *Mg* 40.5.
hneyksl *n.* shame *MvII* 9.5 n.
hóf *n.* moderation *MvIII* 25.3.
hold *n.* flesh *Mg* 43.6; *MvI* 27.3; *MvII* 16.4.
hopp *n.* merriment, merry-making *MvIII* 3.3.
hórdómr *m.* adultery, fornication *MvIII* 18.4.
horfa (ð) *wv. with á* to turn towards, look at, watch *Mg* 21.5 n.
hoskr *a.* wise, sensible *MvI* 23.7.
hreggskrín *n.* storm-shrine *Mg* 49.6 (see List of Kennings, 'Heaven').
hreinlíf *n.* pure life, chastity *MvI* 2.6 (with def. art. as a term for St Andrew)
hreinn *a.* pure, virtuous, good *Mg* 17.4, 25.6, 36.2, 50.6; *VM* 3.8; *MvI* 1.4 n.; *MvII* 3.2, 14.1 (sincere), 18.8, 20.6; *MvIII* 2.1, 2.7, 15.3, 27.4.
hrella (ld) *wv.* to distress *MvI* 19.4.
hringr *m.* ring *Mg* 49.1; *VM* 5.3, 14.1; *MvI* 22.6, 24.5, 26.1; *MvII* 18.2, 20.5.
hristast (st) *wv. md.* to shake, shudder *Mg* 33.5.
hróðr *m.* praise-poem *Mg* 2.2.
hrópa (að) *wv.* to call out loudly *MvIII* 12.1.
hrósa (að) *wv. with dat.* to praise, glory in *Mg* 49.4.
Hrund *f.* name of a valkyrie *MvIII* 5.6 (see List of Kennings, 'Woman').
hrygð *f.* sorrow *Mg* 24.2.
hrygðarfullr *a.* sorrowful *MvIII* 13.5.
hryggja (gð) *wv.* to sadden, grieve; *md. hryggjast viðr* be sorry *MvI* 11.2.
hryggr *a.* sad, sorrowful *Mg* 2.3.
hrynja (hrundi) *wv.* to stream out *Mg* 49.7.
hræðast (dd) *wv. md.* to be afraid, be frightened *Mg* 43.8 n.; *MvI* 13.6.
hræðiligr *a.* frightening, terrible *MvI* 6.1.
hrækja (kt) *wv.* to spit *Mg* 14.2.
hræra (ð) *wv.* to move *Mg* 15.6; *md.* to be moved *Mg* 21.6.
hugarfár *n.* evil disposition *MvIII* 5.2.
hugdýrr *a.* courageous *MvII* 3.1.

**huggan** *f.* comfort, solace *MvII* 14.1.
**hugljúfr** *a.* kind in thought, kindly *MvII* 4.5.
**hugr** *m.* thought *MvIII* 2.4.
**hugrakkr** *a.* brave, bold *MvIII* 26.2.
**húsfrú** *f.* mistress of the house *MvI* 7.2, 8.3.
**huxan** *f.* thought *MvI* 6.1.
**hvað** *pron. n.* what *MvIII* 21.4.
**hvar** *adv.* where *Mg* 22.5; *MvII* 15.6.
**hvarmr** *m.* eyelid *Mg* 49.2, 49.8.
**hve** *adv. interrog.* how *VM* 13.5 n.
**hverfa (hvarf)** *sv.* to turn; to disappear *MvIII* 24.1.
**hverflyndr** *a.* fickle, untrustworthy (*with gen.* regarding?) *VM* 11.6.
**hvergi** *adv.* nowhere, not at all *Mg* 15.5; *MvI* 24.1.
**hverr, hver, hvert** *pron.* (1) who, which, what (*interrog.*) *MvIII* 13.6. (2) each, every *Mg* 24.3, 42.1, 43.8, 48.3; *VM* 16.8, 20.6, 23.4; *MvI* 22.7; *MvII* 4.6, 5.5, 8.2; *MvIII* 5.5, 6.5, 15.2.
**hvesskyns** *adv.* all kinds of *Mg* 48.8.
**hvessu, hversu** *adv.* how *Mg* 29.2; *MvII* 2.5, 20.3; *interrog. MvIII* 14.1, 22.5.
**hví** *adv. interrog.* why *VM* 11.5.
**hvílast (d)** *wv. md.* to take rest *Mg* 35.7.
**hvítr** *a.* white; i.e. unburned *MvI* 25.4; *sup.* most pure *VM* 5.4 n..
**hvólf** *n.* vault *Mg* 22.2 (see List of Kennings, 'Heaven').
**hvórr** *pron.* which of two; *n. hvort VM* 19.7 n. (which one of us); *hvórt* either of two *MvII* 3.8.
**hyggja (hugði)** *wv.* to think, believe *VM* 16.5; to imagine *Mg* 46.6.
**hylja (huldi)** *wv.* to cover, bury *Mg* 35.1 n.
**hyllir** *m.* one who gives favour, favourer *Mg* 10.8 (see List of Kennings, 'Christ').
**hýrliga** *adv.* kindly *Mg* 18.2.
**hýrligr** *a.* gentle, kind *Mg* 33.2.
**hyrr** *m.* fire *MvI* 20.7, 22.3 n.
**hæða (dd)** *wv.* to mock *Mg* 12.7, 14.3.
**hæfilæti** *n.* suitable or proper conduct *MvIII* 15.3.
**hægr** *a.* (1) calm *MvI* 24.6. (2) comfortable *MvIII* 25.3.
**hælast (d)** *wv. md.* to boast *MvIII* 22.6.
**hætta** *f.* danger, risk *VM* 13.5.
**hæveskr** *a.* courteous *MvII* 4.5.
**höfuðborg** *f.* main town *MvII* 6.2.
**höfuðfögnuðr** *m.* chief joy *Mg* 42.2 n.

**höfuðslægð** f. outstanding cunning *MvIII* 13.5 (*adv. dat. or instrumental*).
**höfuðsynd** f. cardinal sin *MvIII* 18.2.
**höldr** m. man, person; *pl.* people *VM* 15.4; humankind *Mg* 13.4.
**höll** f. hall *Mg* 28.1 (see List of Kennings, 'Virgin Mary'), 28.6, 32.6, 36.6; *MvII* 24.7. Cf. **stjörnuhöll**.
**hönd** f. hand *Mg* 31.3; *VM* 8.2 (*acc. sg. hand*); *MvI* 18.4; *í hendr oss* from in our hands *MvIII* 14.1; *á hönd mjer* against me *MvII* 9.6.
**höttr** m. hood *VM* 20.5 n.

**í** *prep.* (1) *with acc.* in, into, for; (*of time*) on, at *Mg* 6.4, 15.2, 35.1, 37.2, 46.2, 46.3, 51.8; *VM* 4.7 n., 8.1, 15.3; *MvI* 14.3, 17.7, 26.2; *MvII* 5.5, 11.2, 12.5, 18.5, 20.2, 24.1 n.; *MvIII* 1.4, 1.7, 3.6, 6.5, 14.1, 24.7. (2) *with dat.* in, on *Mg* 1.8, 5.4, 7.5, 9.8, 15.8, 24.4, 26.7, 28.6, 29.7, 30.2, 30.7, 32.6, 33.6, 34.4, 36.6, 40.3, 49.1; *VM* 1.3, 2.6, 3.1, 3.7, 5.8, 7.8, 9.5, 10.8, 13.4, 14.8 n., 18.6, 22.2, 24.7; *MvI* 3.1, 3.8, 4.2, 8.1, 9.2, 15.1, 16.2, 19.8, 20.4, 23.4, 23.7, 24.2, 25.7, 28.1; *MvII* 4.6, 6.2, 13.8, 17.3; *MvIII* 2.7.
**iðran** f. repentance *Mg* 39.3, 40.7, 48.4.
**iðrast (að)** *wv. md. with gen.* to repent (of) *Mg* 3.8; *MvI* 11.2; *prptc. iðrandi* penitent, repenting *MvI* 29.8; *MvIII* 27.6.
**illa** *adv.* badly, poorly *MvI* 18.5.
**illr** *a.* evil, wicked *MvI* 6.4, 8.7; *MvIII* 23.2.
**illska** f. malice, wickedness *MvI* 5.5.
**ilmr** m. fragrance, scent, perfume *Mg* 9.7.
**inna (nt)** *wv.* to rehearse *Mg* 42.5; to tell, relate *Mg* 11.1; *VM* 2.7; *MvI* 2.7, 29.3 (*pptc. f. acc.*); *MvII* 20.2.
**inniligr** *a.* dear *VM* 8.6.
**ítarligr** *a.* splendid, magnificent *Mg* 3.3, 9.7, 20.1, 28.1, 32.1, 45.5.
**ítr** *a.* glorious, excellent, splendid *Mg* 34.3, 44.8, 51.5; *MvIII* 6.1; *sup.* most glorious *Mg* 26.3, 39.1.

**jafnan** *adv.* always, continually *Mg* 41.4, 47.4; *VM* 2.4; *MvI* 2.4; *MvII* 22.4 n.; *MvIII* 6.2, 17.6.
**jafnvel** *adv.* even *Mg* 33.7.
**jarteign** f. miracle *VM* 2.8, 26.3; *MvI* 2.7, 26.6, 29.3; *MvII* 1.6.
**jáyrði** *n.* consent *VM* 18.4.
**Jesús** m. Jesus *Mg* 5.7 n., 17.7, 19.2, 25.2, 31.6, 35.3, 37.5, 39.6, 51.5; *VM* 25.4.
**jóð** *n.* baby *MvII* 5.8, 8.8, 9.7, 12.2, 17.8.
**jólanótt** f. Christmas night *Mg* 44.3.

## Glossary and Index

**Jón (postuli)** *m.* St John (the Apostle) *Mg* 26.4.
**Jósep** *m.* St Joseph of Arimathea *Mg* 34.3.
**júðar** *m. pl.* Jews *Mg* 8.7, 12.7, 13.4, 21.4.
**jungfrú** *f.* girl, maiden, virgin *Mg* 5.7, 26.3, 39.1.
**jungkæri** *m.* young man *VM* 20.8.
**jöfurr** *m.* prince *Mg* 28.5, 32.5 n., 36.5 n., 49.6 (see List of Kennings, 'Christ').
**jörð** *f.* earth *Mg* 16.7, 20.7, 24.7, 33.5, 48.7; *MvI* 15.4.

**kafadjúp** *n.* great depth *MvIII* 10.3.
**kaldr** *a.* cold *Mg* 1.6; *MvI* 10.1 (bitter); *MvIII* 10.4.
**kalla (að)** *wv.* to claim (*sjer* for oneself) *MvIII* 11.7, 22.7.
**karl** *m.* man *Mg* 33.4.
**karlmaðr** *m.* man *MvI* 13.3.
**kasta (að)** *wv. with dat.* to throw *MvI* 19.6.
**kátr** *a.* cheerful *Mg* 27.5; *MvII* 7.7, 15.7, 19.8.
**kaupmáli** *m.* contract *VM* 16.4.
**kenna (nd)** *wv.* (1) to perceive, notice *MvII* 12.3. (2) to realise *MvIII* 28.7. (3) to teach *Mg* 31.8, 42.5. (4) *md.* to be acknowledged *VM* 1.4.
**kennir** *m.* one who experiences; wearer *MvI* 10.3 n. (see List of Kennings, 'Priest').
**keyra (ð)** *wv.* to drive *Mg* 15.2.
**kinn** *f.* cheek *Mg* 5.4, 15.8, 40.8.
**kippa (pt)** *wv. with dat.* to pull quickly, drag *MvIII* 18.1.
**kirkja** *f.* church *VM* 5.8, 14.8, 22.2; *MvI* 14.3, 26.2; *MvII* 6.4 n., 13.7.
**kjósa (kaus)** *sv.* to choose, select *Mg* 37.4, 51.7.
**klerkr** *m.* cleric *Mg* 5.2; *MvIII* 2.8, 4.6, 5.4, 8.2, 12.2, 16.6, 18.1, 19.4, 25.4, 26.8.
**kljenn** *a.* neat, beautiful *MvII* 6.3.
**klæða (dd)** *wv.* to clothe *Mg* 7.8.
**klæði** *n. pl.* clothes *MvI* 16.1, 24.3.
**klökkr** *a.* moved to tears, tearful *Mg* 40.7, 48.4.
**klökkva (klökk)** *sv.* to sob *MvI* 13.3.
**knje** *n.* knee *VM* 7.8.
**knýja (knúði)** *wv.* to knock, strike; oppress *VM* 13.2.
**koma (kom)** *sv.* to come, arrive *Mg* 9.3, 27.5 n., 35.4, 45.5; *VM* 15.4; *MvII* 10.8 (*pptc.*), 14.8 n., 18.6; *MvIII* 11.1, 11.8, 13.1, 17.1, 24.7; *impers. koma hjer* to happen *Mg* 3.1; *MvI* 7.1.
**kona** (*gen. pl.* **kvinna**) *f.* woman *Mg* 33.4; *VM* 13.8; *MvI* 13.2; *MvII* 3.3; *MvIII* 4.5.

**kóngr, konungr** *m.* king *Mg* 39.7 n.; *VM* 3.3, 4.4, 10.6; *MvIII* 21.6 n. (See List of Kennings, 'Christ'.)

**króna** *f.* crown *Mg* 21.2.

**krakleikr** *m.* contentiousness *MvI* 10.1.

**kraptfimr** *a.* one who is skilful, successful, blessed in one's powers (especially in relation to miracles) *Mg* 27.6 n.

**kraptr** *m.* power *Mg* 28.3, 37.8. (See List of Kennings, 'Holy Spirit'.)

**krefja (krafði)** *wv.* to ask (for) *Mg* 2.6, 30.8, 38.8; *md.* be called on *MvII* 2.8 n.

**kristinn** *a.* Christian *Mg* 23.1, 42.8.

**Kristr** *m.* Christ *Mg* 12.1, 19.1, 25.6, 34.3, 36.2, 44.2, 51.1; *VM* 22.8; *MvI* 3.5; *MvII* 21.4; *MvIII* 8.3, 17.1 n.

**krjúpa (kraup)** *sv.* to creep (with acc., through; sink through?) *MvIII* 10.3; prostrate oneself *MvI* 15.4; *MvIII* 27.1.

**kross** *m.* cross *Mg* 11.4, 13.6, 15.1, 18.1, 34.1.

**kunna (kunni)** *pret.-pres.* (1) to know *Mg* 46.7; *MvI* 28.7, 29.6. (2) *with acc. and gen.* blame s-one for s-thing *MvI* 7.7. (3) *with (að* and) *inf.* to be able, know how to *Mg* 4.5; *VM* 26.4 (*inf. understood*); *MvII* 17.4, 24.2.

**kunnigr** *a.* known *VM* 18.7.

**kunnr** *a.* known, well known, renowned (*with dat.* for s-thing) *Mg* 1.3; *MvI* 6.8; wise *MvI* 4.4.

**kurteiss** *a.* courteous *MvII* 3.4.

**kvalari** *m.* tormentor *MvIII* 17.2.

**kveða (kvað)** *sv.* to say, declare *Mg* 5.1, 23.6, 26.8, 27.2, 29.1, 30.3, 31.4, 35.5, 37.5, 39.1, 46.2, 47.1; *VM* 6.5, 16.7, 21.6; *MvIII* 11.3, 16.2, 17.5, 20.6, 21.1, 22.6, 24.8 n.

**kveðja (kvaddi)** *wv.* (1) to greet *Mg* 10.1. (2) to call, summon *MvIII* 29.6. (3) to address *Mg* 25.2.

**kveðja** *f.* greeting *Mg* 42.2, 47.2 (see List of Kennings, 'Ave Maria').

**kveikja (kt)** *wv.* (1) to kindle, set on fire *VM* 22.3 (*pptc. with varð* inspired); *md.* to be kindled *Mg* 1.7; *VM* 4.2. (2) to invent, start up; *pptc.* upp kveikt *MvIII* 17.3.

**kvelja (kvaldi)** *wv.* to torment *MvI* 16.7; *MvIII* 4.5.

**kvíða (dd)** *wv.* to be worried, anxious *MvIII* 8.1.

**kviðuð** *a. f.* (*pptc.*) pregnant *MvII* 10.4.

**kvikr** *a.* living *MvII* 20.6.

**kvinna** *f.* = *kona* woman *VM* 6.1; *MvI* 5.1, 10.2, 20.6, 23.5; *MvII* 6.3; wife *VM* 8.6.

**kvitta (að)** *wv.* to tell, relate, spread (a story) *MvI* 6.2.

## Glossary and Index 107

**kvón, kvon** *f.* bride, wife, married woman *MvII* 2.8, 8.2. (See List of Kennings, 'Virgin Mary'.)
**kvæði** *n.* poem *Mg* 37.3, 51.2; *VM* 1.7.
**kvöl** *f.* suffering, torment *Mg* 26.6; *MvI* 12.5, 13.4, 21.8; *MvIII* 8.1 (*nauð kvala* = pains of hell), 13.4, 14.4; *pl. kvalir* i.e. hell *MvIII* 24.7.
**kynda (nd)** *wv.* to light (a fire); *impers. kyndir* is lit *MvI* 13.8 n.
**kyndugr** *a.* shrewd, cunning *MvIII* 18.2.
**kynslóð** *f.* family line *VM* 3.8.
**kynstórr** *a.* high-born *MvII* 10.3.
**kyrr** *a.* quiet, collected *MvI* 24.6.
**kyssa (st)** *wv.* to kiss *Mg* 34.5.
**kæra (ð)** *wv.* to complain of, make an accusation about *VM* 21.8.
**kæra** *f.* beloved (wife) *MvII* 3.3, 10.3; *MvIII* 28.3 (vocative with def. art., i.e. the Virgin).
**kærligr** *a.* dear, beloved *MvI* 3.5.
**kærr** *a.* dear, beloved *Mg* 21.6; *MvIII* 13.8, 28.2; *sup. kæstr MvI* 3.6.

**láð** *n.* land, earth *Mg* 10.6, 45.1.
**land** *n.* land *MvI* 4.2; *MvII* 10.4; *MvIII* 2.4 (see List of Kennings, 'Breast').
**langa (að)** *wv. impers. with acc.* one longs for s-thing *Mg* 47.3.
**langr** *a.* long *Mg* 35.6, 40.6; *VM* 9.1; *MvIII* 29.3 n.; *langi frjádagr* Good Friday *Mg* 11.2, 31.7.
**lát** *n.* death *MvI* 9.6.
**láta (ljet)** *sv.* (1) to put, place *MvII* 15.7; *láta ekki í mót* to put nothing against, not to oppose *MvII* 3.7. (2) *with inf.* to let, cause *Mg* 1.7, 25.3, 48.3, 49.5; *VM* 1.5, 19.1; *MvI* 9.1, 25.5, 26.5; *MvII* 17.6, 18.4, 19.2; *MvIII* 8.7, 11.3, 28.6.
**laug** *f.* bath *Mg* 49.8 (see List of Kennings, 'Tears').
**lauga (að)** *wv.* to bathe *Mg* 5.4, 15.8 n., 40.8.
**laun** *n. pl.* reward *Mg* 47.5, 51.7.
**launa (að)** *wv. with dat. and acc.* to repay, reward s-one for s-thing *Mg* 51.3 n.
**lausn** *f.* redemption, salvation *Mg* 23.1, 31.5; remission *MvIII* 25.8.
**lausnari** *m.* Redeemer, Saviour *Mg* 1.2, 8.4, 13.1 n., 34.1; *VM* 1.6. (See List of Kennings, 'Christ'.)
**lauss** *a.* loose, free; unsteady, unrestrained? *MvIII* 21.5.
**leggja (lagði)** *wv.* to lay, place, put *VM* 5.2; *MvII* 11.1, 12.6; *MvIII* 3.5, 30.5; *leggja á síðu* to stab in the side *Mg* 29.5; *leggja niðr* to drop

*VM* 12.3; *pptc.* weighed down *MvI* 10.6; *md. leggjast að* to lie with, have sex with *MvI* 6.5–6.
**leiða (dd)** *wv.* to lead *Mg* 11.6, 12.7, 27.3 (*inf.* with *mun eg*), 46.1; *imp. leittu Mg* 51.5; *md.* to be brought forth *VM* 19.2; *pptc.* led 19.4; impelled (*with dat.* by) *MvI* 10.4.
**leiði** *n.* grave, tomb *Mg* 35.1, 35.8.
**leiðr** *a.* hateful *VM* 12.3.
**leika (ljek)** *sv.* to play *Mg* 47.4; *leika að* to play with *MvII* 11.4, 12.2.
**leikr** *m.* game; love-game? *VM* 4.2.
**leiptr** *n.* lightning *Mg* 1.8, 20.3.
**lengi** *adv.* for a long time *Mg* 14.2, 15.7; *VM* 16.7 n.; *MvI* 25.1; *MvII* 13.3.
**lengr** *adv. comp.* longer *MvII* 18.3.
**lerka (að)** *wv.* to injure *MvIII* 5.4.
**lesa (las)** *sv.* to read, recite *Mg* 52.6; *MvIII* 6.5, 20.7; *lesa út* to recite to the end (or aloud?) *MvIII* 9.5.
**á lesti** *adv.* at last, finally *VM* 8.4.
**leyndr** *a. pptc.* hidden, concealed, secret *Mg* 37.8.
**leynir** *m.* one who hides, hider, concealer *MvIII* 7.7 (see List of Kennings, 'Other').
**leysa (t)** *wv.* to free, redeem *Mg* 26.7; *MvI* 27.2; *MvIII* 2.8, 16.4.
**líða (leið)** *sv.* (1) to flow *MvII* 2.2; *líða að* to press upon, afflict *MvIII* 9.6. (2) to pass by (of time), come to an end *MvII* 14.7, 17.5; *MvIII* 10.4 (*pptc.*), 18.5, 29.4; *impers. VM* 9.1; *líða fram* to go on *Mg* 35.5.
**líf** *n.* life *Mg* 27.3, 29.4, 39.4, 51.3; *VM* 23.8; *MvI* 9.4, 18.3 n., 20.8, 26.3, 27.4 n.; *MvII* 12.4, 17.5, 18.3, 23.6 n.; *MvIII* 10.5, 15.3, 18.5, 20.8, 25.3 n., 26.3; *gen. sg.* as *adv.* alive *Mg* 25.4, *MvII* 19.6 n.
**lifa (ð)** *wv.* to live *Mg* 26.4.
**lifna (að)** *wv.* to come to life, revive *MvII* 19.1 n.
**líftjón** *n.* loss of life, death *MvIII* 7.7.
**liggja (lá)** *sv.* to lie *Mg* 15.7; *MvII* 13.1, 13.3, 20.8; *MvIII* 11.4.
**lík** *n.* corpse *Mg* 34.1, 35.1.
**líka (t)** *wv.* to please *MvIII* 18.6.
**líkami** *m.* body *MvI* 12.8; *MvII* 15.8.
**líkamr** *m.* body *MvII* 13.4 n., 18.5.
**líkn** *f.* mercy, grace *Mg* 26.7, 41.5, 47.8 (relief); *VM* 1.5 n.; *MvII* 16.1, 22.2; *MvIII* 2.6, 30.7. (See List of Kennings, 'Virgin Mary'.)
**líknarmey** *f.* maiden of mercy, merciful Virgin *VM* 19.1.
**líkneski** *n.* image; statue, sculpture *VM* 17.6; *MvI* 17.2.
**líkneskja** *f.* image; statue, sculpture *MvI* 15.6.

## Glossary and Index  109

**líkr** *a. with dat.* like; *sup. n.* most like *Mg* 17.5.
**limr** *m.* limb *MvII* 18.5.
**lín** *n.* linen *MvI* 10.3 n.
**linast (að)** *wv. md.* to be softened, relieved *MvIII* 8.6.
**línband** *n.* band (i.e. supporter, = *skorða*?) of linen *VM* 16.7 n. (see List of Kennings, 'Woman').
**linna (nt)** *wv.* to stop, cease; *linna við* bring to an end *MvIII* 30.8.
**linnr** *m.* serpent; gold? *MvIII* 26.4 n.
**linun** *f.* relief *MvIII* 29.3.
**list** *f.* art, skill *VM* 22.8 (*dat.* with skill, eloquently).
**listugr** *a.* skilled, clever; courteous *MvII* 21.4.
**líta (leit)** *sv.* (1) to look, see *Mg* 13.2, 17.8, 18.3, 19.3, 44.8; *VM* 5.4 (*with af and dat.* to take one's eyes off s-one); *MvI* 25.4; *MvII* 16.2; *MvIII* 10.5. (2) *md. lítast* to see one another, meet *Mg* 18.4.
**lítill** *a.* little, small; *n. lítið MvI* 21.6; *as subst.* little *Mg* 47.5 n.; not much *MvIII* 9.5.
**litr** *m.* colour *MvII* 18.6.
**lítt** *adv.* little, not very (litotes) *MvII* 15.7.
**ljetta (tt)** *wv. with dat.* (1) to stop, cease *Mg* 18.3. (2) to relieve *Mg* 13.5.
**ljettr** *a.* light, easy, effortless *MvII* 2.1.
**ljós** *n.* light *Mg* 9.6.
**ljóss** *a.* light, clear, bright; virtuous *MvI* 3.8.
**ljúfliga** *adv.* gently, willingly, graciously *VM* 23.5 n.
**ljúfr** *a.* lovely, beloved *VM* 17.5, 22.7; *MvII* 21.3; *MvIII* 11.3.
**ljúga (ló)** *sv.* to lie (about or with) *VM* 16.8; *MvIII* 12.4; *ljúga til (adv.) with dat.* to lie to s-one about it *MvIII* 21.5.
**lof** *n.* praise *Mg* 5.1, 11.7, 20.4, 23.7, 31.7; *MvI* 25.3, 26.8; *MvII* 2.1, 19.7.
**lof** *n.* permission *MvIII* 11.2.
**lofa (að)** *wv.* to praise *MvII* 21.3; *pptc.* praised *Mg* 45.3, 52.4; *MvII* 16.1 n., 19.1; *MvIII* 30.7.
**lofðungr** *m.* prince, ruler *Mg* 23.2 n. (see List of Kennings, 'Christ'), 35.5.
**lófi** *m.* palm (of the hand) *Mg* 15.2, 45.8.
**lofskýrr** *a.* shining with praise or glory *MvIII* 28.4.
**lofsöngr** *m.* hymn of praise *VM* 22.7.
**lofsæll** *a.* glorious *Mg* 31.5.
**logi** *m.* flame, fire *Mg* 1.7 n.; *MvI* 23.4, 24.2; *MvIII* 5.3. (See List of Kennings, 'Holy Spirit'.)
**lokka (að)** *wv.* to entice, lure; *prptc. MvIII* 10.6.
**lón** *n.* lagoon *Mg* 49.2 (see List of Kennings, 'Tears').

**Longínús** *m.* St Longinus *Mg* 29.6.
**lopt** *n.* sky *Mg* 13.1; *á lopt* into the air *MvIII* 12.3 (see **bera**).
**lúka (lauk)** *sv. with dat.* (1) *impers.* to finish, end *Mg* 11.8. (2) *md.* to be paid *Mg* 47.6.
**lukka** *f.* good fortune, success *MvI* 26.3.
**lundr** *m.* grove (of trees); tree *Mg* 30.5 n.; *VM* 9.2, 23.6; *MvIII* 26.3. (See List of Kennings, 'Man'.)
**lúta (laut)** *sv.* to bend down (in praying position), pray *VM* 17.5; *MvI* 28.1.
**lútr** *a.* bent, bending down (in prayer) *MvI* 26.4.
**lýðr** *m.* people, humankind *Mg* 5.3 (i.e. lay people), 8.3, 10.8, 12.6, 20.3, 23.1, 26.8, 31.6, 40.5, 41.5, 42.3, 44.4, 47.3; *VM* 20.4, 22.2; *MvI* 2.8, 25.3 n.
**lygð** *f.* lie, falsehood *VM* 12.4.
**lygi** *f.* lie, falsehood *MvIII* 20.3.
**lyndishreinn** *a.* virtuous *Mg* 41.6.
**lýsa (t)** *wv.* (1) to give light to, illumine *Mg* 5.8; *md.* to be illumined, lit up *MvIII* 21.2 n. (2) *with dat.* to disclose, reveal, proclaim *VM* 23.5.
**lystr** *a. pptc. of lysta with inf.* desirous *Mg* 27.4.
**lýti** *n.* fault, blemish; sin *Mg* 3.8; *MvIII* 5.3, 7.8.
**lærðr** *a.* learned *Mg* 5.3 n., 23.7, 31.8, 40.5, 42.6; *MvI* 10.3.
**lærifaðir** *m.* teacher (i.e. Christ) *Mg* 29.5, 51.4.
**lærisveinn** *m.* disciple *Mg* 34.2.
**læsa (t)** *wv.* to lock; *pptc.* shut up, i.e. fettered (by the Devil) *VM* 24.7.
**löð** *f.* a piece of metal with a hole in it (e.g. for drawing wire) *Mg* 35.2 n.
**lög** *n. pl.* laws; *with def. art. lögin Mg* 1.7 n. (cf. **logi**)
**lögmál** *n.* legal prescription, law *MvIII* 15.4.
**löngum** *adv.* for a long time *Mg* 23.8.
**löstr** *m.* fault; sin *MvIII* 12.3.

**maðr** *m.* man, person *Mg* 5.3 n., 14.4, 19.5, 23.7, 31.8, 42.6, 48.1, 48.3, 50.4, 52.5; *VM* 7.3, 11.7, 15.2, 17.7, 24.4, 24.8, 26.6; *MvI* 5.5, 7.7, 12.2, 14.4, 16.8, 17.6, 19.6, 28.3; *MvII* 18.1 n., 23.2; *MvIII* 3.1, 11.7, 14.3, 15.2, 20.6, 22.7, 23.1, 26.5, 26.6, 27.1; husband *VM* 13.6; *MvI* 9.3.
**Magdaljena** *f.* St Mary Magdalene *Mg* 12.3, 34.7.
**magn** *n.* strength, power; effort *MvIII* 3.5.
**mágr** *m.* son-in-law *MvI* 7.7.
**mál** *n.* (1) speech, words, language *Mg* 1.4 (*pl.*); *MvI* 11.4; *MvII* 10.1; *MvIII* 1.8, 29.8. (2) case, suit (in a legal sense) *MvI* 18.7 (*pl.*); *MvII*

7.5; *MvIII* 16.6. (3) affairs, state *MvIII* 3.8. (4) measure (i.e. end) *MvII* 23.6 n.

**máni** *m.* moon *Mg* 26.1, 30.2, 34.8, 41.1, 46.6. (See List of Kennings, 'Heaven'.)

**mannfjöldi** *m.* large crowd *VM* 15.4.

**mannligr** *a.* human *Mg* 46.7.

**manntíðni** *f.* a person's popularity or reputation *MvI* 11.7 n.

**margfalda (að)** *wv.* to multiply *MvI* 26.8.

**margfaldr** *a.* manifold; *sup. VM* 25.1 n.

**margr** *a.* many (a), much *Mg* 17.1, 46.7; *MvI* 19.2, 28.3; *n. as subst.* many things *MvIII* 12.4; *n. as adv. mart* greatly *MvIII* 21.2 n.

**margvíss** a. very cunning, sly *MvI* 6.3.

**María** *f.* St Mary the Virgin *Mg* 4.3, 7.8, 10.1, 17.1, 19.4, 25.1, 28.8, 29.1, 32.8, 33.1, 36.8, 46.1, 47.1, 52.6; *VM* title, 2.5, 8.8, 14.8, 17.4, 20.1, 22.8, 24.6; *MvI* 3.7, 14.3, 15.7, 17.3 n., 20.5, 24.7, 26.7 (*gen. Maríæ*), 28.8, 29.5; *MvII* 6.6, 7.6, 10.2, 13.8, 22.1; *MvIII* 2.6, 6.3, 8.6, 9.7, 11.7, 13.1, 21.7, 26.7, 27.1, 28.1, 29.1, 30.5.

**María** *f.* St Mary Magdalene *Mg* 12.4.

**Maríugrátr** *m.* Lamentation of the Virgin Mary *Mg* title.

**Maríuvísur** *f. pl.* poem about the Virgin Mary *MvI, MvII, MvIII*, titles.

**mark** *n.* (1) mark, sign *Mg* 40.1 n. (see List of Kennings, 'Holy Cross'). (2) site? symbol? cross-shape? *MvII* 13.7.

**máttr** *m.* might, power *MvI* 23.1; *MvIII* 1.1, 27.3; *dat. sg. mætti VM* 10.1.

**máttugr** *a.* mighty *Mg* 6.5, 26.1, 32.3; *MvIII* 1.2.

**máttuligr** *a.* mighty *Mg* 17.3.

**með** *prep.* (1) *with acc.* with *Mg* 7.1; *MvII* 11.2; *MvIII* 11.2, 15.6; by means of *MvII* 24.8. (2) *with dat.* with, together with, through, by (means of) *Mg* 4.2, 9.3, 9.6, 9.7, 10.7, 12.1, 14.1, 17.8, 21.3, 23.4, 24.3, 25.7, 25.8, 27.7, 33.4, 39.2, 39.3, 40.4, 40.6, 41.6, 43.4, 45.6, 47.2, 49.7, 50.8, 52.4, 52.6; *VM* 3.5, 4.3 (between), 5.5, 8.2, 9.8, 12.1, 18.3, 19.5, 22.6; *MvI* 2.3, 4.5, 8.6, 12.4, 15.3, 16.3, 23.3; *MvII* 21.5; *MvIII* 20.4. (3) *adv.* with it *MvII* 10.8; *þar með* in addition *Mg* 12.8.

**meðan** *conj.* while, as long as *Mg* 26.4; *MvII* 13.3; *MvIII* 26.3.

**meðferð** *f.* handling, treatment *VM* 10.7.

**mega (mátta)** *pret.-pres. aux.* can, be able to *Mg* 2.7, 8.1, 13.5, 14.8, 15.5, 16.3, 30.4, 31.2, 33.8, 35.6, 44.8; *VM* 4.5, 5.3, 24.1; *MvI* 2.6; *MvII* 3.7, 4.1, 8.7, 11.6, 14.3, 15.1, 16.7, 18.2, 20.1; *MvIII* 14.1, 21.4, 21.6, 22.5, 28.5 n.

**meginn** *a.* strong, powerful *MvII* 1.6.
**megn** *n.* might, strength, power *VM* 15.8.
**meiðr** *m.* tree *MvIII* 16.5 (see List of Kennings, 'Man').
**meiða (dd)** *wv.* to injure *Mg* 14.3.
**mein** *n.* (1) harm, injury, pain *VM* 10.7; *MvI* 9.8, 16.7, 22.4; *MvII* 12.4 (*with lífs* mortal blow); *MvIII* 4.6, 24.6. (2) sin *Mg* 41.8; *VM* 24.7; *MvIII* 6.7, 8.2, 12.2.
**meina (að)** *wv. with dat.* to do harm to *MvI* 11.7.
**meinafullr** *a.* harmful *MvIII* 13.7.
**meir** *adv. comp.* more, further *Mg* 17.4.
**meiri** *a. comp.* (cf. **mikill**) more, greater *Mg* 22.5, 46.5; *MvI* 22.3, 29.5; *n. as adv. Mg* 21.7, 25.5; *n. as substantive* (i.e. more poetry) *Mg* 3.1.
**meistari** *m.* master, lord *Mg* 43.7 n. (see List of Kennings, 'Christ').
**mekt** *f.* might, strength, power *VM* 22.3; *MvIII* 21.1.
**mektugr** *a.* mighty *VM* 8.5 n.
**men** *n.* necklace *MvIII* 16.5.
**mengrund** *f.* necklace-ground *MvI* 21.8 (see List of Kennings, 'Woman').
**merki** *n.* mark, sign, symbol *Mg* 33.2 n.
**merkiliga** *adv.* in a remarkable way *MvIII* 19.4.
**mest** *adv. sup.* most *VM* 24.7 n.; *MvI* 7.8, 17.3, 28.4; *MvIII* 23.7, 26.5; *sem mest* as much as, as best *Mg* 13.5.
**mestr** *a. sup.* greatest *VM* 22.3; *MvIII* 27.8; very great *VM* 15.3; *MvI* 27.5.
**meta (mat)** *sv.* to measure *VM* 13.5.
**mey = mær** *f.* maiden, young girl, virgin *VM* 26.2; *MvII* 1.7, 18.8, 22.1, 23.3 n., 24.2; *MvIII* 2.5, 8.8, 16.2, 19.3 n., 22.6, 29.1, 30.3. (See List of Kennings, 'Virgin Mary'.)
**meyja** *f.* maiden, young girl, virgin *VM* 8.5; *MvI* 18.7, 27.6; *MvII* 8.7.
**miðnótt** *f.* midnight *MvII* 15.1.
**miðr** *a.* middle, the middle of *MvI* 19.8.
**mikill** *a.* great *Mg* 9.6; *VM* 10.1, 13.5; *MvII* 9.2, 13.7, 14.6; *MvIII* 27.3; *dat. sg. n. as intensifier of a comp.* much *Mg* 21.7, 46.5; *MvI* 22.3.
**mildi** *f. indecl.* generosity, kindness, mercy *Mg* 1.3; *VM* 25.1; *MvIII* 30.4.
**mildingr** *m.* generous man, prince *Mg* 30.1 n. (see List of Kennings, 'Christ').
**mildr** *a.* gentle, kind, generous *Mg* 8.4, 32.3, 38.6, 41.7; *MvI* 1.6 (*sup.*), 14.6; *MvII* 9.7; *MvIII* 19.3.
**milli/á milli** *prep. with gen.* between, among *MvI* 6.4; *MvII* 3.8; *sín á milli* among themselves *MvI* 21.4.

## Glossary and Index 113

**minkast (að)** *wv. md.* to decrease *VM* 10.8.
**minn** *poss. a. 1st pers.* my, mine *Mg* 1.2, 1.8, 10.3, 12.3, 13.8, 14.7, 17.7, 18.7, 21.5, 21.6, 21.8, 26.6, 29.4, 29.6, 31.3, 34.7, 38.5, 39.1, 42.3, 43.6, 43.7, 44.1, 45.6, 46.2, 49.6 n., 51.8; *VM* 1.2, 1.6, 2.2, 7.8, 8.6, 18.2, 19.4, 21.7, 25.8; *MvI* 1.2, 1.8, 16.6, 17.4, 18.1, 18.8; *MvII* 1.5, 7.5, 9.8, 16.4, 16.5, 17.8, 20.3; *MvIII* 2.2, 13.7, 16.7.
**minna (nt)** *wv.* to recall, remember *MvI* 27.5 n. (*prptc., with gen.*), 29.2 (*with acc.*?).
**minnast (nt)** *wv. md. with gen.* to recall, remember *Mg* 24.1, 40.4, 41.4, 42.4, 52.5; *VM* 17.8; *MvI* 1.7, 27.5 n. (*with acc.*); *MvIII* 2.5; *with á and acc. MvIII* 20.5.
**minni** *a. comp.* smaller; *n. as subst.* less *MvIII* 22.8.
**minnigr** *a.* mindful *Mg* 18.8.
**minniligr** *a.* remarkable, splendid *MvI* 13.2 n.
**minning** *f.* memorial token *MvII* 16.3.
**minst** *sup. adv.* very little (i.e. not at all) *MvI* 21.7.
**miskunn** *f.* mercy, grace *Mg* 7.7, 10.3, 22.3; *VM* 17.7; *MvI* 1.7, 3.4, 24.8, 29.6; *MvII* 16.3, 18.1; *MvIII* 12.8; as a term for the Virgin *MvIII* 19.2, 20.5. (See List of Kennings, 'Virgin Mary'.)
**missa (st)** *wv.* to lose *Mg* 33.7, 35.3; *MvI* 29.7; *MvII* 16.6; *MvIII* 24.3.
**mítr** *n.* mitre *Mg* 10.1.
**mjór** *a.* thin, slender, slim *MvI* 21.7.
**mjúklátr** *a.* humble; meek, gentle, kind *MvI* 14.5, 19.5; *MvII* 2.5.
**mjúklæti** *n.* humility *VM* 25.2.
**mjúkr** *a.* soft, gentle, kind *MvI* 16.5; *MvII* 2.3 (supple, eloquent); *MvIII* 6.7 (*við* towards); *sup. VM* 20.1; *MvII* 10.1; *MvIII* 29.2.
**mjög** *adv.* much, very (much) *Mg* 1.1, 17.2; *VM* 11.7, 18.1; *MvI* 23.2; *MvII* 21.1.
**móðir** *f.* mother *Mg* 1.3, 2.2, 3.7, 5.2, 5.6, 6.5, 8.3, 9.5, 10.4, 17.3, 18.7, 19.2, 19.7, 22.6, 23.6, 26.2, 26.5, 27.1, 28.7, 32.4, 32.7, 34.6, 35.5, 36.7, 37.3, 37.5, 41.2, 42.3 n., 46.1, 48.8 n., 51.1, 52.7; *VM* 1.8, 2.6, 7.7, 21.7, 22.4, 25.4; *MvI* 9.7, 16.5, 23.1, 25.2, 28.2, 29.4 n.; *MvII* 1.5, 2.6, 8.8, 11.5, 15.2, 16.5, 19.4, 20.3, 22.2; *MvIII* 27.4, 30.3; i.e. the Virgin *MvI* 19.5; *MvII* 15.5 (*with suffixed def. art.*); *MvIII* 6.8. (See List of Kennings, 'Virgin Mary'.)
**móðurliga** *adv.* maternally, in a motherly way *MvIII* 13.2.
**morð** *n.* murder *MvI* 11.8.
**mót** *n.* meeting, gathering; *til móts* to meet them *MvIII* 13.1; *móti/á móti/í móti/í mót* (1) *as prep. with dat.* (a) against *VM* 14.3, 18.1; *MvII* 23.4. (b) towards, to meet *Mg* 27.5, 45.5. (c) in place of, for

*Mg* 38.5. (2) *as adv.* in opposition, against it/her *VM* 15.7; *MvII* 3.7; hér í móti on the contrary *MvIII* 15.5; in exchange for this *Mg* 47.5.

**muna (mundi)** *pret.-pres.* to remember *MvIII* 11.8.

**mund** *f.* hand *Mg* 13.6.

**mundr** *m.* bride-price, sum paid by the bride-groom *MvI* 4.7.

**munkr** *m.* monk *Mg* 9.4, 41.1.

**munnr** *m.* mouth *MvIII* 21.1 n.

**munu (mundi)** *pret.-pres. aux. with inf.* will, shall (for future or expessing probability or uncertainty) *Mg* 2.6, 3.8, 17.6, 18.5, 26.7, 27.2, 36.1, 42.5, 51.7; *VM* 24.5; *MvI* 6.7, 28.5; *MvII* 9.6, 17.1, 20.4; *MvIII* 16.1, 27.5 (*vb.* to be *understood*), 28.3, 30.7.

**múrr** *m.* stone (for building), stone wall *MvII* 6.5.

**musteri** *n.* (1) temple *Mg* 6.4. (2) church building of great importance, properly a church with *canonici regulares* *VM* 15.3; *MvI* 15.2; *MvII* 6.5 n.

**mynd** *f.* shape, form *MvII* 2.3 (*mynd mærðar* = praise poem).

**mynda (að)** *wv.* to create, make *MvI* 6.3 n., 15.8.

**mæða (dd)** *wv.* to exhaust, weaken, weary; *pptc. MvI* 13.6, 14.2; *prptc.* causing affliction, afflicting *MvI* 9.7 n.

**mæðgin** *n. pl.* mother and son *VM* 18.8.

**mæðr** *f.* mother *MvII* 9.3.

**mægðir** *f. pl.* relationship by marriage *MvI* 4.8.

**mækir** *m.* sword *Mg* 17.5.

**mæla (t)** *wv.* to speak *Mg* 30.1, 31.1 n.; *VM* 20.2; *MvI* 16.4, 18.2; *MvIII* 14.4.

**mær** *f.* (*acc.* **mey,** *gen.* **meyjar,** *dat.* **meyju**) maiden, young woman, virgin *Mg* 6.2, 8.3, 19.7, 28.7, 32.7, 36.7, 43.8; *VM* 2.5, 4.5, 10.2, 21.8; *MvI* 2.5 n., 13.1 n., 14.5, 15.7, 26.4 n., 26.7; *MvII* 7.4; *MvIII* 8.5, 13.8, 28.8. See also **mærr.**

**mærð** *f.* praise, encomium *Mg* 1.1, 51.7; *MvII* 2.4.

**mærr** *a.* famous, glorious, illustrious *MvIII* 8.5 n. (or **mær** *f.*)

**mætr** *a.* valuable, worthy, excellent *Mg* 6.6, 10.2, 16.3; *VM* 7.7 n.; *MvI* 5.2, 13.1, 24.7, 27.2; *MvII* 19.2, 23.3; *MvIII* 25.6; *comp. with dat. Mg* 32.1; *sup. Mg* 5.5, 9.2, 19.8, 26.5, 46.8; *MvII* 2.5; *MvIII* 27.2.

**mögr** *m.* son *MvII* 10.6, 11.5, 12.6.

**mörk** *f.* forest *MvI* 14.3 n.

**Ná** *f.* name of a goddess (= *Gná*) *MvI* 9.5 n. (see List of Kennings, 'Woman').

## Glossary and Index 115

**ná (ð)** *wv. with dat.* to obtain *Mg* 39.6; *with inf.* to manage to *Mg* 7.4.
**náð** *f.* grace *VM* 14.5 *(pl.).*
**Náðarjenus** *a.* Nazarene, of Nazareth *Mg* 39.5 n.
**nafn** *n.* name *VM* 2.4; *MvI* 2.4; *MvII* 8.8, 16.5, 19.1, 22.4; *MvIII* 6.2, 17.6.
**nánd** *f.* proximity *MvII* 4.6.
**nauð** *f.* need, necessity, distress *Mg* 4.8, 29.8; *VM* 10.8 *(pl.)*; *MvII* 2.7, 17.3 n., 17.5 n.; *MvIII* 8.1, 28.7 (i.e. the Last Judgment).
**nauðigr** *a.* under compulsion, against one's will *MvIII* 24.4.
**nauðsyn** *f.* need, necessity *Mg* 39.5.
**nefna (d)** *wv.* to name, call; *pptc.* called *MvI* 2.3; above-mentioned *VM* 14.6.
**neinn** *a.* no *Mg* 19.6; *n. neitt as subst.* nothing *Mg* 35.4.
**nema (nam)** *sv.* (1) to learn *Mg* 42.7. (2) *with inf.* to begin *VM* 5.1; meaningless *aux. VM* 10.1, 13.1; *MvI* 26.1.
**nema** *conj.* unless, except *Mg* 3.6; *MvII* 8.4.
**nest** *n.* provisions, food for a journey *MvIII* 24.3 n.
**niðr** *m.* son *MvII* 11.3 n.
**niðr** *adv.* down, below *VM* 12.3 (*leggja niðr* drop); *MvII* 15.7; *MvIII* 10.1.
**nista (st)** *wv.* to fasten one object to another by piercing, nail *Mg* 11.4.
**nje** *adv.* nor *Mg* 25.4, 26.6; *MvI* 24.4 n.
**njóta (naut)** *sv. with gen.* to enjoy, benefit from *MvI* 24.7.
**nógleikr** *m.* abundance; *gen. sg. as adv.* in abundance *MvI* 2.3.
**nógligr** *a.* enough, abundant *VM* 9.6.
**nógr (gnógr)** *a.* enough, abundant *Mg* 29.7; *MvI* 16.3.
**nógt** see **gnógt**.
**nokkurr** *indef. pron. and a.* a certain *MvII* 3.1; any *Mg* 46.6.
**nótt** *f.* night *MvII* 14.8; *MvIII* 5.5.
**nú** *adv.* now, still *Mg* 36.3; *VM* 9.8 n., 17.2, 24.1; *MvI* 18.1, 29.1; *MvII* 12.8, 16.6; *MvIII* 8.4, 9.2.
**nýr** *a.* new, fresh *MvI* 8.5 n.; *MvIII* 17.4, 24.3 n.
**nýtr** *a.* useful, helpful, beneficial *Mg* 42.8; *VM* 14.5.
**nægja (gð)** *wv.* to be sufficient, enough *Mg* 49.6 n. (*impers.*).
**nær** *adv.* near (by), close *VM* 7.6; *MvII* 7.4; *MvIII* 17.7, 28.7; almost, nearly *VM* 4.6; *MvIII* 4.7, 7.5; *as prep. with dat.* close to *MvIII* 8.5.
**næri** *adv.* close *Mg* 34.2, 51.4; *MvIII* 28.8.
**næst** *adv. with dat.* next to *MvI* 3.5; *MvIII* 6.6 (i.e. after), 30.2.
**næsta** *adv. sup.* almost, virtually *Mg* 29.7, 42.7.
**næstr** *a. sup.* nearest; *eð næsta as prep. with dat.* next to *Mg* 27.8, 46.4.
**nætrrof** *n.* breaking of night, dawn *MvIII* 7.2.

**óast (að)** *wv. md.* to fear, be afraid of *Mg* 33.3.
**óbrunninn** *a. pptc.* unburnt *MvI* 24.8.
**óðr** *m.* poetry *VM* 2.6.
**óðr** *a.* furious, enraged *MvI* 10.5; *n. ótt as adv.* speedily *VM* 4.4.
**of** *adv.* too *MvI* 21.6.
**ofan** *adv.* from above *MvIII* 11.2.
**ofanverðr** *a.* nearing the end *MvIII* 7.2.
**óflekkaðr** *a. pptc.* unblemished, pure *VM* 25.6.
**ofra (að)** *wv.* to offer *Mg* 6.6.
**ofra (að)** *wv. with dat.* to raise, lift up *Mg* 20.4.
**ófæltiliga** *adv.* without fear, undauntedly *MvI* 16.4.
**og** *conj.* and *Mg* 1.4, 3.7, 3.8, 4.3, 4.8, 5.3, 5.4, 6.5, 6.8, 7.8, 8.3, 8.5, 9.1, 9.2, 9.7, 10.3, 11.2, 11.8, 12.3, 12.5, 12.7, 12.8, 13.1, 14.1, 14.2, 14.3, 14.4, 14.7, 15.2, 15.5, 15.7, 15.8, 16.5, 16.7, 18.3, 19.1, 19.3, 19.7, 20.5, 20.7, 21.1, 21.3, 21.4, 23.2, 23.7, 24.1, 24.2, 24.4, 24.5, 24.7, 25.8, 26.8, 28.3, 28.7, 31.8, 32.1, 32.2, 32.7, 33.4, 33.8, 34.2, 34.4, 34.5, 34.7, 36.7, 38.3, 38.7, 39.8, 40.3, 40.8, 41.5, 41.6, 41.7, 42.5, 43.4, 44.7, 45.3, 46.3, 48.2, 48.4, 48.7, 48.8, 49.3, 51.1, 52.6, 52.7; *VM* 1.3, 4.4, 8.8, 9.6, 10.3, 10.7, 13.3, 13.4, 15.2, 21.6, 22.8, 23.2, 23.7, 24.4, 25.4; *MvI* 1.2, 4.6, 8.2, 10.5, 10.6, 11.2, 13.6, 15.4, 16.3, 16.6, 16.8, 19.4, 21.3, 24.6, 25.1, 25.7, 25.8, 26.3; *MvII* 2.6, 3.5, 4.5, 6.6, 7.6, 8.8, 9.3, 9.5, 10.2, 11.4, 14.5, 15.3, 16.5, 18.1, 18.6, 19.3, 19.6, 19.8, 21.2, 21.5, 21.8, 22.2, 23.2, 23.5; *MvIII* 2.2, 8.4, 9.8, 10.2, 12.2, 14.8, 15.3, 16.6, 20.2, 21.4, 23.8, 24.3, 26.5, 28.2, 30.3.
**óglaðr** *a.* unhappy *MvII* 13.5.
**ógndjarfr** *a.* bold in battle *MvII* 5.1.
**ógurliga** *adv.* in a frightening manner, shockingly *MvIII* 17.4.
**okkarr** *poss. a. dual* our *VM* 16.4.
**opinn** *a.* open *MvIII* 1.7.
**opt** *adv.* often, frequently *Mg* 40.3; *MvII* 6.8; *sup. optast* very often *MvII* 7.3.
**orð** *n.* (1) word *Mg* 1.1, 2.6, 3.5, 17.1, 28.4, 29.2, 37.2, 42.4, 42.6; *VM* 1.1, 2.1, 16.8, 20.3, 20.6, 23.4, 26.3; *MvI* 2.3, 11.5; *MvII* 15.8, 24.4; *MvIII* 1.3, 2.1. (2) rumour *MvI* 5.8, 7.1, 8.4.
**orðagnógt** *f.* abundance of words *Mg* 16.4.
**orðasnild** *f.* eloquence *MvI* 1.3.
**orka (að)** *wv. with að and inf.* to have the power to, manage to *Mg* 19.5.
**orka** *f.* strength *Mg* 50.1.
**ósannindi** *n. pl.* untruth, falsehood *VM* 20.7.

## Glossary and Index 117

**óskamey** *f.* chosen maiden or virgin *MvI* 23.6 (see List of Kennings, 'Virgin Mary').
**óttast (að)** *wv. md.* to fear, be afraid of *VM* 10.6; *MvIII* 7.7.
**óttafullr** *a.* full of fear, afraid *MvIII* 9.8.
**óttalauss** *a.* fearless *MvIII* 1.8.
**ótti** *m.* fear *Mg* 24.2.
**óttlauss** (= **óttalauss**) *a.* fearless, courageous *VM* 3.4.

**páskamorginn** *m.* Easter morning *Mg* 38.2, 44.6.
**páter** *m.* (*Latin*) father *Mg* 40.2.
**Pilátús** *m.* Pilate *Mg* 12.6.
**pín** *f.* pain, torment, torture, suffering *MvII* 19.4; *MvIII* 23.5, 29.3 n.
**pína** *f.* torment, suffering *Mg* 13.8, 25.8, 26.6; *MvI* 16.6, 19.3.
**pína (d)** *wv.* to torment *Mg* 8.7, 19.1.
**písl** *f.* torment; suffering, passion *Mg* 4.8 n., 13.2, 14.6, 21.8, 23.2, 30.2, 40.1.
**plaga (að)** *wv.* to take care of, nurse *MvII* 5.8.
**plagg** *n.* that with which s-thing is equipped; bedclothes *MvII* 11.2.
**postuli** *m.* apostle *Mg* 26.4.
**prestr** *m.* priest *Mg* 8.5 n.; *MvI* 10.5.
**próf** *n.* testimony, proof in a trial or lawsuit *VM* 19.2.
**prúðligr** *a.* stately, noble; splendid *Mg* 40.1.
**prúðr** *a.* stately, noble; splendid *Mg* 38.1; *MvI* 3.2; *MvIII* 30.3.
**prýða (dd)** *wv.* to make splendid, adorn *Mg* 23.8, 52.2; *MvIII* 19.7.
**prýði** *f.* ornament, embellishment *Mg* 44.4; splendour *Mg* 46.3.
**prýðir** *m.* one who makes s-thing beautiful, adorner *Mg* 26.8 (see List of Kennings, 'Christ').

**ráð** *n.* (1) decision, undertaking *MvI* 9.2. (2) way of life *MvIII* 15.6, 25.7. (3) affairs, state *MvIII* 5.8. (4) plot, plan of attack *MvIII* 20.1.
**ráða (rjeð)** *sv.* (1) *with dat.* to rule, govern *Mg* 28.7, 32.7, 36.7; *VM* 3.1; *MvI* 3.1. (2) *with dat.* to decide; *impers. pass. því ráðið* it (had been) decided, arranged *VM* 16.6. (3) *with acc.* to contrive *MvI* 8.8. (4) *with að and inf.* to decide *Mg* 12.2; *pptc.* determined *Mg* 27.1; *periphrastic with (að and) inf. Mg* 8.2, 17.4; *VM* 21.2 n.; *MvIII* 20.5.
**ráðtæki** *n.* solution *MvI* 7.5.
**ranglátr** *a.* unjust, unfair *MvIII* 4.1.
**rangr** *a.* false *MvIII* 20.1.
**rann** *n.* house, building *MvIII* 6.3.
**raungrætiligr** *a.* truly sad, very regrettable *MvI* 7.6.

**rausn** *f.* magnificence, excellence; *adv. gen.* splendidly *MvIII* 25.8.
**rausnsamr** *a.* splendid, magnificent *Mg* 48.6.
**regn** *n.* rain *Mg* 38.2.
**regnsalr** *m.* hall of rain *Mg* 48.5 (see List of Kennings, 'Heaven').
**reiðast (dd)** *wv. md.* to become angry *MvI* 10.4.
**reiðimál** *n.* angry language *VM* 23.2.
**reiðiþokki** *m.* angry thought *VM* 12.1.
**reifr** *a.* cheerful; *n. as adv.* in a lively way *MvIII* 20.3.
**reikna (að)** *wv.* to enumerate, count, reckon *Mg* 41.5, 44.5.
**rekkr** *m.* man *VM* 12.1.
**renna (rann)** *sv.* to run, flow *Mg* 49.2; to melt *MvI* 22.8; to spread *MvIII* 20.4; *with dat.* to leave *VM* 23.1; *impers. renna á* to touch *MvI* 24.1; *pptc. runninn* grown *MvIII* 12.8.
**rennir** *m.* one who causes s-thing to run, distributor *MvIII* 4.2 (see List of Kennings, 'Man').
**reyna (d)** *wv.* to try, test *VM* 11.7; *pp.* proven *MvI* 23.3.
**ríki** *n.* kingdom *VM* 3.1, 3.7 n.; realm *VM* 10.3.
**ríkimaðr** *m.* powerful or rich man *VM* 23.1.
**ríkr** *a.* (1) great, powerful, mighty *Mg* 44.7; *VM* 7.4 (*sup.*), 14.2, 15.2; *MvI* 7.5, 23.2; *MvII* 7.1 (*sup.*); *MvIII* 19.5. (2) rich *VM* 12.6.
**rísa (reis)** *sv.* to rise *Mg* 18.5, 27.2, 36.1, 38.1, 44.7; *MvIII* 20.2.
**rist** *f.* instep of the foot *Mg* 15.2.
**rít** *f.* shield *MvI* 21.6 n.; *MvIII* 4.1 n.
**ritning** *f.* writing; written authority *VM* 3.2.
**rjetta (tt)** *wv.* to make correct, amend *MvIII* 25.7.
**rjettindi** *n.* right *VM* 19.4.
**rjettlátr** *a.* just, righteous *MvIII* 12.7.
**rjettr** *a.* right, correct, just *MvI* 12.6; *MvIII* 16.8, 19.6; *n. as adv.* rjett truly *Mg* 30.8; rightly, correctly *VM* 16.5, 20.5.
**rjóðr** *a.* ruddy (of the complexion); red (with anger or shame) *VM* 12.2; *sup.* blushing deeply *MvI* 18.2.
**róg** *n.* slander *MvIII* 17.4, 20.3.
**rót** *f.* root *MvIII* 12.7.
**runnr** *m.* bush, tree *Mg* 35.2 n. (see List of Kennings, 'Man').
**ræða (dd)** *wv.* to speak *MvIII* 19.5 n.
**rækta (að)** *wv.* to care for, take care of *Mg* 27.1.
**ræsir** *m.* prince *Mg* 38.1, 44.8, 48.5 (see List of Kennings, 'Christ').
**röðull** *m.* sun; *in pl.* sun and moon, heavenly bodies *Mg* 3.2, 18.6.

**sá, sú, það** *dem. pron.* the, that, this (one) *Mg* 4.7, 10.5 n., 11.3, 13.4,

14.8 (= such), 17.5, 18.7, 22.5, 25.1, 25.5, 25.7, 30.1, 30.4, 33.1, 38.8, 41.8, 42.4, 42.5, 43.1, 44.1, 44.5, 49.7, 52.8 n.; *VM* 3.3 (= who), 21.5, 22.6, 24.3; *MvI* 1.1, 4.2, 5.4, 7.1, 15.1, 15.7, 23.5, 28.6; *MvII* 1.7, 2.7, 4.6 (= who), 7.2, 7.6, 12.6, 16.3 (= which), 20.7, 22.3; *MvIII* 2.6 (= who), 5.4, 7.6 n., 11.4, 14.6, 16.5, 16.8, 20.4 n., 20.6, 23.3, 25.4, 29.2, 29.4.

**sakasár** *n.* wound that is the result of a fault, sinful blemish *MvIII* 18.7.
**saklauss** *a.* innocent, guiltless *MvI* 7.4, 9.3.
**sál** *f.* soul *Mg* 51.8; *MvI* 27.8; *MvII* 23.6; *MvIII* 16.6, 18.8, 29.8.
**sála** *f.* soul *Mg* 1.4, 44.4.
**samband** *n.* connection, union; *synda samband* sinful union *VM* 18.3.
**sannfróðr** *a.* truly informed, very knowledgeable *MvI* 25.2.
**sannindi** *n. pl.* truth *VM* 21.4, 24.3.
**sannr** *a.* (1) true *Mg* 3.7, 6.8, 14.4, 42.6, 50.4; *VM* 11.3, 24.4 (real), 26.6 n.; *MvI* 2.7, 3.4; *MvII* 23.2; *MvIII* 2.5, 15.2, 21.1, 29.7. (2) *n. as subst. satt* the truth, what is true *VM* 13.3, 21.8; *eð sanna Mg* 4.6 n.; *að sönnu* in truth *Mg* 10.3, 22.7; *MvII* 23.5; *MvIII* 16.7, 20.7. (3) *comp. n. as subst.* more truth, what is more accurate *VM* 19.8.
**sannreyndr** *a. pptc.* proved true *MvII* 23.1.
**sár** *n.* wound *Mg* 19.4, 38.3, 40.4; *MvI* 6.8 n.; *MvIII* 5.2 (*adv. dat.*), 28.6.
**sárleikr** *m.* pain *MvII* 12.3.
**sárliga** *adv.* sorely, bitterly *MvI* 13.7.
**sárr** *a.* (1) sore, painful, grievous, dire *Mg* 26.6, 49.4; *VM* 13.4, 26.5; *MvI* 8.6, 17.7, 24.2; *MvIII* 4.3 (wounded), 17.7, 23.3. (2) *sárt n. as adv.* sorely, bitterly *MvII* 14.5.
**Sátán** *m.* Satan *MvIII* 24.5.
**sátt** *f.* terms of reconciliation, atonement *MvIII* 25.5.
**sáttr** *a.* reconciled, at peace *MvI* 25.8.
**saurlífr** *a.* unchaste *MvIII* 5.1, 14.7.
**sefi** *m.* mind *MvIII* 5.1.
**seggr** *m.* man *VM* 5.2.
**segja (sagða)** *wv.* (1) to say, speak, tell (of) *Mg* 33.2, 39.4; *VM* 7.2, 13.3; *MvI* 6.5, 10.6, 18.6, 21.3; *MvII* 1.7; *MvIII* 6.4, 17.8, 23.6. (2) *pptc.* above-mentioned *VM* 3.7; *MvI* 9.8; *MvII* 4.1. (3) *md.* to declare oneself *MvII* 22.7.
**seimkennandi** *m.* gold-'experiencer', i.e. gold-wearer *MvI* 6.6 (see List of Kennings, 'Man').
**seimstallr** *m.* gold-seat, seat of the gold (ring), i.e. arm *MvI* 25.6 n. (see List of Kennings, 'Other').

**seinast** *adv. sup.* last, finally *Mg* 31.2.
**sekt** *f.* guilt, condemnation, punishment *VM* 26.5.
**sektsárr** *a.* wounded by guilt *MvIII* 28.5.
**sem** *conj.* (a) as *Mg* 2.8, 31.2, 31.6, 44.8; *VM* 18.7, 21.7, 23.8, 26.4; *MvI* 24.6, 29.2 n.; *MvII* 11.8, 24.3; *MvIII* 6.3, 17.2, 24.4, 26.7. (b) as well as, i.e. and *Mg* 9.1, *MvI* 13.2. (c) as if *Mg* 15.6, 17.5, 22.7. (d) *with sup.* as . . . as possible *Mg* 13.5, 42.7. (e) *rel.* who, which *Mg* 2.6, 10.5, 30.8; *MvII* 3.4.
**senda (nd)** *wv.* (1) to send *Mg* 43.3. (2) *md.* to be sent *MvII* 18.7.
**sendir** *m.* sender *MvI* 6.7 n. (see List of Kennings, 'Man').
**senn** *adv.* at once, immediately *MvI* 14.8.
**setja (tt)** *wv.* to set, put, place *MvI* 17.7; to assign, decide *MvI* 12.6; *setja fyr with acc.* to place in charge of *MvIII* 27.3; *pptc.* placed *VM* 6.6, made *VM* 18.4.
**síð** *adv.* late *Mg* 11.8; *um síðir* at last, eventually *VM* 11.2; *MvI* 7.2.
**síða** *f.* side *Mg* 29.5.
**síðan** (1) *adv.* then, afterwards *Mg* 7.1, 11.5, 35.1, 36.3 (since then), 44.5 (after that); *VM* 5.1, 23.7; *MvI* 5.6, 19.1, 25.5; *MvII* 13.1, 19.2, 19.7; *MvIII* 22.3, 23.4 n., 25.5. (2) *síðan er as conj.* after *MvIII* 10.1.
**síðast** *sup. adv.* last of all, finally *MvIII* 18.5, 20.8.
**siðlátr** *a.* virtuous; *sup. MvI* 3.3.
**siðr** *m.* (1) custom *MvII* 10.4. (2) *pl.* conduct, morality *MvIII* 3.1, 4.4, 18.3; *sannr siða* correct in conduct *MvIII* 15.1.
**sig, sín, sjer** *refl. pron.* him(self), her(self), it(self), oneself, themselves *Mg* 13.3 (*poss. dat.*), 23.1, 43.6; *MvI* 7.3, 21.4; *MvIII* 11.7.
**signaðr** *a. pptc. of signa* blessed *Mg* 22.1; *VM* 21.1.
**siklingr** *m.* prince *Mg* 9.6, 31.1. (See List of Kennings, 'Christ'.)
**silkigrund** *f.* ground of silk *VM* 23.6 n. (see List of Kennings, 'Woman').
**silkiskorða** *f.* silk-prop *MvI* 5.8 (see List of Kennings, 'Woman').
**silki-Sól** *f.* Sól (a goddess, personification of the sun) of the silk *MvI* 12.5 (see List of Kennings, 'Woman').
**Símeón** *m.* Simeon *Mg* 6.7.
**sinn, sín, sitt** *a. refl. poss.* his, her, one's, its, their (own) *Mg* 21.8, 22.2, 23.3, 25.8, 26.2, 32.4, 33.8, 38.4, 39.7, 41.3, 45.6, 45.8; *VM* 7.8, 10.7, 11.3, 14.7, 17.8; *MvI* 1.8, 5.3, 7.7, 8.8, 9.3, 11.1, 14.7, 15.3, 26.2; *MvII* 5.8, 10.6, 12.2, 12.5 n., 18.4, 19.4, 20.2; *MvIII* 3.8, 9.1, 15.6, 19.4, 21.3, 24.5, 25.7, 26.4, 27.4.
**sinn** *n.* time *MvI* 10.2; *MvII* 5.5, 12.1; *MvIII* 6.5, 7.1.
**Síón** *m.* Zion, Jerusalem; heaven *MvIII* 20.7 n.

## Glossary and Index

**síst** *adv. sup.* least, i.e. not at all *MvII* 7.7.
**sitja (sat)** *sv.* to sit *Mg* 45.3; *VM* 7.7; *MvI* 19.7, 23.7, 25.4; *MvII* 14.5.
**sjá (sá)** *sv.* to see, look at *Mg* 27.4; *MvI* 15.5, 16.5; *MvII* 8.1, 15.6, 19.3, 23.7 (*pptc. sjeð*); *MvIII* 16.8, 21.4, 22.8; *sjá af* take one's eyes off *VM* 4.5; *MvII* 11.6.
**sjá/þessi, þetta** *dem. pron.* this *Mg* 5.8, 6.7, 21.5, 23.5, 26.7, 29.2, 36.4, 37.3, 41.7, 41.8, 51.2; *VM* 6.6, 18.4, 18.6, 21.2; *MvI* 10.8, 17.1, 23.5; *MvIII* 3.1, 14.3, 18.7, 22.2, 22.7, 26.6, 26.8.
**sjaldan** *adv.* seldom *VM* 4.6, 5.4 n.; *MvIII* 3.2.
**sjálfr** *a.* self, oneself *Mg* 13.1 n.; *MvII* 8.4.
**sjálfráðr** *a.* within one's power *VM* 6.5.
**sjón** *f. pl.* eyes *Mg* 49.2.
**sjúkr** *a.* sick, ill *Mg* 47.6 (*as subst.*); *MvII* 4.2; *MvIII* 29.2 n.; *sjúkr sárleikr* pain of sickness *MvII* 12.3.
**skáld** *n.* poet *Mg* 1.2.
**skapa (að)** *wv.* to shape, form, create; *pptc. MvIII* 28.1.
**skapari** *m.* creator *Mg* 30.6, 32.2, 33.3, 43.5, 50.4. (See List of Kennings, 'Christ'.)
**skaut** *n.* lap *MvII* 12.5 n.
**skepna** *f.* (1) creature, creation *Mg* 2.5, 33.4; *MvI* 1.8. (2) fate, fortune, destiny *Mg* 11.6, 16.6, 20.6, 24.6, 31.4, 45.4, 46.2.
**skera (skar)** *sv.* to cut, carve; *pptc. VM* 17.3 n.; *MvII* 7.3.
**skilinn** *a.* clear, distinct, comprehensible *MvII* 24.4.
**skilja (ld)** *wv.* (1) to separate, part *Mg* 25.3; *VM* 6.4. (2) to know, perceive *MvI* 7.3; *MvIII* 21.6. (3) *md. skiljast við* to separate from *Mg* 8.6.
**skína (skein)** *sv.* to shine *Mg* 33.8; *VM* 26.2 (*prptc.*).
**skip** *n.* boat *MvIII* 7.8.
**skipa (að)** *wv. with dat.* to place *Mg* 27.8, 46.4; to assign, grant *Mg* 38.6.
**skipan** *f.* commandment *VM* 18.2.
**skiptast (pt)** *md. wv.* to be exchanged *MvIII* 25.4.
**skipti** *n.* dealing out, distribution *VM* 10.5.
**skírðr** *a. pptc. of skíra* baptised *Mg* 22.4, 24.2 n., 50.3.
**skjótt** *adv.* swiftly, quickly *MvIII* 9.8.
**skjöldungr** *m.* Skjöldung (a descendant of the Skjöldungs); prince *Mg* 25.3.
**skógr** *m.* forest *MvI* 13.5.
**skorða** *f.* prop, support *VM* 20.6 (see List of kennings, 'Woman').
**skrá (ð)** *wv.* to write *MvIII* 21.8.
**skrifa (að)** *wv.* to write *MvI* 26.5.

**skrín** *n.* shrine *Mg* 1.8 (see List of kennings, 'Heaven').
**skript** *f.* image; statue, sculpture *VM* 17.3; *MvII* 7.3, 15.6.
**skriptagangr** *m.* confession *Mg* 40.6.
**skrúði** *m.* adornment, apparel *Mg* 9.8.
**skrýða (dd)** *wv.* to dress, adorn *Mg* 43.5.
**skulu (skyldi)** *pret.-pres. aux. with inf.* shall, should, must *Mg* 4.4, 5.5, 10.7, 18.8, 26.3, 27.4 (shall be), 27.7, 37.7, 46.1, 47.6 n., 47.8, 48.5, 50.1; *VM* 8.5 (shall be), 12.8; *MvI* 12.7, 14.4, 16.7; *MvII* 9.8; *MvIII* 17.2, 23.5.
**ský** *n.* cloud *Mg* 25.4; *MvIII* 21.5. (See List of Kennings, 'Christ'.)
**skýfold** *f.* land of clouds *Mg* 43.6 (see List of Kennings, 'Heaven').
**skylda (að)** *wv.* to oblige, put under an obligation, require *MvIII* 15.1.
**skylda** *f.* obligation, duty *Mg* 50.3.
**skyldr** *a.* (1) obliged, having a duty *Mg* 20.4; *VM* 26.1. (2) *n. skylt er* it is a duty or obligation, it is obligatory *Mg* 30.1, 42.7; *MvII* 24.3; *MvIII* 24.8.
**skynlauss** *a.* without reason, brutish *Mg* 33.3.
**skýra (ð)** *wv.* to explain *Mg* 4.6, 17.1; *VM* 26.1.
**skýrr** *a.* (1) clear, pure, virtuous; *sup. f. skýrust MvIII* 28.5. (2) clear, distinct; *sup. f. (or n. as adv.?) skýrst VM* 17.4.
**skærr** *a.* clear, bright, luminous; pure; good, excellent *VM* 17.3; *MvII* 7.4, 22.1; *MvIII* 27.7, 28.1; *sup.* most excellent *MvII* 24.3; *MvIII* 28.2.
**skör** *f.* multitude, crowd *MvIII* 21.5 n.
**slá (sló)** *sv.* to strike *Mg* 12.8.
**slíkr** *a.* (1) such *Mg* 48.1; *MvIII* 6.7, 14.2; *n. as subst.* such a thing or such things *Mg* 17.4; *MvIII* 18.6. (2) this *Mg* 49.4; *MvI* 8.4, 23.2, 26.6; *MvII* 10.1, 13.4, 15.8; *MvIII* 20.2, 30.6; *n. as subst.* (*pron.*) this *Mg* 8.2, 21.4, 49.3; *VM* 7.2, 14.2; *MvIII* 19.8.
**slæmr** *m.* concluding section of a *drápa Mg* 37.2.
**smíð** *f.* work of art, art form, structure *Mg* 37.4.
**smíðast (að)** *wv. md. with upp* to be made up *MvI* 5.6.
**snemma** *adv.* early *Mg* 42.1.
**snild** *f.* skill with language, articulacy, eloquence *MvIII* 30.4.
**snjallr** *a.* clever, skilful *VM* 15.6; good, helpful *MvII* 8.6.
**snót** *f.* woman *MvI* 9.2.
**so** = **svó** *Vm* 11.5.
**sól** *f.* sun *Mg* 15.1, 23.3, 27.2, 31.1, 33.7, 37.4, 39.7, 43.2, 52.1; cf. **silki-Sól**.
**sómalauss** *a.* dishonourable *MvIII* 18.4.
**sómi** *m.* honour *Mg* 52.2.

**sonr, son** *m.* son *Mg* 6.1, 6.7, 7.1, 12.5, 21.6, 24.1 n., 25.6, 40.3, 45.6; *VM* 21.2, 25.8; *MvII* 8.2, 14.6, 23.5 n.; *MvIII* 16.7, 29.7. (See List of kennings, 'Christ'.)
**sorg** *f.* sorrow, grief *Mg* 15.5; *VM* 13.2; *MvI* 8.5 n., 14.7, 17.8; *MvII* 17.4; *MvIII* 12.6.
**sorgaðr** *a.* sorrowful *MvII* 6.2.
**spekt** *f.* wisdom *Mg* 4.4.
**spenna (nt)** *wv.* to clasp, entrap, hold fast *MvI* 16.2.
**spillast (lt)** *wv. md.* to be spoiled *MvIII* 4.4.
**sprakki** *m.* woman *MvI* 7.4 n.
**sprund** *n.* woman *Mg* 8.7, 25.7; *VM* 5.2, 9.2; *MvII* 20.4.
**spyrja (spurði)** *wv.* (1) to ask *VM* 11.4, 14.1. (2) to hear, be informed of; *sem frá er spurt* of whom there is report *MvII* 3.4.
**spöng** *f.* metal plate *MvII* 5.2 (see List of kennings, 'Woman').
**stá** *vb.* (= **standa**) to stand *MvII* 13.8.
**staddr** *pptc.* positioned, present *VM* 5.6.
**staðarmenn** *m. pl.* people of the town *MvII* 14.2.
**staðr** *m.* place *Mg* 13.8; *MvIII* 1.4; town *MvII* 3.2.
**stál** *n.* steel *Mg* 15.3; i.e. sword *Mg* 22.7.
**standa (stóð)** *sv.* to stand, be (standing) *Mg* 51.4; *MvI* 2.2; *MvII* 6.4, 7.4, 15.6; *MvIII* 13.2; *with acc.* come upon *MvIII* 7.6; *standa í gegnum* to be stuck in or through *Mg* 17.7, 22.8; *standa til* to require, warrant, permit *MvIII* 15.8; *standa upp* to get up (from bed), arise *MvII* 15.2; *MvIII* 6.8.
**stef** *n.* refrain *Mg* 16.2, 28.4.
**stefna (d)** *wv.* to summon *VM* 14.6.
**sterkr** *a.* strong, powerful *Mg* 24.4; *MvIII* 4.6 n., 8.2 (dire).
**stíga (stje)** *sv. with upp* to ascend *Mg* 45.1.
**stillir** *m.* controller, ruler *Mg* 16.1, 20.3, 21.2, 26.2, 28.1, 34.8, 35.8 n., 52.1. (See List of Kennings, 'God' and 'Christ'.)
**stinnoddaðr** *a.* stiffly pointed *Mg* 15.3.
**stinnr** *a.* stiff, strong *Mg* 22.7.
**stirðr** *a.* stiff, rigid *MvII* 15.3, 20.8.
**stjett** *f.* way, path, track *Mg* 26.1, 37.1 (see List of Kennings, 'Heaven'); attitude *MvIII* 19.6.
**stjörnuhöll** *f.* star-hall *Mg* 16.1 (see List of Kennings, 'Heaven').
**stólpi** *m.* pillar, column, post *Mg* 13.3 n. (see List of Kennings, 'Holy Cross').
**stórligr** *a.* great, mighty *Mg* 15.4.
**stórr** *a.* great, mighty *VM* 14.4; *MvIII* 24.6.

**stórstraumr** *m.* great stream, current or river *MvIII* 7.3.
**strangr** *a.* strong, powerful *MvIII* 7.4 n.
**stríð** *n.* grief, sorrow, pain *Mg* 11.8, 19.7; *MvI* 12.3; *MvII* 9.2; *MvIII* 9.6, 23.4.
**strönd** *f.* strand, beach, shore *Mg* 41.1 (see List of Kennings, 'Heaven').
**stund** *f.* length of time, while *Mg* 35.6, 40.6; time, hour *Mg* 50.7; *VM* 5.5 n.
**styggja (gð)** *wv.* to offend, blaspheme *MvIII* 17.6.
**stýra (ð)** *wv. with dat.* to steer, direct *Mg* 28.7, 32.7, 36.7; *VM* 2.1.
**stýrir** *m.* controller, ruler *Mg* 10.1, 18.2, 33.2 n. (See List of Kennings, 'Bishop' and 'Christ'.)
**styrkja (kt)** *wv.* to strengthen, support *VM* 6.6.
**stökkva (stökk)** *sv.* to spurt *Mg* 19.2; to take to flight *MvIII* 22.1.
**stöpull** *m.* tower *MvII* 6.6.
**sunna** *f.* sun *Mg* 9.5, 11.3, 35.2.
**súrr** *a.* sour *Mg* 30.7.
**sútafullr** *a.* full of sorrow, sorrowful *MvII* 12.5 (*with svanni*); *sup. MvII* 7.8.
**svanni** *m.* woman *Mg* 7.2; *VM* 5.7, 22.6; *MvI* 15.2, 20.2; *MvII* 12.6 (*with f. a.*).
**svara (að)** *wv.* to answer *VM* 7.4.
**sveinn** *m.* (1) boy, young man *VM* 3.8, 4.5, 5.3, 5.8, 6.5; *MvII* 11.1, 12.4, 13.1, 15.2, 18.8, 20.6. (2) servant *MvIII* 24.6.
**sveit** *f.* body of people, host, troop, company *Mg* 8.3, 22.4; *VM* 19.6; *MvI* 6.5, 23.4, 27.1; *MvII* 22.8; *MvIII* 11.3, 22.4.
**sveiti** *m.* blood *Mg* 17.8.
**sveldr** *a. pptc. of svella* swollen *MvI* 22.2.
**sverja (sór)** *sv.* to swear (an oath) *VM* 14.4.
**svik** *n. pl.* falsehood, treachery *Mg* 49.3.
**svíkja (sveik)** *sv.* to deceive *MvIII* 23.8.
**svinnr** *a.* clever, intelligent *Mg* 42.4 n.; *VM* 3.7, 5.7.
**svipta (pt)** *sv. with dat.* take away; *pp. with dat.* freed from *VM* 26.7; deprived of *MvIII* 24.2 n.
**sviptuðr** *m.* one who takes away *MvIII* 18.3 (see List of Kennings, 'Other').
**svó** *adv.* so, thus *Mg* 3.1, 10.4, 15.7, 18.6, 22.1, 34.6, 35.5, 38.6, 46.8, 47.1 (*gjör svó vel* please); *VM* 3.2, 6.3 (therefore), 11.4; *MvI* 3.1 (similarly?), 6.7 (so much), 18.2, 27.4 n.; *MvIII* 9.6 (so hard, so quickly), 14.7, 15.1, 19.5; also *Mg* 12.3; *svó að* so that *Mg* 2.7, 43.8 n., 50.7 n.; *VM* 20.3; *MvI* 2.5, 8.5, 10.4, 20.7; *MvII* 11.7, 12.7, 18.5 n.;

*MvIII* 1.3, 2.1, 8.6; *svó* . . . *að* so . . . that *Mg* 29.7–8; *VM* 11.5–6 (written *so*); *MvI* 22.5–6; *MvII* 17.5–6; *MvIII* 27.5–7; *svó as conj.* so that *Mg* 49.6; *MvI* 13.6 n.

**sýna (d)** *wv.* (1) to show *Mg* 1.5, 38.3; *VM* 19.5, 24.3; *MvI* 21.2, 23.3. (2) *md.* to be revealed, show oneself *Mg* 9.5; *MvII* 4.1.

**synd** *f.* sin *Mg* 3.4, 25.7, 39.3, 50.8; *VM* 26.7; *MvI* 13.8; *MvII* 23.1; *synda samband* sinful union *VM* 18.3.

**syndaauki** *m.* increase of sins *Mg* 49.3.

**syndafullr** *a.* sinful *MvIII* 10.2 n., 14.8.

**syndalausn** *f.* redemption of or from sins *Mg* 39.8, 48.6.

**syndalauss** *a.* sinless, without sin *Mg* 23.4.

**syndlauss** *a.* sinless, without sin *MvI* 5.4.

**syndugr** *a.* sinful *Mg* 19.6 n.; *MvI* 20.6; *MvII* 22.7.

**syngja (söng)** *sv.* to sing *Mg* 11.7, 31.7; *MvI* 25.1; *MvIII* 19.8.

**syrgja (gð)** *wv.* to mourn, grieve; *syrgja að* to weep for *MvII* 6.8.

**systir** *f.* sister *Mg* 12.2, 34.7.

**sýta (tt)** *wv.* to grieve over *Mg* 3.8.

**sækja (sótta)** *wv.* (1) to go (to a place) *MvI* 17.1; *sækja til* to attend *MvII* 6.1 n. (2) to pursue, attack *MvI* 19.2; to accuse *MvI* 9.4 (*pptc.*).

**sæld** *f.* happiness, blessedness *MvI* 7.3 n. (*descriptive gen.*).

**sæll** *a.* blessed *Mg* 19.3, 28.8, 32.8, 36.8, 52.1; *VM* 20.2; *MvI* 2.5 n., 28.8 n.; *MvII* 1.7, 8.1, 18.7; *MvIII* 22.3, 22.6; *comp. sælli Mg* 16.5, 20.5, 24.5; *sup. sælstr Mg* 3.7; *MvI* 18.1; *MvII* 7.5.

**sæmd** *f.* honour *MvII* 24.6 (see List of Kennings, 'Virgin Mary').

**sæta (tt)** *wv. with dat.* to be faced with *MvI* 11.4 n.

**sæta** *f.* woman *Mg* 17.2, 46.8; *VM* 6.2, 11.1, 14.3, 17.1, 21.1; *MvI* 3.3, 7.6, 13.7 n., 19.1, 25.5 n., 27.1; *MvII* 1.8, 7.7, 13.2.

**sæta** *f.* sweetness *Mg* 9.7.

**sæti** *n.* seat, dwelling *Mg* 2.4, 9.4 (see List of Kennings, 'Heaven' and 'Virgin Mary').

**sætleikr** *m.* sweetness, kindness *VM* 19.5; *MvI* 23.3.

**sætr** *a.* (1) sweet *Mg* 9.2; *VM* 5.1, 26.8; *MvI* 2.6, 27.2; *MvII* 16.8; *MvIII* 16.2; *sup. Mg* 19.3. (2) pleasant, delightful *Mg* 11.7, 33.7. (3) *n. as adv. sætt* sweetly *MvI* 25.1; *MvII* 19.3; dearly *MvI* 5.3 n.

**sætta (tt)** *wv.* to reconcile, make peace, atone; *prptc. MvIII* 25.6.

**sögn** *f.* report, account, story *VM* 14.3.

**sök** *f.* offence, guilt, sin *MvIII* 4.3, 23.3; charge *MvIII* 17.7.

**sökkva (sökk)** *sv.* to sink *MvIII* 10.1.

**söngr** *m.* (1) song *Mg* 23.8 n., 24.4, 40.3; *MvIII* 21.3. (2) Mass *MvII* 6.1.

**taka (tók)** *sv.* (1) to take *Mg* 23.2 n., 23.3, 34.1; *VM* 26.5; *MvII* 15.4; *MvIII* 13.6; to take hold *Mg* 13.6 n.; *taka í* to take hold of *VM* 8.1. (2) *with inf.* to begin (sometimes as a meaningless aux.) *Mg* 6.2, 21.6, 29.4, 41.5; *VM* 10.3, 20.1; *MvII* 4.8, 5.6, 7.1, 21.6. (3) *md.* to take place *MvI* 4.8.

**tákn** *n.* (1) symbol *MvII* 16.1 (see List of Kennings, 'Virgin Mary'). (2) miracle *MvIII* 30.7.

**tala (að)** *wv.* to talk, speak *Mg* 18.6, 34.6, 46.8; *MvII* 7.1; *MvIII* 13.8; *tala við* to speak to, address *Mg* 10.4, 22.1; *VM* 5.7.

**tállaust** *adv.* without deceit *VM* 6.8 n.

**tár** *n.* tear *Mg* 5.4, 15.8, 24.4, 37.6, 39.2, 40.4, 48.2, 49.4, 52.6; *VM* 13.4; *MvI* 15.1, 16.2; *MvII* 7.6, 10.2, 17.2.

**teiti** *f.* cheerfulness *Mg* 43.4.

**telja (taldi)** *wv.* to count, number, reckon *Mg* 6.7, 43.1; *pptc. adv. gen. taldra daga* after a fixed number of days *Mg* 6.4; *md.* to be counted *MvIII* 10.8.

**tíð** *f.* (1) time *VM* 9.1; *MvIII* 20.8 n. (2) *in pl.* the seven canonical offices or hours *MvIII* 6.6, 9.1.

**tíðast** *adv. sup.* most often *VM* 24.6.

**tiggi** *m.* prince, king *VM* 10.4.

**tiginn** *a.* of high rank, noble *Mg* 8.6, 9.1.

**tign** *f.* nobility, status *VM* 10.3; sublimity *MvIII* 8.3.

**tigna (að)** *wv.* to honour *Mg* 48.5.

**tignarmeyja** *f.* noble maiden or young woman *VM* 6.7.

**til** *prep. with gen.* (1) to, towards, at (*direction, destination*) *Mg* 13.2, 13.8, 18.2, 27.3; *VM* 1.1, 14.7 (before), 22.3; *MvI* 13.5 n.; *MvII* 6.1; *MvIII* 13.1. (2) about, concerning *VM* 13.3. (3) to, for, as (*purpose*) *Mg* 1.1, 2.8, 12.5, 23.1, 23.7, 28.4, 31.5, 36.4, 44.4, 48.6; *VM* 12.4; *MvI* 15.8, 17.5; so as to bring about *Mg* 4.8. (4) *as adv.* to, for *MvIII* 15.8; for it *MvII* 24.4 (see **fá**); *MvIII* 3.4 (see **gefa**); for this *Mg* 47.3; about it *MvIII* 21.6 (see **ljúga**).

**tilkall** *n.* claim *VM* 15.6.

**tína (d)** *wv.* to bring forward, relate *Mg* 8.2.

**tínir** *m.* gatherer; compiler, determiner *Mg* 46.2 (see List of Kennings, 'Christ').

**tírargjarn** *a.* eager for glory *Mg* 6.3.

**tjá (ð)** *wv.* to describe *Mg* 30.1; *VM* 15.5.

**tjald** *n.* tent *Mg* 35.8 (see List of Kennings, 'Heaven').

**tjecum** (*Latin*) (be) with you *Mg* 47.4.

**traustr** *a.* trustworthy, reliable *VM* 7.5.

**trautt** *adv.* hardly, scarcely *MvII* 11.8.
**tregafullr** *a.* sorrowful *MvII* 7.2.
**tregbjóðr** *m.* reluctant preacher *MvIII* 9.1 (see List of Kennings, 'Other').
**tregi** *m.* sorrow *VM* 15.5; *MvII* 13.2.
**treysta (st)** *wv. with dat.* to rely upon *Mg* 8.5 n.; *VM* 2.3; *MvI* 17.3; *treysta á with acc. MvIII* 8.3.
**trje** *n.* tree *Mg* 13.4 (see List of Kennings, 'Holy Cross').
**trú** *f.* (1) troth *VM* 6.7. (2) Christian faith *MvIII* 9.2.
**trúa (ð)** *wv.* to believe *MvIII* 29.6; *prptc. MvIII* 8.4; *with dat.* to believe, trust in *Mg* 18.7; *with acc. Mg* 8.5 n.
**tunga** *f.* (1) tongue *Mg* 19.5, 47.3; *MvI* 5.7; *MvII* 20.1; *MvIII* 21.3. (2) language; *forn tunga* Ancient Hebrew; The Old Testament *Mg* 6.3 n.
**tveir, tvær, tvau** *card. num.* two *Mg* 2.7, 12.2.
**tvennr** *a.* double *MvIII* 9.4.
**tvistr** *a.* sad *MvII* 16.6.
**týna (d)** *wv. with dat.* to lose *Mg* 51.3.
**tæmast (d)** *wv. md. with dat.* to fall to s-one, devolve upon s-one *VM* 9.4.

**um** *prep. with acc.* (1) around *Mg* 49.1. (2) over, through(out) *VM* 9.1; *MvI* 23.8; *MvII* 24.7; *MvIII* 3.2; *um aldr, um aldir* for ever *MvI* 1.3; *MvIII* 1.6; *um aldr og æfi* for time and eternity *Mg* 45.3; *um síðir* eventually, at last *VM* 11.2; *MvI* 7.2. (3) regarding, concerning, about *MvI* 23.2; *MvIII* 3.8, 18.1; with regard to *MvIII* 5.8.
**umgaupnandi** *m.* one who holds a thing in the palm of his/her hand *Mg* 2.5.
**umhverfis** *prep. with acc.* round about, around *MvI* 20.2.
**unað** *n.* happiness, contentment *MvIII* 2.3.
**und** *f.* wound *Mg* 17.7, 38.3.
**undan** (1) *prep. with dat.* away from, out of, to escape *Mg* 7.2, 51.6. (2) *adv.* out of it *VM* 20.7.
**undir** *prep. with acc.* underneath *Mg* 13.6; as *MvIII* 25.5.
**undra (að)** *wv.* to be surprised, wonder, marvel *Mg* 8.1.
**ungimaðr** *m.* young man *VM* 4.3.
**ungr** *a.* young *VM* 3.3, 7.1; *MvII* 13.3.
**unna (unni)** *pret.-pres. with dat.* to love *Mg* 25.5; *VM* 6.1, 23.7; *MvI* 5.1, 6.8; *MvII* 11.5; *MvIII* 26.5; *prptc. unnandi* loving *MvII* 12.1; *MvIII* 19.2; *as noun* lover, husband *MvI* 4.4; *md.* to love one another *MvII* 3.5.
**unnusta** *f.* loved one *VM* 11.8.
**unz** *conj.* until *MvII* 14.7.

**upp** *adv.* up *Mg* 18.5, 27.2, 36.1, 45.1, 45.8; *VM* 3.5; *MvI* 5.6; *MvII* 14.5, 15.2, 19.3; *MvIII* 6.8, 9.7, 12.8, 17.3, 18.1, 20.2, 21.2 n.
**upphaf** *n.* beginning *VM* 1.1; *MvIII* 21.7.
**uppi** *adv.* up *MvIII* 3.3 (see **hafa**).
**úr** *prep. with dat.* out of, from *Mg* 40.7; *VM* 26.5 n.; *MvI* 11.8, 24.5, 27.3; *MvIII* 4.7, 29.5.
**út** *adv.* out, forth *Mg* 37.8, 49.8; *MvI* 19.1; *MvII* 7.8; to the end *MvI* 29.1; *MvIII* 9.5.
**utan** *prep. with acc.* without *MvII* 19.4; *fyr utan MvIII* 25.2.

**vagga** *f.* cradle *MvII* 11.2.
**vagn** *m.* 'Wain', the constellation Ursa Major *Mg* 38.7.
**vakta (að)** *wv.* to watch, observe *MvIII* 6.4.
**vald** *n.* power *Mg* 46.3; *MvI* 20.5; *MvII* 24.8; *MvIII* 1.5, 13.6.
**valdandi** *m.* ruler *MvIII* 1.6 (see List of Kennings, 'God').
**valdi** *m.* ruler (= Christ) *Mg* 6.4.
**valdr** *m.* ruler *Mg* 8.6.
**vanda (að)** *wv.* to do s-thing carefully or meticulously; *pptc.* beautifully made *Mg* 2.4.
**varla** *adv.* scarcely, hardly *MvII* 11.6.
**vatn** *n.* water *Mg* 49.5 (see List of Kennings, 'Tears').
**vaxa (óx)** *sv.* to grow *MvI* 6.1.
**vazfall** *n.* river *MvIII* 5.7.
**vefja (vafði)** *wv.* to wrap *Mg* 34.4.
**vega (vó)** *sv.* to slay, kill; *pptc. MvI* 12.2.
**vegligr** *a.* magnificent, distinguished, noble *VM* 11.1.
**vegr** *m.* honour, glory; *á veg* in glory *Mg* 45.4.
**vegr** *m.* (1) way, road, path *MvIII* 13.4. (2) *(á) þann veg* in this way, thus *VM* 22.6; *MvII* 7.2.
**veita (tt)** *wv.* to grant, give *Mg* 3.3, 5.1, 5.5, 37.1, 47.8, 50.5, 52.3; *VM* 19.6; *MvI* 14.8, 29.5; *MvII* 1.3, 2.1, 14.2, 17.2, 22.4, 23.1, 23.8; *MvIII* 1.5, 19.1.
**vel** *adv.* well, very, quite *Mg* 47.1; *VM* 7.6, 16.6; *MvI* 4.4; easily *MvII* 16.7.
**veldi** *n.* (1) power, might, influence (in the community) *MvII* 4.8. (2) kingdom *Mg* 35.7.
**velferð** *f.* prosperity *MvII* 4.7.
**velja (valdi)** *wv.* to choose *Mg* 13.4, 14.6; *pptc.* chosen *Mg* 28.2; choice *MvII* 24.5.
**vera (var)** *sv.* to be *Mg* 3.1, 10.2, 11.1, 13.7, 15.6 n., 16.2, 16.5, 16.7,

# Glossary and Index 129

16.8, 17.1, 17.5, 18.5, 18.8, 19.1, 20.1, 20.3, 20.5, 20.7, 20.8, 22.7, 24.5, 24.7, 24.8, 25.5, 27.1, 27.5, 29.3, 29.8, 30.1, 32.2, 34.2, 35.3, 36.1, 39.3, 42.6, 42.7, 43.8, 44.7, 47.6, 48.1, 49.1, 49.3, 50.3, 50.4; *VM* 5.6, 6.3, 7.5, 9.5, 11.4, 11.5, 13.5, 16.2 n., 17.3, 18.1, 18.7, 25.1, 26.1; *MvI* 1.6, 4.1, 5.4, 7.4, 7.5, 11.8, 12.5, 13.5, 15.8, 17.7, 19.3, 22.5, 23.1, 25.8; *MvII* 2.4, 3.4, 4.6, 9.4 (exist), 12.8, 14.6, 15.1, 16.3, 21.7, 22.1, 24.3; *MvIII* 2.6, 4.6, 4.7, 6.4, 8.5, 12.7, 14.7, 15.2, 15.4, 16.8, 21.8, 23.2, 23.6, 24.8, 25.8, 26.7, 27.8, 28.1, 28.8, 29.2, 30.2.

**verða (varð, urðu/vurðu, orðið)** *sv.* (1) to come into being, come about, arise *MvI* 8.7, 11.8. (2) to become *Mg* 3.5, 38.4; *VM* 4.7, 8.7, 18.5; *MvI* 9.2, 10.5, 18.3 (*pptc.* spent); *MvII* 4.7; *MvIII* 4.3. (3) *aux.* with *inf.* must, have to, be obliged to *MvII* 9.2; *MvIII* 18.8. (4) *aux.* with *pptc.* forming the passive *VM* 22.1; *MvII* 10.3, 24.5; *MvIII* 10.2, 11.6.

**verk** *n.* deed *Mg* 24.4, 40.1; *MvI* 3.8; *MvIII* 2.8, 15.7, 26.8, 30.6 (poem).

**verki** *m.* poem *Mg* 2.3.

**vernda (að)** *wv.* to defend, protect *MvIII* 19.3.

**verr** *m.* husband *MvII* 9.8.

**vess** *n.* verse (i.e. Ave Maria) *Mg* 52.6 (see List of Kennings 'Ave Maria'); *MvIII* 22.2.

**vestr** *a. sup.* worst *MvI* 7.8; *MvIII* 14.6.

**við, viðr** *prep.* (1) *with acc.* (a) with, against, towards, to, on *Mg* 10.4 n., 22.4, 24.2; *VM* 5.2, 5.7, 15.6, 19.8; *MvI* 10.3; *MvII* 5.2 n., 15.8, 23.2; *MvIII* 3.7 (amidst), 4.2, 12.8, 16.1, 26.4, 30.8. (b) close to *Mg* 35.8. (c) (separate) from *Mg* 8.8, 25.4; *VM* 6.4. (c) with respect to, about *MvIII* 6.7, 8.1, 12.4. (2) *with dat.* (a) at, on, on the point of *Mg* 29.8 (for), 30.2; *MvI* 27.8 n. (b) with, together with, along with *Mg* 12.2. (c) *ganga við* see **ganga** *VM* 23.3, *MvI* 11.6. (3) *adv. viðr* about it *MvI* 11.2; *þar við* with that *MvIII* 4.4.

**við** *pron. 2nd pers. dual* we *Mg* 18.4; *VM* 8.7.

**viðköstr** *m.* pile of wood *MvI* 20.4.

**viðr** *m.* wood, bush, tree *Mg* 1.6; *MvI* 25.6 (see List of Kennings, 'Man').

**viðr** *prep. and adv.* see **við**.

**víðr** *a.* wide *MvI* 20.3.

**viðrkvæmiligr** *a.* suitable, appropriate, becoming *Mg* 37.2.

**víf** *n.* woman *Mg* 6.5, 39.4; *VM* 23.8, 26.8; *MvII* 8.3, 8.6, 11.1, 21.3, 24.6; *MvIII* 4.8, 25.1 (bride). (See List of Kennings, 'Virgin Mary'.)

**víg** *n.* killing, homicide *MvI* 11.8.

**vild** *f.* wish, desire *MvI* 1.6.

# 130  Glossary and Index

**vili** *m.* will, wish *Mg* 10.7, 12.6, 16.4, 23.3, 39.7, 44.3; *VM* 6.4; *MvI* 18.8; *MvII* 3.6; *MvIII* 15.8.
**vilja (vildi)** *wv.* to be willing, want, wish *Mg* 2.1, 3.6, 4.5, 7.3, 8.4, 35.7, 38.6, 38.8, 42.1; *VM* 2.3, 2.7, 20.8; *MvI* 1.5, 8.3, 14.6, 28.6; *MvII* 1.6, 3.8, 5.4, 14.1; *MvIII* 3.3.
**villr** *a.* astray, erring *MvI* 21.4; *MvIII* 5.7.
**vín** *n.* wine *Mg* 30.7.
**víndrykkr** *m.* wine-drinking *MvIII* 3.6.
**vinna (vann, unnu)** *sv.* to work, perform, bring about, cause, make, do *Mg* 7.4; *VM* 22.7; *MvI* 5.7, 20.6; *prptc. as noun* alls vinnandi maker or causer of everything *VM* 1.2; *md.* to be achieved *MvIII* 22.8.
**vinr** *m.* friend *Mg* 10.2.
**virða (rð)** *wv.* (1) to value, regard *Mg* 21.7. (2) *md.* to deign *VM* 8.7 (*subj.*).
**virðar** *m. pl.* men, people *Mg* 14.5; *MvI* 21.3.
**virkr** *a.* careful, dutiful *VM* 14.8, 22.2; dear, beloved *MvII* 6.4.
**virktafríðr** *a.* very beautiful *VM* 11.2 n.
**vísir** *m.* prince *Mg* 14.5, 27.2. (See List of Kennings, 'Christ'.)
**vísliga** *adv.* with certainty, for certain *Mg* 13.2.
**víss** *a.* certain, sure *MvIII* 2.7; *n. as adv.* víst certainly, in truth *VM* 6.3, 7.5.
**vit** *n.* wits, intelligence, sense, consciousness *MvII* 18.6; *MvIII* 4.7.
**vita (vissi)** *pret.-pres.* to know (of) *Mg* 22.5; *VM* 16.1, 18.1; *MvI* 10.7; *MvIII* 6.3.
**viti** *m.* beacon *VM* 20.6 (see List of Kennings, 'Gold').
**vitja (að)** *wv.* to go to, visit *VM* 11.1.
**vitni** *n.* witness, testimony *VM* 3.2, 21.5, 24.2.
**vitnisburðr** *m.* testimony *VM* 22.1.
**vitnisvísur** *f. pl.* testimonial poem *VM* title.
**vitrast (að)** *wv. md.* to manifest oneself *Mg* 4.4.
**vjer, vær** *pron. 1st pers. pl.* we *Mg* 27.3, 34.5, 48.5, 48.6; *MvI* 29.6 n., 29.7; *MvII* 22.7, 23.3, 23.8; *MvIII* 6.3, 14.1, 29.4, 29.6.
**vóðamaðr** *m.* dangerous man, terrible man *Mg* 7.3.
**vóði** *m.* harm, damage; *adv. dat.* dangerously *MvIII* 5.8 n.
**vón, von** *f.* hope, expectation *Mg* 25.5; *VM* 26.6; *MvII* 14.6 (*það er mikil von* that is only to be expected); *MvIII* 2.7, 26.7 (*sem vón var* as was to be expected). (See List of Kennings, 'Virgin Mary'.)
**vóndr** *a.* bad, evil, wicked *Mg* 24.3.
**vórkunn** *f.* compassion, pity *MvII* 17.1.

# Glossary and Index 131

**vórkynna (nd)** *wv. with dat. and acc.* to pity, have sympathy or compassion for s-one for s-thing *Mg* 39.2.
**vórr** *poss. a.* our *Mg* 12.4, 14.4, 28.8, 32.2, 32.8, 34.1, 36.8; *VM* 6.3 (*referring to the speaker, i.e. with sg. meaning*); *MvI* 27.8; *MvII* 22.6; *MvIII* 1.4, 2.6, 15.7, 28.6, 28.7.
**vóttr, vottr** *m.* witness *VM* 7.5, 8.8, 13.3, 14.7, 16.1; *MvIII* 20.1.
**vægð** *f.* mercy *MvI* 21.3.
**vænn** *a.* (1) good, noble, beneficial *Mg* 48.2; *VM* 14.7. (2) beautiful *Mg* 37.1; *MvII* 6.8, 11.1, 17.1 n.
**vænta (nt)** *wv.* to hope *Mg* 2.3.
**vær** see **vjer**.
**völdugr** *a.* powerful, mighty *MvI* 20.5 n.
**völlr** *m.* level ground, plain *MvI* 20.3.
**völna (að)** *wv.* to shrivel *MvI* 24.4 n.
**Vör** *f.* name of a goddess *MvII* 15.4 (see List of Kennings 'Woman').
**vörðr** *m.* guardian *MvII* 1.1 (see List of Kennings, 'Christ').
**vörnun** *f.* abstinence (*with gen.* from s-thing) *Mg* 24.3 n.
**vörr** *f.* lip *VM* 20.2.

**yðvarr** *poss. a.* 2nd pers. pl. your *Mg* 39.4, 39.5.
**yfir** *prep. with acc.* over, across *MvIII* 5.7, 7.3.
**yfirbót** *f.* atonement *MvII* 23.4.
**yfirmaðr** *m.* superior *MvIII* 4.2.
**yfirskínandi** *prptc.* overshining *VM* 2.2.
**yfirþjóðkóngr** *m.* supreme king *Mg* 28.5, 32.5, 36.5. (See List of Kennings, 'Christ'.)
**ýmiss** *a.* various *Mg* 23.8 n.
**yndi** *n.* delight, joy, pleasure *Mg* 3.4, 23.4, 39.3, 39.8, 41.6; *VM* 5.5; *MvI* 5.4, 15.8.
**ynniligr** *a.* lovely *VM* 26.4.
**yrða (rt)** *wv.* to address *MvIII* 22.3 n.
**yrkja (orti)** *wv.* to compose (poetry) *Mg* 2.7.
**ýtar** *m. pl.* people, humankind *Mg* 11.1, 42.8, 52.3; *MvI* 29.1.
**ýtir** *m.* pusher *MvI* 21.5 (see List of Kennings, 'Man').

**þá** *adv.* then, at that time, after that *Mg* 9.6, 19.3, 19.8, 21.3, 34.2, 50.5, 51.4, 51.7; *VM* 8.1, 16.5, 22.5 n.; *MvI* 7.3; *MvII* 10.7, 21.1; *MvIII* 21.8 n.; *þá as conj.* when *MvIII* 23.6; *þá er* when *Mg* 43.5; *VM* 16.2, 24.5–8 n.; *MvI* 25.3, 27.6, 28.4, 29.7; *MvII* 5.7, 20.5.
**þaðan af** *adv.* from then on, thereafter *MvII* 21.5; *MvIII* 26.1.

**þagna (að)** *wv.* to fall silent, stop speaking *VM* 21.1.
**þakka (að)** *wv. with dat. and acc.* to thank someone for something *Mg* 23.5; *MvI* 26.3.
**þakkir** *f. pl.* thanks *VM* 22.5; *MvIII* 26.2.
**þangað er** *adv.* to where *VM* 17.2.
**þanninn** *adv.* in this way, thus, as follows *VM* 21.4 n.
**þar** *adv.* there *VM* 4.2, 17.6; *MvI* 15.5, 25.4; *MvIII* 13.1, 21.8 (*þar á* on it); *þar er* where *MvII* 6.3, 6.7, 7.3, 13.7 (to where); *þar með* in addition *Mg* 12.8; *þassem* (= *þar sem*) whereas, although *MvI* 10.7; *þar við* with that *MvIII* 4.4.
**þarfnast (að)** *md. wv.* to lack, want, be without *VM* 19.3 n.
**þassem** see **þar**.
**þegar** *adv.* immediately, straight away *VM* 15.7; *MvI* 11.3; *MvII* 21.1; *MvIII* 12.2; *as conj.* when, as soon as *MvIII* 3.4, 6.8, 10.5, 22.1.
**þegn** *m.* man, soldier *Mg* 21.1, 41.3; *VM* 15.8; *MvIII* 3.5.
**þekkr** *a.* agreeable, pleasing *Mg* 37.4.
**þella** *f.* pine *VM* 9.7; *MvI* 22.6; *MvII* 13.5. (See List of Kennings, 'Woman'.)
**þengill** *m.* prince, lord *Mg* 4.7, 8.8, 20.2, 43.2. (See List of Kennings, 'Christ'.)
**þerfiliga** *adv.* profitably; humbly (?) *MvIII* 26.1.
**þeygi** *neg. adv.* yet not; certainly not, not at all *MvII* 24.2.
**þeyr** *m.* thaw wind *Mg* 44.6.
**þið** *pron. 2nd pers. dual* you (two), you both *Mg* 3.6, 51.2; *VM* 18.7.
**þiggja (þá)** *sv.* to accept *Mg* 2.3; to receive *Mg* 46.5; *VM* 10.4; *MvIII* 11.4.
**þikkja** see **þykkja**.
**þinn** *poss. a. 2nd pers. sg.* your *Mg* 1.2, 1.3, 6.1, 6.7, 7.1, 7.5, 10.8 n., 28.4, 37.3, 51.8; *VM* 1.3, 1.6, 2.4, 11.8, 18.2, 19.4, 25.8, 26.2; *MvI* 2.4, 17.2, 17.4 n., 18.8, 27.7, 28.7, 29.2; *MvII* 1.5, 9.3, 16.4, 22.4, 22.8, 23.5, 24.1; *MvIII* 1.5, 29.7, 29.8, 30.8.
**þjer** *pron. 2nd pers. pl.* you *Mg* 22.5, 31.3 (in addressing God), 40.5, 47.8; *VM* 6.4 (*honorific pl. alternating with sg.*); *MvIII* 11.3, 11.5, 11.8, 13.6, 19.6, 23.1, 23.5, 23.7.
**þjóð** *f.* people, humankind, the public *Mg* 4.6 n., 17.2, 19.6, 22.4 (*pl.*), 23.6, 26.2, 29.1, 33.1, 40.4, 47.2, 48.8; *MvI* 25.8 (*pl.*); *MvII* 21.2 (*pl.*), 22.5; *pl.* multitudes *Mg* 30.6 n., 36.3; *MvI* 10.7, 28.2. (See List of Kennings, 'Angels'.)
**þjóna (að)** *wv.* to serve *MvII* 21.6.
**þjónn** *m.* servant *MvIII* 13.7.

## Glossary and Index 133

**þó** *adv.* though, yet *Mg* 1.6; *MvII* 19.8; *MvIII* 12.4; *þó að* although *MvI* 18.5.
**þola (d)** *wv.* to endure, suffer *Mg* 4.8.
**þora (ð)** *wv.* to dare *VM* 7.2; *MvI* 11.3.
**þótt** *conj.* (1) although, though *Mg* 46.7, 49.2; *MvII* 23.3. (2) seeing that, since *MvII* 17.3 n.
**þrár** *a.* persistent *MvIII* 3.5; *n. as adv.* constantly, continually *MvII* 6.1.
**þraut** *f.* distress, trouble; trial *MvI* 28.1.
**þrautgóðr** *a.* good in trouble, helpful *MvII* 2.6.
**þrenning** *f.* Trinity *VM* 1.4.
**þrennr** *num. a.* triple, threefold *VM* 1.3.
**þreyja (þráði)** *wv.* to yearn; *prptc.* patient, suffering *MvI* 26.4.
**þriði** *ord. num.* third *Mg* 18.4, 44.5.
**þrif** *n. pl.* prosperity *MvII* 21.5.
**þrjóta (þraut)** *sv. impers. with acc.* to fail *MvIII* 10.5.
**þróast (að)** *md. wv.* to grow, increase *MvII* 4.8.
**þróttr** *m.* endurance, strength, fortitude *MvI* 23.6.
**þræll** *m.* servant *MvI* 28.8.
**þræta (tt)** *wv.* to dispute, quarrel, argue about *MvIII* 16.2; *þræta á móti* to contradict *VM* 15.7.
**þræta** *f.* dispute; *þræta máls* contradiction of her speech or in her case *MvI* 11.4.
**þröngr** *a.* tight *Mg* 21.1.
**þú** *pron.* 2nd *pers. sg.* you *Mg* 1.1, 1.5, 1.7, 3.2, 7.1, 10.5, 16.2, 18.8, 25.4, 26.3, 26.5, 27.4, 27.6, 27.8, 37.8, 46.1, 46.4, 51.1, 52.3, 52.4; *VM* 6.2 (*alternation of sg. and pl. referring to an individual*), 8.5, 11.7, 12.3, 13.5, 19.3, 20.5, 25.1, 26.5; *MvI* 18.4, 27.2, 28.1, 28.3, 28.7; *MvII* 22.5, 22.6, 24.5; *MvIII* 1.1, 14.3, 16.1, 22.8, 27.1, 27.3, 27.6, 29.1, 30.5; *suffixed to verbs -tu/-tú/-du/-ðu Mg* 6.2, 7.6, 10.2, 16.1, 18.5, 18.8, 27.5, 49.5, 50.5, 51.5; *VM* 1.1, 1.5, 2.1, 11.5, 16.1, 19.1, 19.5, 25.6; *MvI* 16.5, 27.5, 29.5; *MvII* 1.1, 2.1, 7.5, 8.6, 9.4, 16.2, 16.7, 17.1, 17.6, 22.1, 23.1, 23.8; *MvIII* 1.5, 2.1, 8.5, 14.1, 22.5, 27.8, 28.1, 28.3, 28.6, 28.8, 30.2.
**þungr** *a.* heavy, harsh *MvIII* 20.1.
**þurfa (t)** *pret.-pres. with gen.* to need *VM* 24.8; to be in need *MvI* 28.4.
**þurr** *a.* dry; *n. as adv. Mg* 49.1.
**þverra (þvarr)** *wv.* to decrease, diminish, wane *Mg* 29.4.
**þverinn** *a.* defiant *MvIII* 14.4 n.
**því** *adv.* therefore, for this reason *Mg* 36.3; *MvI* 17.7, 21.7; *with comp.* by so much, the *Mg* 29.3; *því, því að as conj.* because, for *Mg* 21.6 n.,

27.5; *VM* 2.3, 2.5 n., 9.3; *MvI* 6.7, 14.5 n.; *MvIII* 27.2, 29.5; *því*... *að* for this reason... that *MvI* 17.1–3.
**þvóttdagr** *m.* Saturday *Mg* 36.2.
**þýða (dd)** *wv.* to indicate, explain *Mg* 31.6.
**þýðr** *a.* kind, gentle *Mg* 41.7.
**þykkja/þikkja (þótti)** *wv.* (1) to seem *VM* 16.5; *MvII* 12.8. (2) *md.* to think oneself *MvII* 24.1.
**þykkjustórr** *a.* arrogant *MvIII* 3.6.
**þyrnir** *m.* thorn *Mg* 21.2.
**þysta (st)** *wv. impers. with acc.* to be thirsty *Mg* 30.3.
**þögn** *f.* silence *MvII* 1.4.
**þörf** *f.* need, necessity *MvI* 16.6.

**æ** *adv.* ever, continually *Mg* 29.3.
**æði** *f.* frenzy *MvI* 8.2.
**æðri** *comp. a.* higher (in dignity), nobler; more powerful (*with dat. of comparison*) *Mg* 16.5, 20.5, 24.5.
**æfi** *f.* lifetime *MvI* 18.3; age *Mg* 45.3.
**æra** *f.* honour *MvI* 25.7.
**ærligr** *a.* honest *MvI* 5.1.
**æsa (st)** *wv.* to stir up, excite; *md.* to become enraged *MvI* 10.5; *pptc.* made violent *Mg* 35.3.
**æsiligr** *a.* intense, violent, vehement *MvI* 22.5.
**æskiselja** *f.* desirous giver *MvI* 14.1 (see List of Kennings, 'Woman').
**æstr, æztr (æðstr)** *a. sup.* highest, noblest *VM* 16.1; *MvI* 2.1; *MvIII* 2.3.
**ætla (að)** *wv.* to intend *Mg* 3.1; *VM* 12.5.

**öðlingr** *m.* prince *Mg* 3.2, 18.6. (See List of Kennings, 'Christ'.)
**öl** *n.* ale *MvI* 14.1 n.
**öld** *f.* (1) age; *um aldir* for ever *MvI* 1.3. (2) people, humankind *Mg* 28.2, 39.2, 50.3 (*pl.*); *MvI* 21.1, 26.8 (*pl.*).
**önd** *f.* soul *VM* 26.7; *MvII* 18.7; *MvIII* 10.7, 24.2; *missa önd* die *MvI* 29.7.
**öngr = engi.**
**öngvit** *n. pl.* unconscious state, unconsciousness *Mg* 15.4.
**örlátr** *a.* generous *MvII* 4.4.
**örr** *a. with gen.* generous (with something) *Mg* 1.4 n.

# LIST OF KENNINGS

**Angels**
dýrð himna glory of the heavens *Mg* 45.7.
þjóð stjettar mána people of the path of the moon *Mg* 26.1–2. See also *stjett mána* under 'Heaven'.

**Ave Maria**
kveðja engils greeting of the angel *Mg* 47.2.
kveðja móður grams greeting of the mother of the prince *Mg* 42.2–3. See also *móðir grams* under 'The Virgin Mary'.
vess Maríu verse of Mary *Mg* 52.6.
(söngr) Síóns song of Zion *MvIII* 20.7–8 n.

**Bishop**
gætir góðra klerka keeper of good clerics *Mg* 5.1–2.
gætir munka keeper of monks *Mg* 9.4.
stýrir merkja controller of symbols *Mg* 33.2.
stýrir mítra controller of mitres *Mg* 10.1.

**Breast (or heart)**
land hugar land of thought *MvIII* 2.4.

**Christ**
bragningr hvólfs byrjar prince of the vault of the wind *Mg* 22.1–2. See also *hvólf byrjar* under 'Heaven'.
deilir skepnu dealer of destiny *Mg* 11.6, 31.4, 45.4. Cf. *deilir skepnu* under 'God'.
dróttinn líknar lord of mercy *VM* 1.5.
dróttinn strandar mána lord of the shore of the moon *Mg* 41.1–2. See also *strönd mána* under 'Heaven'.
fylkir sunnu king of the sun *Mg* 11.3.
fögnuðr allra bragna joy of all humankind *Mg* 7.6.
geymir vagns keeper of the Wain (constellation; the Plough) *Mg* 38.7.
gætir aldar keeper of humankind *Mg* 28.2.
gætir engla keeper of angels *Mg* 10.2, 19.8.
gætir himna keeper of the heavens *Mg* 6.6, 47.7, 50.2.
herra hlýrna lord of heavenly bodies *Mg* 30.3–4.
hilmir hlýrna ruler of heavenly bodies *Mg* 2.1.
hilmir sólar ruler of the sun *Mg* 15.1.

**hilmir sunnu** ruler of the sun *Mg* 35.2.
**hilmir vænnar stjettar bjartrar sólar** ruler of the beautiful path of the bright sun *Mg* 37.1 and 4. See also *stjett bjartrar sólar* under 'Heaven'.
**hirðir bryggju mána** shepherd of the jetty of the moon *Mg* 46.5–6. See also *bryggja mána* under 'Heaven'.
**hyllir lýðs** favourer of humankind *Mg* 10.8.
**jöfurr hreggskríns** prince of the shrine of the storm *Mg* 49.6. See also *hreggskrín* under 'Heaven'.
**kóngr skýja** king of clouds *MvIII* 21.5–6.
**kóngr sólar** king of the sun *Mg* 39.7.
**lausnari lopts og himna** redeemer of the sky and heavens *Mg* 13.1.
**lofðungr hauðrs sólar** prince of the land of the sun *Mg* 23.2–3. See also *hauðr sólar* under 'Heaven'.
**meistari alls** master of everything *Mg* 43.7.
**mildingr hauðrs mána** prince of the land of the moon *Mg* 30.1–2. See also *hauðr mána* under 'Heaven'.
**prýðir engla** adorner of angels *Mg* 26.8.
**ræsir borgar regna** prince of the stronghold of rains *Mg* 38.1–2. See also *borg regna* under 'Heaven'.
**ræsir borgar þeyja** prince of the stronghold of thaw winds *Mg* 44.6 and 8. See also *borg þeyja* under 'Heaven'.
**ræsir regnsals** prince of the hall of rain *Mg* 48.5. See also *regnsalr* under 'Heaven'.
**siklingr grundar sunnu** prince of the sun's field *Mg* 9.5–6. See also *grund sunnu* under 'Heaven'.
**siklingr sólar** prince of the sun *Mg* 31.1.
**skapari allra manna** creator of all humankind *Mg* 50.4.
**skapari skýfoldar** creator of the land of clouds *Mg* 43.5–6. See also *skýfold* under kennings for heaven.
**skjöldungr hauðrs skýja** prince of the land of clouds *Mg* 25.3–4. See also *hauðr skýja* under 'Heaven'.
**son(r) guðs** son of God *Mg* 6.1, 12.5, 24.1, 40.3.
**stillir hauðrs mána** controller of the land of the moon *Mg* 34.8. See also *hauðr mána* under 'Heaven'.
**stillir himna** controller of the heavens *Mg* 28.1.
**stillir hlýrna** controller of heavenly bodies *Mg* 21.2.
**stillir sólar** controller of the sun *Mg* 52.1.
**stillir tjalds heiðar** controller of the tent of the heath *Mg* 35.8. See also *tjald heiðar* under 'Heaven'.

# Kennings 137

**stillir veldis himna** controller of the heavenly kingdom *Mg* 35.7–8 n.
**stillir þjóðar stjettar mána** controller of the people of the moon's path *Mg* 26.1–2. See also *þjóð stjettar mána* under 'Angels' and *stjett mána* under 'Heaven'.
**stýrir engla** controller of angels *Mg* 18.2.
**tínir skepnu** gatherer of fate *Mg* 46.2. Cf. *deilir skepnu* above and under 'God'.
**vísir dýrðar** prince of glory *Mg* 14.5.
**vísir sólar** prince of the sun *Mg* 27.2.
**vörðr dóms dýrðar** guardian of the court of glory *MvII* 1.1. See also *dómr dýrðar* under 'Heaven'.
**yfirþjóðkóngr allra jöfra** supreme king of all princes *Mg* 28.5, 32.5, 36.5.
**þengill grundar engla** prince of the field of angels *Mg* 20.2. See also *grund engla* under 'Heaven'.
**þengill himna** prince of the heavens *Mg* 4.7, 8.8.
**þengill sólar** prince of the sun *Mg* 43.2.
**öðlingr bjartra röðla** prince of the bright stars (sun and moon?) *Mg* 3.2, 18.6.

## Fiends

**herr kvala** host of torments *MvIII* 14.4.

## God

**auðgreinandi** distributor of riches *MvI* 1.4.
**deilir skepnu** dealer of destiny *Mg* 16.6, 20.6, 24.6. Cf. *deilir skepnu* under 'Christ'.
**dróttinn skríns leiptra** Lord of the shrine of lightnings *Mg* 1.7–8. See also *skrín leiptra* under 'Heaven'.
**stillir stjörnuhallar** controller of the star-hall *Mg* 16.1. See also *stjörnuhöll* under 'Heaven'.
**stillir leiptra** controller of lightnings *Mg* 20.3.
**valdandi ástar** ruler of love *MvIII* 1.6–7.

## Gold

**blóm bríma** flower of fire *VM* 12.5 n.
**brimglóðir** embers of the sea *VM* 15.1
**fjarðlog** flame of the fjord *MvIII* 14.5.
**glóðir græðis** embers of the sea *MvI* 9.5.
**viti hattar** beacon of the hood *VM* 20.5–6 n.

## Heaven

**borg regna** stronghold of rains *Mg* 38.2.
**borg þeyja** stronghold of thaw winds *Mg* 44.6.
**bryggja mána** jetty of the moon *Mg* 46.6.
**dómr dýrðar** court of glory *MvII* 1.1.
**grund engla** field of angels *Mg* 20.2.
**grund sunnu** field of the sun *Mg* 9.5.
**hauðr mána** land of the moon *Mg* 30.2, 34.8.
**hauðr skýja** land of the clouds *Mg* 25.4.
**hauðr sólar** land of the sun *Mg* 23.2–3.
**hreggskrín** shrine of storms *Mg* 49.6.
**hvólf byrjar** vault of the wind *Mg* 22.2.
**regnsalr** hall of rain *Mg* 48.5.
**skýfold** land of clouds *Mg* 43.6.
**skrín leiptra** shrine of lightnings *Mg* 1.8.
**stjett bjartrar sólar** path of the bright sun *Mg* 37.1 and 4.
**stjett mána** path of the moon *Mg* 26.1.
**stjörnuhöll** star-hall *Mg* 16.1.
**strönd mána** shore of the moon *Mg* 41.1.
**sæti dægra** seat of days and nights (of day-time and night-time?) *Mg* 9.4.
**tjald heiðar** tent of the heath *Mg* 35.8.

## The Holy Cross

**mark píslar** sign of the passion *Mg* 40.1–2.
**stólpi hjálpar** pillar of salvation *Mg* 13.3.
**trje hölda** tree of humankind *Mg* 13.4.

## The Holy Spirit

**andi guðdóms** spirit of the Godhead *VM* 25.3.
**kraptr guðdóms** power of the Godhead *Mg* 28.3.
**logi dróttins skríns leiptra** flame of the Lord of the shrine of lightnings *Mg* 1.7–8. See also *dróttinn skríns leiptra* under 'God' and *skrín leiptra* under 'Heaven'.

## Man

**álmbörr** bow-tree *MvIII* 17.5.
**auðgætandi** keeper of riches *MvI* 5.2.
**beiðir borða** commander of ships (or shields) *VM* 23.3–4.

**fleinhristandi** shaft-shaker *Mg* 11.4.
**fleygir fjarðlogs** flinger, i.e. distributor of the fjord-flame *MvIII* 14.5.
  See also *fjarðlog* under 'Gold'.
**hirðir hringa** keeper of rings *VM* 14.1.
**hirtir manna** punisher (i.e. ruler) of people *VM* 11.5 and 7.
**hlynr branda** maple-tree of swords *Mg* 8.1.
**lundr geira** grove of spears *Mg* 30.5.
**lundr auðs** grove of riches *VM* 9.2–3, 23.6–7.
**lundr linna** grove of gold? *MvIII* 26.3–4 n.
**meiðr mens** neck-ring tree *MvIII* 16.5.
**rennir rítar** flinger, i.e. distributor of the shield *MvIII* 4.1–2.
**runnr laðar** bush of the metal plate *Mg* 35.2 n.
**seimkennandi** gold-'experiencer', i.e. gold-wearer *MvI* 6.6. Cf. *kennir líns* under 'Priest'.
**sendir sárs** sender of wounds *MvI* 6.7–8.
**viðr seimstalls** tree of the gold-seat (i.e. arm) *MvI* 25.6.
**ýtir rítar** pusher of the shield *MvI* 21.5–6.

*Priest*

**kennir líns** 'experiencer' (i.e. wearer) of linen *MvI* 10.3. Cf. *seimkennandi* under 'Man'.

*Tears*

**laug hvarma** bath of the eyelids *Mg* 49.8.
**lón hvarma** lagoon of the eyelids *Mg* 49.2.
**vatn hjálpar** water of salvation *Mg* 49.5.

*The Virgin Mary*

**blóm himinríkis** flower of the heavenly kingdom *MvIII* 30.1.
**brúðr bragnings hvólfs byrjar** bride of the prince of the wind-vault *Mg* 22.1–2. See also *bragningr hvólfs byrjar* under 'Christ' and *hvólf byrjar* under 'Heaven'.
**brúðr guðs** bride of God *MvII* 11.7.
**brúðr himins** bride of heaven *MvIII* 12.5.
**drottning sætis dægra** queen of the seat of days and nights *Mg* 9.2 and 4. See also *sæti dægra* under 'Heaven'.
**gimsteinn vífa** gemstone of women *Mg* 39.4.
**grund anda guðdóms** ground/site of the spirit of the Godhead *VM* 25.3. See also *andi guðdóms* under 'The Holy Spirit'.

# 140    Kennings

**hásæti gætis aldar** high seat of the keeper of humankind *Mg* 28.2.
See also *gætir aldar* under 'Christ'.
**hásæti mjúklætis** high seat of humility *VM* 25.2.
**hjálp fljóða** salvation of women *MvII* 17.8.
**hjálp og miskunn manna** salvation and mercy of humankind *MvII* 18.1.
**höll stillis himna** hall of the controller of the heavens (i.e. when he was in her womb) *Mg* 28.1. See also *stillir himna* under 'Christ'.
**kvón guðs** bride of God *MvII* 2.8.
**líkn og hjálp lýðs** mercy and salvation of humankind *Mg* 41.5.
**líknarmey dróttins** virgin of mercy of the Lord *VM* 19.1.
**mey guðs** virgin of God *MvII* 24.2, *MvIII* 8.8.
**miskunn manna** mercy of humankind *VM* 17.7, *MvII* 18.1.
**móðir dróttins** mother of the Lord *Mg* 5.2, 5.6, 6.5, 17.3, 22.6, 23.6, 34.6, 48.8, *MvI* 23.1.
**móðir dróttins strandar mána** mother of the lord of the shore of the moon *Mg* 41.1–2. See also *dróttinn strandar mána* under 'Christ' and *strönd mána* under 'Heaven'.
**móðir grams** mother of the prince *Mg* 42.2–3.
**móðir guðs** mother of God *Mg* 52.7, *VM* 2.6, 22.4, *MvI* 25.2, 29.4.
**móðir gætis engla** mother of the keeper of angels *Mg* 19.7–8. See also *gætir engla* under 'Christ'.
**móðir hilmis hlýrna** mother of the ruler of heavenly bodies *Mg* 2.1–2. See also *hilmir hlýrna* under 'Christ'.
**móðir Jesú(s)** mother of Jesus *Mg* 19.2, 37.5, *VM* 25.4.
**móðir lofðungs** mother of the prince *Mg* 35.5.
**móðir miskunnar** mother of mercy *Mg* 10.3–4.
**móðir siklings grundar sunnu** mother of the prince of the field of the sun *Mg* 9.5–6. See also *siklingr grundar sunnu* under 'Christ' and *grund sunnu* under 'Heaven'.
**móðir yfirþjóðkóngs allra jöfra** mother of the supreme king of all princes *Mg* 28.5 and 7, 32.5 and 7, 36.5 and 7. See also *yfirþjóðkóngr allra jöfra* under 'Christ'.
**óskamey dróttins** chosen virgin of the Lord *MvI* 23.6.
**sæmd vífa** honour of women *MvII* 24.6.
**sæti heilags anda** seat of the Holy Spirit *Mg* 2.4.
**tákn líknarinnar** symbol of mercy *MvII* 16.1.
**víf Guðs** bride of God *MvIII* 25.1.
**vón hjálpar** hope of salvation *VM* 26.6.

## Woman

**auðbrík** panel of riches *VM* 7.4.
**auðspöng** (metal) plate of riches *MvII* 14.3.
**baugnorn** ring-Norn *MvII* 6.7.
**Bil auðar** Bil of riches *MvI* 14.6.
**brík baugs** panel of the ring *MvI* 26.5–6.
**brík blóms bríma** panel of the flower of fire *VM* 12.5–6 n. See also *blóm bríma* under 'Gold'.
**brík brimglóða** panel of sea-embers *VM* 15.1–2. See also *brimglóðir* under 'Gold'.
**brúðr baugstalls** see *MvI* 23.7–8 n.
**Dís driptar** Dís of snow (i.e. silver; perhaps a half-kenning) *MvII* 15.5–6.
**faldreið** carrier (i.e. wearer) of the head-dress *VM* 12.8.
**Fríðr falds** Fríðr of the head-dress *VM* 3.5–6.
**gátt hrings** door-post of the ring *MvII* 18.2.
**gullskorð** gold-prop *MvII* 10.7.
**Hildr hrings** Hildr of the ring *MvI* 24.5.
**hlíð hrings** hill-side of the ring *MvII* 20.5.
**Hlín hrings** Hlín of the ring *VM* 5.3, *MvI* 26.1–2.
**Hrund gulls** Hrund of gold *MvIII* 5.6.
**línband** band (i.e. resting-place? that which is bound?) of linen *VM* 16.7 n.
**mengrund** necklace-ground *MvI* 21.8.
**Ná glóða græðis** Ná of sea-embers *MvI* 9.5. See also *glóðir græðis* under 'Gold'.
**silkigrund** ground of silk *VM* 23.6.
**silkiskorða** prop of silk *MvI* 5.8.
**silki-Sól** Sól of silk *MvI* 12.5.
**skorða vita hattar** prop of the hood-beacon *VM* 20.5–6 n. See also *viti hattar* under 'Gold'.
**spöng gulls** (metal) plate of gold *MvII* 5.2.
**Vör gulls** Vör of gold *MvII* 15.4.
**þella auðar** pine (tree) of riches *MvII* 13.5.
**þella guðvefs** pine of costly cloth *VM* 9.7.
**þella hringa** pine of rings *MvI* 22.6.
**æskiselja öls** desirous giver of ale *MvI* 14.1 n.

## Other

**baugstallr** ring-seat (i.e. arm) or seat of the shield-boss (shield) *MvI* 23.8 n.
**frændi Áróns** Aaron's relative (i.e. Moses) *Mg* 1.5.
**leynir lýta** hider of sins, secret sinner *MvIII* 7.7–8.
**seimstallr** seat of gold (i.e. arm) *MvI* 25.6.
**sviptuðr siða** destroyer of morality *MvIII* 18.3
**tregbjóðr trúar** reluctant preacher of the faith, i.e. cleric.

# BIBLIOGRAPHY AND ABBREVIATIONS

BK = Kahle 1898.

BK n. = explanatory notes in BK.

BK t.n. = textual notes in BK.

*Biskupa Sögur*, 1858–78, ed. Jón Sigurðsson and Guðbrandr Vigfússon I–II, Kaupmannahöfn.

Clayton, Mary, 1990, *The Cult of the Virgin Mary in Anglo-Saxon England*, Cambridge.

Cormack, Margaret, 1994, *The Saints in Iceland. Their Veneration from the Conversion to 1400*, Bruxelles.

Crane, Thomas Frederick (ed.), 1925, *Liber de miraculis sanctae Dei genitricis Mariae. Published at Vienna in 1731 by Bernard Pez*, Ithaca.

EK = Kock 1946–49.

Finnur Jónsson (ed.), 1918, *Jón Arasons religiøse digte*, København.

Finnur Jónsson, 1920–24, *Den oldnorske og oldislandske litteraturs historie* I–III, København.

Fr. = Fritzner, Johan, 1886–96, *Ordbog over det gamle norske Sprog* I–III, Oslo.

Gautier de Coincy, 1857, *Les miracles de la sainte Vierge*, ed. Alexandre Eusébe Poquet, Paris.

HS = Sperber 1911.

HS n. = explanatory notes in HS.

Jacobus a Voragine, 1890, *Legenda aurea*, ed. Theodor Graesse, Osnabrück.

John of Garland, 1946, *Stella Maris*, ed. Evelyn Faye Wilson. The Mediaeval Academy of America Publication No. 45, Cambridge, Massachusetts.

Jón Helgason, 1932, 'Nokkur íslenzk handrit frá 16. öld', *Skírnir* 106, 143–68.

Jón Helgason (ed.), 1936–38, *Íslenzk miðaldakvæði. Islandske digte fra senmiddelalderen* I–II, København.

JÞ = Jón Þorkelsson, 1888, *Om digtningen på Island i det 15. og 16. århundrede*, København.

Kahle, Bernhard (ed.), 1898, *Isländische geistliche Dichtungen des ausgehenden Mittelalters*, Heidelberg.

Kalinke, Marianne, 1996, *The Book of Reykjahólar. The Last of the Great Medieval Legendaries*, Toronto.

KLNM = *Kulturhistoriskt lexikon för nordisk medeltid*, 1956–78, 1–22, Malmö. (Cited by volume and column number)

Kock, Ernst A. (ed.), 1946–49, *Den norsk-isländska skaldediktningen* I–II, Lund. (Cited by volume, page, stanza and line number)

Kålund, P. E. K., 1889–94, *Katalog over den Arnamagnæanske håndskriftsamling* I–II, København.

Kålund, P. E. K. (ed.), 1906–11, *Sturlunga Saga efter Membranen Króksfjarðarbók udfyldt efter Reykjarfjarðarbók* I–II, København.

*LP* = *Lexicon Poeticum Antiquæ Linguæ Septentrionalis, Oprindelig forfattet af Sveinbjörn Egilsson*, rev. Finnur Jónsson, 1931, København.

Meissner, Rudolf, 1921, *Die Kenningar der Skalden. Ein Beitrag zur skaldischen Poetik*, Hildesheim.

*Mg* = *Drápa af Maríugrát*.

*Ms* = Unger, C. R. (ed.), 1871, *Maríu saga. Legender om Jomfru Maria og hendes Jertegn*, Christiana.

Mushacke, W. (ed.), 1890, *Altprovenzalische Marienklage des xiii. Jahrhunderts*, Halle.

Mussafia, Adolfo, 1886–98, *Studien zu den mittelalterlichen Marienlegenden*. Sitzungsberichte der kaiserliche Akademie der Wissenschaften in Wien, Pts. 1–5, Wien.

*MvI–III* = *Maríuvísur I–III*.

Neuhaus, Carl (ed.), 1886, *Adgar's Marienlegenden nach der Londoner Handschrift Egerton 612 zum ersten Mal vollständig herausgegeben*, Heilbronn.

*NN* = Kock, Ernst A., 1923–44, *Notationes norrœnæ: Anteckningar till Edda och skaldediktningen* I–XXVIII, Lund. (Cited by section number)

Noreen, Adolf, 1923, *Altisländische und altnorwegische Grammatik*, Halle (Saale).

OI = Old Icelandic.

*PL* = Migne, J. P. (ed.), 1844–64, *Patrologiae cursus completus, Series Latina*, 1–221, Parisiis. (Cited by volume and column number)

Schottmann, Hans, 1973, *Die isländische Mariendichtung: Untersuchungen zur volkssprachigen Mariendichtung des Mittelalters*, München.

Skj A = Jónsson, Finnur (ed.), 1908–15, *Den norsk-islandske skjaldedigtning*, A I–II, tekst efter håndskrifterne, København. (Cited by volume, stanza and line number)

Skj B = Jónsson, Finnur (ed.), 1908–15, *Den norsk-islandske skjaldedigtning* B I–II, rettet tekst, København. (Cited by volume, stanza and line number)

Sperber, Hans (ed.), 1911, *Sechs isländische Gedichte legendarischen Inhalts*, Uppsala.

Stefán Karlsson, 1970, 'Ritun Reykjarfjarðarbókar. Excursus: Bókagerð bænda', in *Opuscula* IV. *Bibliotheca Arnamagnæana* 30, 131–40.

Stefán Karlsson (ed.), 1983, *Guðmundar sögur biskups* I: *Ævi Guðmundar biskups. Guðmundar saga A*, Kaupmannahöfn.

Vincent of Beauvais, 1624, *Bibliotheca mundi Vincentii Burgundi. Speculum quadruplex, naturale, doctrinale, morale, historiale*, Douai.

VM = *Vitnisvísur af Maríu.*

Widding, Ole, 1961, 'Om de norrøne Marialegender', in *Opuscula* II,1. *Bibliotheca Arnamagnæana* 25,1, 1–9.

Widding, Ole, 1967, 'Norrøne Marialegender med Rhinegnene som hjemsted', *Arv* 23, 143–58.

Widding, Ole, 1969, 'Nogle norske Marialegender', *Maal og Minne*, 51–59.

Widding, Ole, 1995, 'Norrøne Marialegender på europæisk baggrund', in *Opuscula* 10. *Bibliotheca Arnamagnæana* 40, 1–128.

Widding, Ole and Hans Bekker-Nielsen, 1961, 'The Virgin bares her Breast: An Icelandic Version of a Miracle of the Blessed Virgin', in *Opuscula* II,1. *Bibliotheca Arnamagnæana* 25,1, 76–79.

Wolf, Kirsten, 1994, 'The Cult of Saint Anne in Iceland', in *The Ninth International Saga Conference. Akureyri. 31 July – 6 August 1994*, 863–77.

Wrightson, Kellinde, 1994, 'Changing Attitudes to Old Icelandic Marian Poetry', in *Old Norse Studies in the New World*, ed. Geraldine Barnes, Margaret Clunies Ross and Judy Quinn, Sydney, 138–53.

Wrightson, Kellinde, 1995, 'Marian Miracles in Old Icelandic Skaldic Poetry', in *Treasures of the Elder Tongue*, ed. Katrina Burge and John Stanley Martin, Melbourne, 87–99.

Wrightson, Kellinde, 1997a, '*Drápa af Maríugrát*, the Joys and Sorrows of the Virgin and Christ, and the Dominican Rosary', *Saga-Book* XXIV:5, 283–92.

Wrightson, Kellinde, 1997b, 'The *Lærðir Menn* of the Old Icelandic Marian Lament *Drápa af Maríugrát*', in *Sagas and the Norwegian Experience. Preprints of the 10th International Saga Conference Trondheim 3–9 August 1997*, 685–92.

Wrightson, Kellinde, 1997c, 'The Jilted Fiancée: The Old Icelandic Miracle Poem *Vitnisvísur af Maríu* and its Modern English Translation', *Parergon. Journal of the Australian and New Zealand Association for Medieval and Early Modern Studies* New Series 15, 117–136.